𝕰𝖝𝖕𝖊𝖗𝖎𝖒𝖊𝖓𝖙𝖆𝖑 𝕰𝖉𝖚𝖈𝖆𝖙𝖎𝖔𝖓 𝖘𝖊𝖗𝖎𝖊𝖘

EDITED BY M. V. O'SHEA

MODERN PSYCHOLOGIES
AND EDUCATION

EXPERIMENTAL EDUCATION SERIES

Edited by M. V. O'SHEA

MODERN PSYCHOLOGIES AND EDUCATION

BY

CLARENCE E. RAGSDALE, Ph.D.

ASSISTANT PROFESSOR OF EDUCATION
THE UNIVERSITY OF WISCONSIN

With an Introduction by

M. V. O'SHEA

PROFESSOR OF EDUCATION
THE UNIVERSITY OF WISCONSIN

New York

THE MACMILLAN COMPANY

1932

SET UP, ELECTROTYPED, AND PRINTED IN THE UNITED STATES OF AMERICA
BY T. MOREY & SON

To

MINNIE E. RAGSDALE

PREFACE

It is usually recognized that there are sharp differences of opinion among psychologists; but the extent and the fundamental nature of the points of disagreement are commonly ignored. Students in teacher-training institutions, who are able to get only a minimum acquaintance with psychology, are often confused by the divergent views the nature of which they do not clearly understand. Teachers who feel that they need to bring their knowledge of psychology up to date are at a loss to know where to turn to get a survey of the whole of modern psychology. This book is written to meet the needs of these students and teachers.

At the present time there are many new departures in education and there is much criticism of established institutions. In this volume I have given an evaluation of many educational movements. Criticisms are always directed from one or another of the recognized psychological points of view. The book shows what one ought logically to think of present education, if one adopts and consistently maintains any one of the contemporary attitudes in psychology.

The discussion remains impartial throughout. Nevertheless, I have shown the directions in which psychological and educational thought of the present day is tending. Whether the trends are desirable or undesirable I have left to the judgment of the reader.

For advice in the preparation of this volume I am indebted to Professor M. V. O'Shea. My greatest psychological debt is to my former teacher, Professor Max F. Meyer.

C. E. RAGSDALE

MADISON, WISCONSIN
December, 1931

vii

TABLE OF CONTENTS

PART I

Psychological Theories Underlying Education

PART II

CURRENT EDUCATIONAL PROBLEMS VIEWED IN THE LIGHT OF MODERN PSYCHOLOGIES

EDITOR'S INTRODUCTION

Probably all persons who read these lines will readily agree that interest in psychology has been increasing constantly during the past two decades and also that confusion in regard to psychology has been gaining ground in spite of the efforts of its votaries to make it intelligible and consistent. Psychology has become a favorite topic of conversation among teachers, social workers, professional people of all sorts, and laymen. If one attends an educational convention anywhere in the United States, one can hear speakers striving to expound psychological principles and apply them to educational procedures. Also, if one listens to the talk in a drawing room it will be noted that guests are praising or condemning one or another school of contemporary psychology. Physicians are introducing psychological courses into the programs of medical colleges; lawyers are inquiring about psychological books to read so that they may pursue their profession in accordance with the supposed laws of human nature; parents are asking for lists of books on psychology that they may study so that they can understand their children and train them up in the way in which they should go; social workers want to learn about the latest discoveries in psychology; and so it goes. One would expect that out of all this enthusiasm for and activity in psychology there would be available by this time a large body of principles that would be universally accepted; but this expectation—or hope, perhaps—has not yet been realized.

Four or five decades ago there was well-nigh universal

agreement among students of human nature regarding most of the so-called laws of the mind, because all who were engaged in elaborating psychological systems approached this task from the same general standpoint and adopted the same method—introspection. But with the development of scientific interest and the widespread adoption of objective methods of investigation, people began to lose confidence in the accuracy and adequacy of introspective procedure in discovering the nature and functions of the human mind. When men began to be discontented with the findings and elaborations of introspective psychologists, the one-time unity of opinion regarding the constitution and modes of operation of the mind began to collapse. Upon the ruins, so to speak, of the introspective structure there arose a large assortment of schools or systems of psychology. Inevitably there developed disharmony and discord in the psychological field. In due course, the conceptions of human nature advanced by one school were denied *in toto* by other schools, with the result that laymen, and also some of the brethren in the psychological fold, wandered far afield in respect to psychological facts and interpretations. General interest, however, was only intensified by the struggle that everyone came to appreciate was going on among the devotees of and the dilettantes and fakirs in psychology.

If one discusses any psychological problem these days with his colleagues or friends he must at the outset let it be known whether he is a Structuralist, a Functionalist, a Behaviorist, a Purposivist, a Freudian, an Adlerian, a Jungian, a Gestaltian, or some variety of one or more of these schools or systems. If one opens up on a psychological theme in any gathering to-day and reveals the school with which he takes sides, he is certain to arouse lively competitive and defensive reactions among those in his audience who claim adherence to a different school. The present writer has not for some time been in any group of teachers, laymen, or psychologists among whom psychological discussion was in progress that he has not observed some of the members assuming defensive attitudes, no matter from what point of view any speaker might be endeavoring to explain the human mechanism. In the university with which the writer is connected, there have recently been as many as six distinctive schools of psychology, each being expounded by a partisan and each having adherents and votaries among students. The followers of one school have manifested but slight confidence in the tenets of any other school.

It will be granted by all readers that it would be highly desirable to show, if possible, in what respects the different schools of psychology are in accord and in what respects they differ in their conceptions of human nature. This is the problem which Professor Ragsdale attacks in this volume. First of all, he presents in a simple and brief way the essentials of each school of psychology, and makes it clear how each school has arisen in the development of modern psychologies. Then he points out similarities and dissimilarities in the tenets of the various schools. He discusses the question,—In laying out an educational program, or in class-room teaching, or in ministering to those who are ailing, or in persuading and dissuading persons in regard to any belief or line of conduct, to what extent are the different schools of psychology in agreement in respect to fundamental principles of procedure? He succeeds in showing that, although the various schools may hold divergent or contrasted views regarding the origin or bases of human traits or activities of any sort, when it comes actually to dealing with human beings so as to accomplish desired results, there is considerable unity among the outstanding schools. Any reader who will go through this book cannot fail to be convinced by Professor Ragsdale's clear exposition that discord among the psychologists of to-day is more largely in their fundamental conceptions of the technique of mental activities than in methods of procedure in order to secure certain outcomes in influencing the behavior of individuals and especially of the young.

Faithfully and without prejudice or bias, Professor Ragsdale reveals the distinctive attitudes, points of view, and conceptions of each recognized school of psychology. The reader may conclude by the time he finishes this book that the author leans rather in the direction of the objective or behavioristic than of any other school; but even so, he does not permit his own convictions to affect his portrayal and evaluation of all schools that are treated herein. It may be appropriate to note in this connection that the editor of this volume finds somewhat more comfort and satisfaction in the functional and biological type of psychology than in any other. He believes that the individual is more largely influenced by hereditary contributions derived from the survival and persistence of useful developments in the race than do the behaviorists, for instance. While he confesses to these leanings he may say that, at the same time, he regards himself as quite largely a behaviorist or objective psychologist. This matter is mentioned here by way of introducing the assertion that any reader who is eager to find out the clearest and most satisfactory conception of human nature will not be able to take a stand absolutely with the Structuralist, or the Functionalist, or the Freudian, or the Objectivist, or the Gestaltian, or the Purposivist School, when each stands rigidly upon the details of its particular system and refuses to acknowledge any merit in what is offered in any other system. The author of this volume, while he gains more comfort from the objective than any other variety of psychology, is what might properly be called an eclectic psychologist. The discussion in this volume will probably be regarded as evidence of the fact that the author and the editor, in common, no doubt, with most of those who will read the book, cannot be thrust into one school of psychology and held there securely. It is the belief of the present writer that *Modern Psychologies and Education* will, among other accomplishments, help to bridge the gap between the different schools of psychology so that there will develop among them greater agreement than there has apparently existed during the past decade or more.

Professor Ragsdale has written this book partly for the purpose of revealing the points of view and the attitudes of the various schools of psychology, but primarily for the purpose of showing how educational procedures are affected by the principles presented in each school regarded separately, and in all the schools regarded collectively. The last half of the book is devoted to a somewhat detailed discussion of the treatment of current educational problems and pressures viewed from the standpoint of contemporary psychologies. The reader will not fail to note that many of these educational problems are so complicated that one cannot be dogmatic, in the present state of our psychological knowledge, in prescribing how the problems can be solved most effectively and with the least disturbance and waste. The problems which Professor Ragsdale discusses have been propounded to him by many students, alike of psychology and of education. It can be confidently asserted that he has made a sincere and gratifying effort to apply to these perplexing present-day pressures all the wisdom that can be distilled from all the systems of psychology.

So this book can be heartily commended to those who wish to make a survey of contemporary psychologies as expounded by their leading exponents, and also to those who are charged with the care and culture of the young and who are seeking for guidance from those who, it is believed, understand human nature and know how to shape it one way or another according to the aims, ideals, and wishes of teachers, parents, social workers, and all others who have anything to do in molding the lives of the younger generation.

M. V. O'SHEA

THE UNIVERSITY OF WISCONSIN
December, 1931

MODERN PSYCHOLOGIES
AND EDUCATION

MODERN PSYCHOLOGIES AND EDUCATION

CHAPTER I

CHILD NATURE AS THE BASIS FOR EDUCATIONAL THEORY

I. Pre-scientific Views of Childhood and of Education

The Child as a Miniature Adult. Critical examination of the educational systems of the past and the present shows the important part played by the current concept of the nature of childhood. As the attitude of philosophers and scientists toward the nature of the child has changed, the fundamental characteristics of education have been altered. Underlying all thinking concerning the nature of childhood up until the most recent development of the sciences of biology and psychology was the view that the child is essentially a little man. It was assumed that in its physical, mental, moral, and spiritual characteristics the child was merely a miniature adult.

Physically the Child Is Not a Miniature Adult. It was believed by some biologists that the father transmitted to the mother a perfectly formed little human being, complete in all its parts but infinitely small. The function of the mother was believed to be merely that of protecting and feeding this miniature human being until it was sufficiently large to begin an independent life at the time of

1

birth. Becoming an adult was merely a matter of enlarging and strengthening parts which were already present.

We know quite well that physically children are very different from adults. If a child of one year were merely enlarged to the height and weight of an adult, it would be a great monstrosity; its head would be much too large, its legs and arms much too short, and its trunk too long and thick. In the same way, a child of eleven or twelve years has legs and arms which are too long when compared with the adult proportions. Becoming an adult requires a readjustment of the proportions of the different parts of the body and not a mere increase in size of the body as a whole.

It Has Been Believed that the Child Is Mentally an Adult in Miniature. Psychologically the view that a child is a miniature adult is tied up with belief in the existence and importance of a large number of instincts. These instincts are supposed to be mental characteristics which are passed on from generation to generation as a matter of racial inheritance. An instinctive tendency has only to mature to become functionally active. If the stimulus for the instinctive action is lacking, it is frequently supposed that the person will hunt for a situation which will give opportunity for making the instinctive response. Each child is supposed to have his full quota of instincts characteristic of the human race. If any of these instinctive tendencies fail to appear it indicates that the normal course of development has been interfered with. The chief function of education is to arrange environmental conditions in such a way that each of the instinctive tendencies may appear at its appropriate time. It is assumed that these instinctive tendencies are unmoral in character. They may be either good or bad, dependent upon the kind of situation which calls them forth.

Philosophically this attitude toward the nature of childhood showed itself in the view that man possesses many intuitions, that is, that he contains within himself a great amount of knowledge which is inborn and not obtained from any outside source. Knowledge of the important moral principles, for example, was considered to be intuitive. There was considered to be an absolute morality with which every human being was natively acquainted. He did not have to learn to distinguish between right and wrong, but became able to do so as soon as his mental and spiritual development had reached a high enough level, that is, as soon as he had reached an age when he could be held "accountable" for his actions.

Accountability was ordinarily thought to have its beginning in the child when it learned to talk, and was fully developed by the time of sexual maturity. The beginning of accountability with talking was based on the traditional view that language is the expression of the soul. When the soul had mastered the body sufficiently to talk, it was believed to have become mature enough to be to some extent responsible for its actions. This view, that talking is an affair of the soul, can be understood if we refer to the popular attitude toward the first work which was done in teaching deaf mutes to talk. It had formerly been believed that deaf mutes were incapable of talking, because, through some unfortunate accident, they had not been given a soul at birth. They were considered to be in every respect on the level of animals who had no souls. Toward the beginning of the nineteenth century, certain work was done in teaching deaf mutes to talk. When these efforts met with some success, the effects were considered to be truly miraculous. The explanation, which was accepted by the majority of people, was that somehow a soul had been given to these unfortunate creatures who previously had possessed none.

The date at which children have traditionally entered school is doubtless based upon this view of the reaching of a stage of accountability for their actions. When talking is fairly well established, that is, when the child is about six years old, it is assumed that he has begun to be responsible for his actions. We therefore send him to school to be trained and drilled in the correct modes of behavior. If he fails to learn he is simply stubborn and disobedient and must be punished.

The date at which accountability was supposed to be fully established—sexual maturity—was based upon the social importance of that event. Its importance was further emphasized by the traditionally negative attitude of Christian theology toward the facts of sex.

Beliefs concerning Inborn Moral Nature. When we believe that a child is essentially a little man, we may assume that this little man is essentially evil, that he is essentially good, or that he is neither good nor bad. The attitude of the ancient Greeks seems to have been that the child was a little adult who was neither good nor bad, but was inclined toward goodness. The Christian theology has usually assumed that the child is a little man who is inherently bad. He is wholly evil in his inner nature, but is put into this world so that he can be made over and fitted to live in the world to come. The chief function of Christian education, therefore, is to restrain and discipline human nature to the end that the child will become better and better as he grows older and will eventually reach perfect goodness in the world to come.

St. Augustine believed, for example, that human nature is wholly evil because Adam chose to disobey God, and thereby corrupted the whole human race. The first man transmitted his sinful nature to his offspring so that it is now impossible for man not to sin. Adam's sin is thus a hereditary sin which is found in each human being. Presumably a child is wholly bad, although still too small and weak to engage in sinful actions of any great consequence. As he grows and matures he must be subjected to disciplinary training to help him in overcoming his original sinful tendencies.

Discipline and Restraint Are Educational Consequences of the Belief that the Child Is a Bad Little Man. This view, that the child is essentially bad, dominated education from the beginning of the Christian era until comparatively recent times, in fact it still dominates much of our modern educational effort. Under this view the method of education consists in fixing upon the child the habits and ways of life which are considered desirable in the adult, as soon as he is old enough to be held accountable for his actions. The attitude of Christian theologians toward the spontaneous and natural actions of children can be illustrated by a quotation from the discipline of the Methodist Episcopal Church of America in 1792:

". . . we prohibit *play* in the strongest terms. . . . The students shall rise at five o'clock . . . summer and winter. . . . Their recreation shall be gardening, walking, riding, and bathing without doors, and the carpenter's, joiner's, cabinet-maker's or turner's business within doors. . . . A person skilled in gardening shall be appointed to overlook the students . . . in this recreation. . . . A Master . . . shall always be present at the time of bathing. Only one shall bathe at a time; and no one shall remain in the water above a minute. No student shall be allowed to bathe in the river. A *Taberna Lignaria* (carpenter's shop) shall be provided . . . with all proper instruments and materials, and a skillful per-

son . . . to overlook the students at this recreation. . . .
The students shall be indulged with nothing which the
world calls *play*. Let this rule be observed with the
strictest nicety; for those who play when they are young,
will play when they are old."

Education Has Been Dominated by Institutions—Reli-
gious, Political, and Industrial. This idea that the inner
nature of the child must be made over for an institution
has been adopted and applied, not only by the church, but
by the political and industrial institutions as well. It is
commonly assumed that the only reason why the state
is justified in providing for public education is that citizens must be made who will fit into the dominant political
system. In a democracy, for example, we are justified in
educating children solely because educated citizens are
needed for the proper conduct of a democracy; in a monarchical system of government, education is concerned
with training citizens who will fit into a monarchical system; in the Soviet Republic, education is concerned with
producing citizens who have communistic ideas which fit
in with the dominant political system. Sometimes in education industrial aims are emphasized; the aim has been
to produce citizens who will be good workers in some form
of industry. When these social, political, or industrial
aims are emphasized, there is added to the theological
belief that the child must be made over and fitted for
life in the next world, the more immediately practical aim
concerned with making the child over and fitting him for
life in his present world.

Up to the present, religious, political, and industrial
institutions have had the deciding part in determining the
aims and the content as well as the method of education.
During recent years the influence of all these institutions
has been summarized in the statement of the ultimate

aim of education as *social efficiency*. While the belief that the aim of education is social efficiency has grown out of this earlier view, that the child is essentially a little man who is inherently bad, it is not wholly incompatible with the more modern scientific view of the nature of childhood, which we will describe later.

Rousseau Introduced the View that the Child Is a Good Little Man. The older view of the nature of childhood and education was not seriously challenged until the advent of Rousseau in the eighteenth century. The child is, for Rousseau, still a little man, but, being unspoiled by the customs and conventions of adults, he is a *better* man than the adults who are attempting to mold him to their pattern. For the first time since the beginning of the Christian era it was announced that nature is right.

The belief that the child is a "good little man" has introduced freedom and liberality into education. If the child is perfect in every respect, the problem of education is merely that of providing him with an opportunity to develop according to his own inner tendencies. The less he is interfered with by parents and teachers the better. An education which permits him to develop with a minimum of interference will be the ideal. The procedure in education is at once changed upon the acceptance of this view. Restraint of all kinds becomes obnoxious. The child must be free. He must discover and observe on his own account rather than imitate. He must study natural objects rather than words. Books are likely to contain the conventions of the adult world which surrounds him. The child must be freed from these as far as possible. Natural objects are unspoiled by man; the child may, therefore, associate with them and learn from them without danger of contamination. We can summarize the educational views of Rousseau by saying that the child must be permitted to develop according to his own inner bent and disposition.

The physical body is of importance as well as the mind. The physical body is a natural possession of the child and as such is good. It must be given an opportunity to develop to the fullest extent possible. The writings of Rousseau, therefore, furnish the starting point for our modern attitude toward physical education. It is true that there had been an interest in physical development before the time of Rousseau. This interest sprung from the same sources as the other attitudes toward education. Physical development was considered desirable for the making of soldiers to uphold the state. Physical development was considered entirely from the standpoint of the necessities of the state rather than from the viewpoint of the welfare of the individual.

The Doctrine of "Self-Activity" Has Been Developed by the Followers of Rousseau. These principles have been embodied in the writings and in the schools of many educators since the time of Rousseau, and have gradually modified the whole of education. Basedow, Pestalozzi, and Froebel were among the pioneers in this movement. Basedow founded, in 1774, a school known as the Philanthropnum in which he attempted to make education practical in content and playful in method. Pestalozzi attempted to develop the negative and contrary attitude of Rousseau into a consistent and positive system of education. In 1775 he founded a school in which he attempted to combine industrial and intellectual training. He conceived of education as a natural development of innate powers. His method consisted of an analysis of sense perceptions from which clear ideas were developed by a series of graded exercises. The function of the teacher was to provide material for sense perceptions, to ask questions leading to close observation, and to aid in summing up the results of the observations. "He only takes care that no untoward influence shall disturb nature's march of development." His function is permissive, while the child's is active. When introduced into this country, the Pestalozzian schools quickly became highly formalized, and contained as much restraint and discipline as the schools which they were intended to replace. The Pestalozzian method became simply a method for memorizing facts by an object method of teaching.

Froebel likewise believed that the child contained within himself the germs of all his future possibilities. He would develop by a process of self-activity if given appropriate materials with which to concern himself. Unfortunately Froebel determined the characteristics of children and the nature of his kindergarten "gifts" and "occupations" on the basis of symbolical and metaphysical values rather than by a direct study of the facts of child life.

From the writings of these four, Rousseau, Basedow, Pestalozzi, and Froebel, there have developed two important doctrines: (1) that the child's spontaneous and natural activities are the chief factors in his education, and (2) that the child passes through definite stages of development, each calling for its own type of activity and furnishing the essential basis for the next stage of development. The program of study demanded by these two principles has led to the modern scientific movement for child study. It has brought the development of the modern view that the child is not a little man at all, but is a creature of an entirely different sort, living its own life in its own way, with adulthood as a remote goal.

II. Scientific Attitudes toward Child Nature and Education

The Scientific Study of Childhood Begins with G. Stanley Hall. G. Stanley Hall brought together the earlier tendencies in education in an address before the National Council of Education in 1901, and in his numerous books. He extended the recapitulation theory of biology to include childhood and not merely embryological development, and merged it with the culture-epoch theory of the Herbartians. The recapitulation theory and the culture-epoch theory serve to emphasize and make concrete the principle of Rousseau that the child passes through definite stages of development.

The recapitulation theory, as formulated by the biologists, states that any animal, in its individual physical development, rehearses in general outline the evolutionary development of that species of animals. The human embryo at various stages in its growth shows anatomical characteristics which remind us of the anatomical structure of various lower animals. The so-called gill slits in the neck of the embryo, for example, are reminiscent of that period of racial development in which our ancestors were water-dwelling animals. It is supposed, however, that this recapitulation is essentially complete in human beings by the time of birth.

The culture-epoch theory of the Herbartians states that children, in their mental development, pass through stages roughly corresponding to the cultural stages in the development of the human race after it became human. The child, for example, is supposed at one time to be in a cultural stage corresponding to savage life. He is supposed at this time to be interested in using bow and arrow, in fighting, running, hiding, and other activities characteristic of the life of savages. At a later time his interests change to the barbarian, or other higher cultural levels. These cultural stages in development are supposed to represent the normal course of intellectual growth in children. Each stage is supposed to be essential and unavoidable. The right procedure in education should then be one which leads the child on from one cultural stage through the next, following the same order in which these cultural stages appeared in the human race. This theory is based upon the assumption that the habits of one generation are transmitted by a kind of mental inheritance to the next generation. The theory is, of course, in direct contradiction to the present rejection of the belief that acquired characteristics can be transmitted to the next generation through the germ plasm.

G. Stanley Hall finds in child life many stages corresponding to the stages of biological and cultural development of the human race. He finds in the child the swaying movements which remind him of the swimming of the fish; movements of the arms and legs which remind him of the climbing of monkeys; interest in hunting which reminds him of the primitive interests of the human race. His studies of child life and his recommendations concerning education take this principle of recapitulation as a point of departure. His great contribution to education is not concerned with his detailed recommendations, since this principle of recapitulation as applied to education has been largely discarded; he has contributed rather to the interest in a fact-finding study of child life. He gave a great impetus to the child study movement which has led others to apply scientific techniques to child study without the bias of the recapitulation and the culture-epoch theories.

A New Concept of Childhood Has Grown Out of the Scientific Movement. During recent years educational psychologists have minimized or ignored the recapitulation theory in the form proposed by its child study advocates. While the embryo roughly repeats the phylogenetic series, there are large omissions in this series; moreover the recapitulation is complete by the time of birth. Studies in inheritance throw great doubt upon the germinal transmission of acquired characters, and thus discredit the culture-epoch theory, which asserts that the individual inherits, and thus lives over again, the cultural experiences of his ancestors. In a like manner, modern views of heredity and individual physical and physiological development lead to the giving up, or at least the profound modification of the formerly accepted psychological views of instinct. These changes in biology and psychology have made necessary a new, fact-finding study of child life.

This new child study makes use of the objective techniques of biology and psychology and discards the metaphysical assumption of Rousseau and his followers that the child is *an adult in miniature* which needs only to unfold and grow to become an ideal man or woman. For Rousseau and his followers, the environment exercises a passive, permissive rôle. This view gained support from the early work of students of heredity and genetics. The more recent opinion among biologists, as held by Child and Jennings, is that the *environment enters actively* into the changes that take place in the developing individual. This view is confirmed by modern students of psychology, notably the behaviorists. For child study, we can accept Weiss' definition of psychology: "The science which studies the development of the animal-like infant into the civilized adult." At any point in his development, whether as germ cell, embryo, or infant, the child may be considered as raw material out of which an adult is being made by the surrounding physical and social forces. The character of the raw material is a matter of great consequence and deserves the fullest investigation; *but interest in the nature of childhood must not blind the educator to the fact that the environmental processes by which changes are effected are active means by which the child becomes an adult.*

Restraint and Freedom in Existing Educational Systems Are an Outgrowth of Conflict between the Older Views of Child Nature. American education to-day is dominated by the two older views of the nature of childhood. The prevailing influence has been, and still remains, the belief that the child is a miniature adult, but with many evil tendencies which must be repressed and redirected in order to make a "socially efficient" individual. Based upon this view we have schools with fixed courses of study, formal group instruction, and rigid discipline. There is in every curriculum a group of "required" courses, based upon the assumption that they contain information or skills which every child must acquire, but which he would probably overlook if left to his own devices. They must be forced upon him. If the child is "normal" and wishes to learn, it is assumed that he has only to apply himself. Method of teaching may, therefore, become formalized and does not require much adaptation to the varying character of students or subject matter. The value of training in method and technique of teaching is minimized; the teacher is just a taskmaster. Discipline is rigid, not merely to meet the practical requirements of the school, but because it is believed the students must have a training in obedience to law. Their own unrestrained impulses would lead them into every manner of evil; their desires must be disciplined and redirected into useful channels. No school at the present time embodies all these principles, although it is only a few years since schools everywhere attempted to do so. That there has been departure from this view of education as a process of discipline and restraint is due to the impact upon the educational system of the view of child nature, proposed by Rousseau and his followers, that the child is essentially good.

Many of the recent movements in education have as their professed object the liberation of the child to follow his own inclinations. Instead of fixed courses of study, we must have electives; instead of formally planned instruction, we must have incidental and informal learning; instead of rigid discipline, student self-government and freedom from all restraint. The contrast is between education as a process of disciplining and seasoning by external direction, and education as a process of development from within. If we accept the one view, restraint, direction, and guidance are the essential features of education and without them we should never have the properly educated man or woman; if we accept the other view, restraint and external supervision are educationally indefensible, unless a minimum of each is considered necessary to avoid danger of irreparable harm to the developing individual as a result of his temporary inability to meet practical situations.

Dissatisfaction with Present-day Education Is Due to the Conflict between the Older Views of Child Nature. The conflict between these two views of childhood and of education, together with the seeming impossibility of consistently applying either view, is responsible for much of the unrest and agitation which characterizes our whole educational system, from the pre-school group to the university. School systems at the present time represent a compromise between these two views, a state of affairs which pleases the advocates of neither. Within any one institution there exist side by side electives and required

courses, some measure of self-government and freedom
and restrictive rules and regulations.   When a student
undertakes a course his reading and study are narrowly
prescribed; or perhaps a "project" method is used in
which the student is seemingly given freedom in selection
of material studied.   Such freedom is usually narrowly
limited by the "suggestions" of the teacher and by the
material available for instruction.   It matters little so
far as freedom of choice is concerned whether the teacher
directly limits and prescribes the students' study, or
whether it is limited just as surely and directly by the
type of instructional material provided.   Many of the
so-called progressive schools have merely substituted limitations imposed by materials for limitations imposed by
a teacher and have introduced scarcely anything of the
freedom which is their professed aim.   They have substituted study of materials and objects in nature for the
study of textbooks in the belief that by so doing they are
introducing freedom.   However, variety in physical and
social surroundings is not so easily obtained as variety
in books.   The truly progressive school would use each
type of material to supplement and explain the other,
and would recognize that widening the environment may
introduce freedom where changing the type of environment
merely substitutes one kind of restriction for another.

The true value of an object method of teaching is to
be found not in any introduction of freedom or liberality
into education but rather in its avoidance of purely verbal
or symbolical knowledge. The person who has only a verbal
knowledge of any subject is likely to make many foolish
mistakes which could be avoided if his knowledge were
based upon first-hand familiarity with the objects and
natural processes to which words refer. One of the true
values of laboratory instruction in science (which is sim-

ply one means for using an object method of teaching) is to give this first-hand acquaintance which will help students to avoid absurd errors in reasoning and thinking. Laboratory instruction is not intended to make learning more rapid or more certain; it is not intended to give more opportunity for initiative; it is not intended to introduce more freedom; but it is intended to be a method of teaching which aids students in sticking close to the facts and avoiding unjustifiable and unwarranted generalizations.

Some educational institutions incline more toward the disciplinary idea in education and some more toward the idea of freedom and liberality. Among the universities, for example, some are recognized as being distinctly conservative, retaining a large number of required courses in the curriculum, holding fast to a group plan of instruction largely based upon lectures, textbook reading, and quizzes. They have many rules governing the conduct of students, such as scholastic requirements for participation in extra-curricular activities, bans on the driving of automobiles by students, and fixed hours at which women students must be in their rooming houses and dormitories at night. On the other hand, these same institutions have been forced to introduce a certain number of electives and to relax somewhat their supervision of the social life of students. Other institutions, which pride themselves upon their liberality and upon the lack of restraints imposed upon students, still retain required courses in the curriculum and a comparatively large number of rules and regulations concerning the social and extra-curricular activities of their student body. In each case the situation is felt to be a compromise between what is desirable and what is forced upon the institution by practical considerations. The same situation is true in high schools and elementary schools. The result is that no one is satisfied with present educational institutions. It seems impossible that anyone can ever be satisfied, so long as we hold to either of these two views of the nature of education, based upon the underlying assumption that children are miniature adults who are either good or bad in their original nature.

Growing Out of the Scientific Movement a New Conception of Education Is Developing. Growing out of the recent scientific study of childhood by educators and scientists there has developed an entirely new conception of the nature of children which has made possible a wholly new approach to the problems of education. This view is that children are not miniature adults at all, but are an entirely different kind of creature. They are creatures who will later become adult men and women, it is true, but for the time being they are living a life of their own and can, in a sense, be thought of as being an entirely different species of animal.

This attitude can be understood if we think of children as being the raw material out of which adults are being made in much the same sense that wood and iron are the raw material out of which automobiles are made. We may compare the school to a factory. Just as in the automobile factory, it is the business of the workers to take the raw materials, which are wood and iron, and by using certain tools and certain methods of manufacture turn out finished automobiles, so in our schools and other educational agencies it is the business of teachers, parents, and others to take the raw material, in the form of children, and make adult men and women of them by using any available tools and materials. For those interested in education, the tools and materials which are available are the various activities included in the cur-

riculum, the physical equipment of educational institutions, the playgrounds, motion picture theaters, churches,
and the like.

In our attempts to transform children into civilized
adults, certain difficulties are encountered which are not
found in the automobile factory. In the automobile factory there are fixed hours of work, during which skilled
workmen are employed to treat the raw material in certain definite ways. When the working hours for the day
are ended, the factory is locked up and placed under the
care of a watchman until the next day. No one from the
outside is permitted to come in and interfere with the
work which is in progress. In our educational efforts a
very different situation exists. If we confine our attention
for a moment to the schools, we find that the teachers,
as workmen, are occupied about six hours daily at their
task of transforming raw material, in the form of children,
into civilized adults. After working hours they have no
further control over the children, who are in the process
of being transformed into adult citizens. After school
hours the children go home to parents, who take their
turn at the process of making adults out of them; or the
children play on the streets, or go to a motion picture
theater, and come in contact with endless numbers of
influences of every kind and description. The net result
from the standpoint of efficiently transforming children
into civilized adults is comparable to the result which
would be obtained in an automobile factory, where the
working day was six hours in length, but where, for the
remainder of the day, the factory doors were left wide
open, with the invitation freely extended to anyone who
cared to do so, to come in and take whatever material
and tools he happened to find, to make anything in which
he happened to be interested. It might very well be

true that every one who came to the factory would be interested in turning out some useful article, but the net result would be an indescribable kind of confusion. The workman who to-day left a bit of steel which he had begun to fashion into a crank case or a cylinder, might, on his return to-morrow, find that someone else had taken this same bit of material and begun to fashion it into some other article, such as a lawn mower or a doorbell. In spite of the fact that each of these things is a useful article, the failure of the different workers to coöperate would prevent either of them from accomplishing any very useful result.

We are faced with just that situation in education at the present time. We have teachers, parents, social workers, business men, and others, all trying to make useful citizens out of children, but each proceeding in his own way, with little regard for the efforts of the others. The thing needed to make education efficient is coöperation among the various educational agencies. It is true that steps in this direction are being taken; the organization of parent-teacher associations, for example, is an important movement of this kind; but there is still a long way to go before this kind of coöperation will be sufficiently close to eliminate many of the difficulties which are characteristic of our present-day educational efforts.

Conflicting Educational Opinions Can Be Reconciled When the Scientific Attitude Is Adopted. When we adopt the view that children are raw material out of which we are trying to make civilized adults, all our dissatisfaction with rules and regulations on the one hand, and freedom and liberality on the other tends to disappear into nothingness. We are now concerned only with discovering the nature of the raw material with which we are working, and the right tools and processes to use, in making it into the finished product. It is highly important that we know the nature of children, just as an engineer, constructing a bridge, must know the nature of the steel and wood which he uses, and understand its ability to withstand stresses and strains, the wear and tear of wind and water, and changes in temperature. The bridge engineer does not attempt to do things with steel and wood which are incompatible with the nature of these materials, neither does he take the absurd attitude that the wood and steel must be left to themselves to make a bridge without interference by workmen. Our educational efforts must be based upon an understanding of the nature of children, but we must not be afraid to use whatever processes of manufacture are found to be desirable for the efficient making of adult men and women. If a given rule or regulation, such as a ban on student automobiles, or a scholastic requirement for intercollegiate athletics, or corporal punishment for children in the grade school, is found to be a useful tool, we must not hesitate to use it because of any philosophical or sentimental belief that children must be left to develop according to principles of self-activity. If we find that electives in the curriculum, that removal of restraints and regulations are efficient devices in a given situation, we must not hesitate to remove the restrictions in order to gain the desired results. Freedom and liberality on the one hand, and restraints and regulations on the other become merely processes of manufacture, which are to be used for transforming children, considered as raw material, into adult citizens as a finished product. We need not hesitate to use whatever method seems worth while.

A school system which contains rules and regulations together with opportunities for self-determination and self-expression does not represent a compromise if these devices are being wisely used to accomplish the making of good citizens. From this point of view educators and the public can be satisfied with school systems just to the extent that they are being intelligently and efficiently conducted. They will not judge school systems on the basis of any preconceived idea that there must be *restraint* or that there must be *freedom*, but will look upon these two things as being merely manufacturing processes which are to be used as needed.

The Scientific Attitude toward Education Is Not Yet Widely Adopted. There are few educators to-day who have advanced beyond a compromise between the two older views of the nature of childhood and of education. Many educators do not recognize the possibility of anything except a compromise, or the outright acceptance of one or the other of these two views. J. K. Hart, in his *Social Interpretation of Education* states that there is an old school and a new. He finds two presuppositions underlying the old school—"The first is that the child is a natural barbarian, or even a bit of an animal, and he must be humanized and civilized. . . . The second assumption is that 'education' is something already in existence; it is made up of patterns of behavior, and a certain content of culture; it is sacredly treasured in schools; and the individual, if he is to get it at all, must go to a school to get it." Hart believes that this program of the old school demands institutional tyrannies, against which children rebel, and which adults ridicule, in spite of the fact that most communities still go on paying for the support of schools of this type. The fundamental presuppositions underlying the new school are of a different kind. "The first of these is that children are young human beings and, if given adequate chance, will naturally develop into adult human beings in good time. The second assumption is that education is an affair of the specific individual; as a process it lies entirely within his experience, even within the mind of the specific child; it must never be imposed upon him from without."

It is clear that Hart is referring to the old disciplinary concept of education as the "old school," and to the concept worked out by Rousseau, Pestalozzi, Froebel, and their followers as the "new school." He entirely ignores the whole modern movement for the scientific study of childhood, and the attitude toward human nature and education which is an outgrowth of modern psychology and experimental education. Hart is not alone in his disregard of modern psychological and educational movements. His attitude is typical of the majority of educated adults in any community and even of many teachers and educators themselves. Nevertheless the scientific movement is becoming more and more important.

III. Summary

An important factor underlying the development of educational systems has been the current belief concerning the nature of childhood. Three different attitudes toward children have been held during the Christian era. Historically the first is the view that the child is a miniature adult who is essentially evil in his inner nature. The second view is that the child is a miniature adult who is essentially good in his inner nature. The third view is that the child is essentially different from adults in his physical and mental characteristics; he is distinguished from the young of other species of animals only by the fact that he can be made into a civilized adult by the application of proper environmental pressures.

The educational system which grew out of the first of these three views of the nature of childhood required the constant use of discipline and restraints, as essential parts of educational procedure. Religious, political, and industrial institutions came to dominate education. This domination was finally summed up in the statement of the ultimate aim of education as "social efficiency." This movement in education carries behind it the weight of opinion of the entire Christian era, and still dominates the thinking of the majority of educated adults in America.

The second view of the nature of childhood has culminated in the so-called progressive schools of the present day. It has led to the statement of the aim of education as the harmonious development of all the powers of the individual. The keynotes of this type of educational theory are tolerant understanding and creative self-expression. It is believed that personality develops from within; it cannot be imposed from without. Schools which are based upon this theory must contain a maximum of freedom and pupil initiative, and a minimum of control by the teacher.

The conflict between these two incompatible attitudes toward education has resulted in a widespread dissatisfaction with the educational systems of the present day. Those who hold to the first view of the nature of childhood are displeased with the necessity for introducing freedom and liberality into school work. Those who hold to the second view are dissatisfied because they find it impossible to dispense entirely with rules, regulations, and restraints. Educational systems to-day incline toward one or the other of these two viewpoints, but are in every case a compromise between them.

The third view of the nature of childhood, that the child is in every respect different from the adult, but that he is the raw material out of which a civilized adult can be made with proper treatment, has grown out of recent scientific developments in biology and psychology. Because of its newness, and because of the widespread ignorance of modern biology and psychology, this viewpoint has not yet produced any fundamental changes in educational systems. Its advocates believe that when it is widely applied the great dissatisfaction with education will disappear. Education will then no longer be a compromise between two conflicting opinions which require restraint on the one hand and freedom on the other. Restraint and freedom will then become merely two devices, which are to be used, with as much intelligence as possible, in fashioning men and women out of boys and girls regarded as raw materials. Dissatisfaction then will have no other basis than failure to discover and adopt the best techniques. Conflict of educational opinion will be based upon differences concerning the best educational devices, rather than upon more fundamental differences in educational theory. Conflict of opinion concerning devices can be settled by the use of scientific methods of investigation, while conflict in underlying educational theory can be settled only by a fundamental change in our whole approach to the problems of human life. The scientific movement in education represents such a new approach to the fundamental problems of human life. This scientific attitude toward human nature is in accord with the approach which has come to dominate our views of the natural world outside of man.

CHAPTER II

THE NATURE AND FUNCTION OF MODERN PSYCHOLOGY

I. THE MIND-BODY RELATIONSHIP IN MODERN PSYCHOLOGY

As a preliminary to understanding the different schools of psychology, it will be a good plan to examine their underlying philosophical assumptions, particularly with respect to the relation supposed to exist between mind and body.

Psycho-physical Parallelism Has Been Popular among Psychologists. According to this view, mind is supposed to be quite distinct from body. It is supposed to be of an entirely different kind of substance, in every respect the opposite of physical matter. It is supposed that every mental event is accompanied by a physical event. There is, however, no causal relation existing between the two. Mental events are supposed to have no influence whatever upon bodily activity. Bodily activity is never caused by mental activity, but is somehow always found present whenever mental activity occurs. On the other hand, bodily activity can never be the cause of mental activity. The two things have somehow existed together from the beginning, running along parallel, in such a fashion that whenever the thought of moving the hand occurs the hand somehow moves. This view of the mind-body relationship, as we shall see more in detail later, is typical of the view of psychology which we shall call structuralism. It is a view which is very widely held among the functionalists.

Interactionism Is the Common-sense Attitude. A second view of the relationship existing between mind and body, which maintains the same dualism, assumes the possibility of interaction between the two. Professor Mc-Dougall is the leader of this group of psychologists. He maintains that, however far neurologists and physiologists may go in explanation of the processes which occur in the body, there is, nevertheless, a mind or a soul in addition. This is a purely spiritual thing, utterly different in every respect from the body. It interacts with the body, being affected by it and likewise affecting it. That is, the thought of a bodily activity may be a real *cause* for the occurrence of the bodily activity, while bodily change, such as a movement of the arm or a pressure on the skin, may be the real cause for some mental activity. This view corresponds very closely to the views of animism, as held among primitive peoples. It is the view which is undoubtedly commonly accepted among the majority of people, both educated and uneducated, who have had no special training in philosophy or psychology.

Epiphenomenonalism Has Few Adherents. A third dualistic theory minimizes the importance of mind. Mind is held to be a by-product or an epiphenomenon. It occurs whenever neural activity takes place, but is thought to have no particular importance. It is to be compared to a noise produced by an engine while running. It is something which is necessarily present, which the untrained observer might be led to believe to be essential to the activity, but which is in reality a mere by-product of the more important and fundamental activities underlying it. This theory is not very widely held at the present time but has been replaced by the double-aspect hypothesis.

The Double-aspect Hypothesis Is a Popular Form of Monism. According to this hypothesis mind and body are not really different at all. They are one and the same thing, which may be seen in two different ways. This view may be illustrated by reference to the fable of the two blind men and the elephant,—the one, on touching the elephant's ear, exclaimed that the elephant was like a fan, and that it was broad and thin and flat; the other, on touching the elephant's leg, remarked that the elephant was like a tree, since it resembled in every way a tree's trunk. According to the double-aspect hypothesis we sometimes observe human activity in such a way that we are led to call it mental, while at other times we observe the very same activity in a different fashion and call it physical and physiological. One of the leading advocates of this view at the present time is Professor Warren.

The Double-language Hypothesis Is Growing in Favor. A second monistic view, very similar to the double-aspect hypothesis, is the double-language hypothesis,—mind and body are supposed to be identical. We have, however, during the course of human history developed two languages for talking about human activity. The one language makes use of such terms as "consciousness," "images," "sensations," and the like. When we talk in such terms we take the mental or the spiritual view of life. We have developed a second language in which we have such terms as "nerve," "muscle," "stimulus," and "response." The situation is exactly parallel to that of an American and a German who on meeting speak the one German words and the other English. They may find some difficulty in understanding one another until they have learned each other's language, although they may both be talking about the same objects which are present before them.

Materialism and Idealism Are Very Similar. The extreme monistic view is represented by materialism on the one hand and idealism on the other. Idealism is not represented by any important psychological system at the present time, and will not be considered here. Materialism, however, has many representatives among present-day psychologists. This theory has been popularized in recent times by the behaviorists and the objective psychologists. According to these psychologists there is only one kind of material and one kind of event in the world. This material is best thought of as being physical, and human activity is best thought of as being purely physical or physiological. The great evangelist of this view was John B. Watson, although many other psychologists at the present time are adherents of the materialistic view of human activity. The problem of the mind-body relationship is solved by discarding mind and retaining bodily activity. The word "mind," which is a part of our popular language, is supposed to refer to nothing more than bodily activity, particularly that part of bodily activity which appears in the form of language.

The Trend toward Materialism in Science. This tendency in modern psychology, to discard the view that there is a capricious, willful, incomprehensible, and non-material mind which directs human behavior, corresponds to a similar tendency which has reached its goal in the better developed sciences of physics and chemistry. Primitive peoples were vitalists in their view of the activity of all the physical objects in nature. They attributed consciousness to everything and assumed that it was the spirit, living within, which produced the activities observed in nature. Trees had spirits which caused them to grow; the wind was the manifestation of a spirit personality; storms were the activity of an angry god; and even the stones had souls. In addition to assuming that the objects in nature were controlled by spiritual forces living within them, primitive man assumed that these spirits were more or less capricious, willful, and unpredictable in their action.

With the development of scientific understanding of natural forces, the spirits were gradually driven out of sticks and stones. This elimination of spirits from physical objects is, however, comparatively recent. At the time of Galileo, nature was still thought of as having a distinct personality. The expression that nature had a "horror of a vacuum" was not figurative in the sense that it is for us to-day, but was taken as showing the real nature of a spiritual personality. While the development of science in the eighteenth and nineteenth centuries effectively banished spirits from physical nature, especially as the capricious causes of natural phenomena, physical science *has never proved* that such spirits do not exist. If a person wishes to maintain that there is a spirit in a bar of iron, which causes that physical substance to act in the way it does, there is seemingly no way to disprove his belief. Instead of concerning themselves with disproving the existence of spiritual forces in nature, physicists and chemists, astronomers and meteorologists have gone about their business of explaining the occurrence of natural events in which they are interested, with simply *no reference* to the existence of animistic forces. They have found that they can satisfactorily explain the movement of the planets, the occurrence of a thunderstorm, the falling of a physical body, and the occurrence of chemical changes in terms of natural law, without including, as a part of their explanation, the existence of an in-dwelling, non-material spirit.

During the past two centuries there has been a similar

development in biological science, which has, however, not been quite so complete and convincing. The discovery of the circulation of the blood, increased knowledge of anatomy and physiology, the formulation of the theory of organic evolution, and other biological discoveries have gone far toward banishing spirits as the causes of animal activity and establishing the reign of natural law. The work of Pasteur, and the formulation of the germ theory of disease, have practically banished evil spirits as the cause of disease. Nevertheless, it is still commonly believed that many forms of insanity are the perverted activity of an inner soul or non-material mind. Driving the spirits out of animals and men has been a difficult task. Some biologists are still vitalists in the sense that they believe it necessary to assume the existence of some guiding force or entelechy of a non-material nature which controls and directs the natural growth processes of an animal, and which has controlled and directed the course of animal evolution. Such vitalists are, however, in the minority. Most biologists look upon the course of racial and individual development as occurring in a purely mechanical way, according to the working of natural laws.

Materialism Underlies Objective or Behavioristic Psychology. It seems that psychology is now in a stage of development through which other sciences have passed. Whether the outcome will be the same as in the physical and chemical sciences is still an open question. Many psychologists believe that this will be true. The school of psychologists, who have adopted this point of view, are commonly called behaviorists or objective psychologists. They believe that human activity can be completely explained in physical and chemical terms. A soul, consciousness, or mind, if it is to be regarded as anything more than a special form of intra-organic stimulation as yet poorly understood, is ignored. *No attempt is made to disprove the existence of such a non-material entity.* It is realized that such proof is impossible.

The mere fact that we have many words in our language which assume the existence of such non-material forces, makes the education of the public to this point of view much more difficult, but does not in any way prove the existence of such non-material forces. There are many examples in the development of human thought of the discarding of beliefs in such forces, even though the words themselves have been retained. The word "ghost" is still in common usage. It is only a few years since the existence of ghosts was widely accepted. Many people were thoroughly convinced that they had seen ghosts, just as to-day many people are thoroughly convinced that they have evidence of the existence of a non-material mind or consciousness. Objective psychologists believe that the word "mind" is the same type of word as "ghost." It refers to a non-material being which has no existence or at least no importance as an explanatory factor in human actions. The objective psychologists believe that the words "mind," "conscious," "idea," "image," "sensation," and the like may continue to be used in literary and poetical expressions, just as the word "ghost" has persisted in such places, but that they have outlived their usefulness as scientific terms.

II. The Place of Psychology among the Sciences

The Field of Psychology Is Not Clearly Defined. There are almost as many definitions of psychology as there are psychologists. It is hardly worth while to quote these definitions or to try to reach any reconciliation of them. The only result of such an attempt would be the addition of one more to the number of definitions. When we attempt to arrive at any statement of the function of psychology as a science in modern life, we find much confusion of opinion, although many demands are made upon psychology by people in many different lines of work. There is more or less general agreement that psychological science is basic to the understanding of the social sciences, such as politics, economics, sociology, education, and history. It is also agreed that psychology is closely related to the biological sciences, especially to physiology and neurology. There is a growing opinion among the pessimistically inclined that psychology, as a science, is in process of dissolution, that it will eventually disappear by being absorbed into the social sciences on the one hand and into the biological sciences on the other.

When we examine modern science as a whole, we find that the lines between sciences, even in the older established sciences of physics and chemistry, are beginning to break down. Modern scientists are interested in working out special problems, rather than in advancing the interests of a special science. When a scientist attempts to find the solution to a problem which requires experimentation of both physical and chemical nature, he does not hesitate to carry on physical research, which seems to be basic to his problem, merely because he is a chemist. Likewise a man who is primarily a sociologist does not hesitate to carry on psychological research when such research has a bearing upon the special problems in which he is interested. He will frequently find it necessary to conduct such psychological research as a part of his efforts in studying social problems, because psychology as a science is not yet well developed. Psychologists, too, in investigating the problems in which they are especially interested, frequently find serious gaps in knowledge of physiology and neurology, so that they are forced to investigate problems which properly belong in the field of these two sciences.

Psychologists Are Interested in Social Behavior of Individuals. In spite of the fact that others than psychologists are making investigations in the field of psychology, and that psychologists are making investigations in biological sciences other than their own, there seems to be a definite type of problem in which psychologists as a whole are interested. This type of problem is concerned with the behavior of human beings which has more than a purely personal value or importance. The physiologist may investigate such activities as digestion, circulation, and breathing, which are important particularly to each person as an individual. Psychologists, on the other hand, investigate such activities as talking, playing, and sense perception, which are of importance, not merely to individuals, but to other members of the social group in which an individual lives. The kind of behavior, then, in which psychologists are primarily interested seems to be behavior which has social value. Sociologists, on the other hand, are interested in the social behavior of human beings which arises particularly out of group life. They are interested in the development of institutions, group customs, and the like, and are only secondarily interested in the members of the group as individuals. This study of the members of a group as individuals is the peculiar field of psychology.

The interest of physiologists, psychologists, and sociologists in the processes of food-getting will illustrate the difference in their approach to the problems of human action. The physiologist is interested in those phases of food-getting which are concerned primarily with the well-being of the particular individual. He is concerned with studying the peristaltic activity of the intestines, the secretion of the digestive juices, the absorption of food into the blood and its utilization by muscles and other bodily organs. These processes furnish the background for the individual's behavior in social situations, but are studied in every case as purely individual functions with no relation to the individual's place as a member of a social organization. The psychologist is interested in those food habits which require the use of the individual's body in such a fashion that he comes into contact with his environment and becomes an object of interest to other people. The psychologist studies the course of development of feeding habits, such as getting food to the mouth by the use of the hands, the use of the eyes, nose, and other sense organs in the discovery of food. These are activities which are always studied as a part of the behavior equipment of a particular person; they are, however, items of behavior which are not purely personal, since they bring the individual into contact with other people. The development of these habits, likewise, is commonly the outgrowth of training, which is dependent upon the existence of parents, teachers, and others who are interested in the individual's welfare. The sociologist is interested, not so much in these personal habits, as in the social organization which grows out of them. He is interested in the type of social, industrial, and political institutions which are dependent upon food habits for their existence.

III. Determinism in Psychology and in Every-day Life

The Principle of Scientific Determinism Is Generally Accepted by Psychologists. In spite of the fact that there are several rather well-defined viewpoints in modern psychology, there are certain general principles which are common to psychology as a whole. Every type of modern psychology adopts the scientific viewpoint of human life, which consists essentially of the conviction that human activity is in accordance with natural law. Even though a psychological system may assume the existence of mind as a non-material agency which is useful in adapting man to his environment, no psychological system of importance, with a single exception, is willing to grant to mind any power which is independent of natural law. The single exception is the psychological system developed by the Catholic Church, which makes special allowance for a theological concept of freedom of the will demanded by the Church. All modern psychology assumes that one human being affects another only by means of physical stimuli which are applied to sense organs. The physical activity of human beings can be explained by the natural growth processes and the natural changes which take place in the individual's body, especially in his nervous system in response to external stimulation. Some psychological systems assume an interaction between mind and body in such a fashion that a mental event may influence the course of physical activity. When it happens, however, that an idea or a thought influences physical activity, it is assumed that this influence occurs in accordance with natural law and that the idea or thought did not arise in a purely spontaneous fashion. Nowhere within a human being, either in his physical body or in his "mind," is there anything of the nature of an independent occurrence of a mental or physical activity which has no cause. There is nothing in the nature of a "self-starter" within our physical structure or within our mind.

Behaviorism Is Not the Only Deterministic Psychology. Many people have misunderstood modern psychology and have attributed this view, that no human activity occurs without a sufficient cause in the way of preceding activity or external physical stimulation, to that particular movement in psychology which is called "behaviorism." It should be pointed out that this view is not peculiar to behaviorism but is common to all modern systems of psychology. According to all the modern psychological systems, behavior could be predicted if we had sufficient knowledge of the stimulating conditions and of the nature of the person concerned. This predictability, which is the outgrowth of conformity with natural law, is not, however, incompatible with freedom of a certain kind. Whatever acts a person performs depend upon the internal nature of the person, as well as upon the external situation which is present at the time. Freedom may be taken to mean merely this dependence of activity upon our own internal nature. If freedom is defined in this way, then conformity to natural law does not mean lack of freedom; it means rather lack of capriciousness, willfulness, or irresponsibility, it means the presence of constancy, responsibility, and dependability in human nature.

Determinism Is Commonly Assumed in Child Training. It would be a very disastrous thing for modern life if human behavior were not highly predictable. When a mother trains her child to tell the truth, she proceeds on the assumption that, after a certain amount of training, the child will no longer be free to tell the truth or to lie whenever an opportunity arises. She assumes, rather, that the result of her training will be the production of such an effect in the child's nature that it will no longer be free to lie, but can respond only by telling the truth. When in school we teach a child that four plus three is seven, and give it repeated opportunity to practice making this combination of numbers, we do so on the theory that after a certain amount of practice the child will no longer be free to obtain any other result from the addition of four and three than the one desirable result of seven. If in spite of all the training of the mother concerned with truth-telling, or the training of the teacher concerned with the addition of numbers, the child is still free to do as it pleases, home training and formal education have no meaning or value.

Determinism Is the Basis for Many Business Relations. The whole of modern business is regulated upon the assumption that human beings are consistent. The extension of credit to a man by a bank is based upon the assumption that a man will continue in his business dealings to act in the future as he has in the past. It is assumed that, if the man has been financially successful in the past, he will continue to be successful in the future; that, if he has shown good judgment in the past, he will continue to show such good judgment in the future; that, if he has been honest in the past, he will continue to be honest in the future. It is just this fact, that human actions can be rather definitely predicted, which makes all modern business, social, and political life possible. That we sometimes fail in predicting the behavior of our business associates and friends is due, not to the fact that they are free at any moment to do "anything they please," but to the fact that we do not have a sufficient knowledge of their inner nature and of the external situations which influence their actions. If we had a complete understanding of the internal nature of our friend and business associate, if he were thoroughly familiar with the situation in which he finds himself, if we ourselves had gained a sufficient understanding of the natural laws which govern human action, we could predict his behavior with a high degree of certainty. It is clear that the belief that the principle of causation is at work in human actions is an integral part of our every-day life.

A large part of business is concerned with the directing of human activity and the securing of certain types of conduct in business associates. Such problems as the selection and training of employees, advertising and selling, vocational guidance, and human relations in industry may be approached from the scientific, or from the popular point of view. Business men have been solving such problems for centuries without the aid of psychology. They have been reasonably successful, just as means of transportation were successfully used without the natural science view of mechanics, and just as teachers developed considerable skill without the aid of a scientific knowledge of human nature. The psychological approach to business and industrial problems represents merely a means for increasing accuracy and efficiency in meeting the human problems. It is new, and requires a technical language with which the average educated adult is not familiar, while the popular and teleological point of view is familiar to all, and is an inseparable part of our ordinary language. The most immediately practical procedure, in making use of the scientific approach to the human factors in the business and industrial world, would seem to be the employment of specialists to apply scientific methods. The general adoption of the attitude of modern psychology must wait upon a widespread education along scientific lines.

Education in Psychology Should Begin in the Elementary Schools. Up to the present we have believed that education in psychology must wait until students have reached college age. It is very common, in colleges, to find that freshmen are not considered sufficiently mature to master the mysteries of psychology. In some universities the study of human behavior is delayed until the junior or senior year. Because of this fact, that the attempt to understand human nature in a scientific way is delayed until such a late period in education, only a few people come into any close contact with the scientific explanation of human actions. We can expect the population at large to gain the scientific attitude toward human nature only when the fundamental principles of psychology are included in the scientific curriculum of elementary schools and high schools. There is apparently no reason why such information cannot be included in these early years along with scientific information concerning geography, astronomy, physics, biology, and other sciences.

From the Psychological Standpoint the Treatment of Criminals Is an Educational Problem. In the treatment of criminals, the application of the psychological point of view is beginning to produce some effect. Punishment was formerly regarded as the securing of vengeance against the offender and as a warning to others. It is doubtful whether we can justify, from the standpoint of ethics, punishment of an individual for the sake of the effect of the punishment upon other people. If we center our thinking about the effect of punishment upon the person who has committed an offense, we may turn our thinking in either of two directions. We may believe that he has committed a crime because he "wanted to," that is, we may believe that he has a non-material mind, which is free to choose either the good or the bad thing, but that in this particular instance it has chosen wrongly. When we proceed to imprison him, and make his body uncomfortable for the sake of reforming his mind or soul, we are guilty of absurdity, for we have supposed that his mind is free either to commit a crime or to refrain, regardless of what happens to his body. Punishment, then, degenerates into needless torture, or the securing of revenge. From such a viewpoint, the more cruel and inhuman the punishment, the better it attains its purpose. Much of the opposition to prison reform of the present day is based upon such a view. This attitude seems to be inherent in the popular and teleological conception of human activity. If, on the other hand, we regard criminal activity as the result of physical causes, existing within the nervous and other bodily structure of the criminal and in his environment, we have only to discover the proper physical remedies and apply them, to bring about a reformation of the criminal. Punishment, from this point of view, consists of reëducation, that is, the breaking of bad habits, and the replacing of these bad habits with habits which are socially useful. In the United States we are attempting to apply this point of view in many of our prisons.

Much of the dissatisfaction with the management of our prisons and much of the failure in prison administration is due to the fact that this point of view has been only partially understood and applied. The application of this point of view requires that the wardens, keepers, and others concerned with the conduct of penal institutions shall be trained primarily as teachers, who have the direction of a highly specialized kind of education. There should exist, in connection with our universities, departments concerned with the training of teachers for the reëducation of criminals.

The Transition from the Popular to the Scientific Attitude Causes Temporary Confusion. Although we have made half-hearted attempts to apply the psychological attitude to the treatment of convicted people, we have only just begun to incorporate this attitude into criminal law. The legislators who are responsible for the passing of laws are, for the most part, wholly ignorant of the scientific approach to human action and continue to make use of the popular teleological point of view. They fashion criminal laws upon the theory that punishment is a form of revenge, or a means of warning prospective criminals. Laws permitting parole and indeterminate sentence are about the only indications of the application of a more scientific point of view on the part of legislators. The judges stand between the legislators, on the one hand, and the prison officials on the other. The judges are required to follow laws which have been framed from the older point of view. Although many of them as individuals recognize the value of the scientific attitude, they are limited in their application of this attitude to the use of parole, suspended sentences, indeterminate sentences, and the like.

The confusion in popular thinking, which can result when an attempt is made to understand human activity in terms of causation, can be understood by reference to the famous Loeb-Leopold murder case in Chicago. Here it was urged that the death penalty should not be inflicted, because the two murderers had been led to the commission of the crime by a sequence of events which made it impossible for them to do anything else. Just this same statement can be made concerning the activity of any criminal whatever when we adopt the natural science point of view concerning human actions.

When we adopt this point of view we are, however, not kept from punishing criminals, but are, on the other hand, given an indication of what the nature of punishment should be. Punishment should consist of a kind of reëducation, that is, of the introduction of new causal factors of such a character that the criminal will sooner or later become incapable of repeating the previous crime.

The introduction of these new causal factors can have this effect because we recognize that any particular crime occurs as a result of the interaction between the make-up of the criminal and the particular environmental circumstances to which he has been subjected. The make-up of an individual can be changed by a process of reëducation, so that, in the future, the same environmental circumstances will not lead to the crime, but to some socially acceptable action. For example, a man who is in need of money may solve his problem by robbing a bank. The course of punishment will then be concerned with the making of such changes in this man that, at a future time, when he needs money, he will find some acceptable means for securing it, such as engaging in some useful occupation. Our attitude toward criminals should be very much that which we take toward a broken-down automobile. We do not take revenge on the automobile by locking it up in storage for a period of months, but we take it to a garage, where an expert mechanic repairs it. When the mechanic assures us that it is once more in condition for use, we take it out. We should likewise send a criminal to an institution which has as its special job the task of making him over. He should remain there until the people in charge of the institution can assure us that he is once more capable of returning to normal life and activity. It is true that, in human affairs, it is usually difficult to determine when this process of reeducation has been completed, but this practical difficulty should not stand in the way of an attempt to follow out the proper line of action.

One of the important reasons for disorders in prisons, and general inefficiency in the administration of criminal law in the United States at the present time is probably the conflict between these two points of view. We are making a transition from the older teleological viewpoint to the more recent scientific attitude. While making this transition we get into many difficulties, which are not experienced in such a country as England, where the transition has scarcely begun. When the transition has been completed, however, we can expect a much better social result than that which existed under the older viewpoint.

Politics from the Standpoint of the Psychologists. In politics the teleological conception of human life is still almost unchallenged. The monarchical system assumes that each individual is directed by a soul, which is, however, inferior to the specially endowed soul of the monarch. This conception makes for intolerance in politics. Democratic institutions assume that each individual has a soul which directs his activities, but this soul is as good as every other soul. Extended to its logical conclusion, this view leads to anarchy or communism, for each individual must be either absolutely free and independent or a system must be created in which all are exactly equal. From the scientific point of view, each individual has a certain physical body which, coming into contact with relatively standardized living conditions, leads him to act very much like other individuals. If the extremes are eliminated (defectives and geniuses), this similarity is great enough to permit individuals to live together in a democratic society, especially when all receive a certain common training. The unusual individuals may also take their place in society, if they receive special training to fit them for some specialized activity. This view of human life emphasizes the necessity for universal education as a training for citizenship and the necessity for individualized instruction as the method by which good citizens can be created.

Psychology in Religion. At first thought it would seem that in religion the psychological point of view has no place. Religion deals with the welfare of the soul, an entity which is unknown to science. Religion is, nevertheless, interested in training the individual in certain forms of bodily activity, such as moral acts, ceremonials, and knowledge of religious history. These are educational problems and the psychological point of view has the same value that it has in all education.

IV. SUMMARY

When we examine the philosophical assumptions which underlie modern psychology, we find two alternative points of view. Some systems assume a dualism of mind and body. Mind and body are two very different kinds of substances which may exist in a kind of parallelism, each having no influence upon the other, or they may be assumed to interact, each sometimes causing changes in the other. During recent years the general tendency has been to discard this dualism in favor of some form of monism. The important types of monism are: (1) the double-aspect hypothesis, which assumes that mind and body are merely different ways of looking at the same substance; (2) the double-language hypothesis, which assumes that we have developed two languages, one a mental language, the other a physical or physiological language, both referring to the same substance; (3) idealism, which assumes that mind is the only reality; (4) materialism which assumes that matter is the only reality. With the development of behaviorism in psychology, there has been a strong trend toward materialism as a pure form of monism.

Psychology seems to be concerned with the careful and systematic study of human actions which have more than a purely individual importance.

In studying human actions, psychologists have arrived at the conclusion that the law of cause and effect is operative in the same fashion in which it is found in the natural sciences. They have concluded that there is a kind of determinism in human affairs. Whatever we do is supposed to be the immediate result of the interaction between our physical make-up (in the case of materialists) or of our psycho-physical make-up (in the case of dualists) and the environmental conditions of the moment. The application of this point of view to the problems of education, business, law, politics, and religion is well under way. In many cases it has created a temporary confusion, which can be overcome only when the new point of view is fully understood and accepted. The acceptance of this point of view must be delayed until the fundamental principles of psychology have found their way into the course of study of elementary schools and high schools as well as the colleges and universities, to which psychology as a science is now confined.

CHAPTER III

SURVEY OF THE MODERN PSYCHOLOGIES

I. Introduction

Schools of Psychology Are Not Sharply Defined. There are several more or less well defined points of view in modern psychology. The assigning of names and the classification into schools is certain to do some violence to the facts, but some classification is desirable in the interests of economy in thinking. Frequently a man who is classified as belonging to one school might with good reason be also assigned to another.

From the multiplicity of points of view, six are chosen as being most important. Three of these—Structuralism, Functionalism, and Behaviorism (or Objective Psychology)—have a close historical and theoretical relationship. They have dominated the thinking of psychologists in America during the twentieth century. They are characterized by their attempt to understand human (and animal) mind and behavior by the processes of analysis and classification which are common to all the natural sciences. They tend to become mechanistic in their explanations. A fourth school—purposive psychology—has fewer adherents among psychologists but has much appeal to the common sense of the average educated adult. It is based upon an opposition to the materialistic and mechanistic tendencies in the first three named schools. Psycho-analysis is an importation from Europe. It has grown out of the study of nervous and mental disorders and is popular among psychiatrists and social workers.

The most recent psychological system is the Gestalt psychology, introduced from Germany during the last decade. It is characterized by an opposition to the analytical procedures of the other psychological schools.

II. STRUCTURAL, FUNCTIONAL, AND BEHAVIORISTIC (OBJECTIVE) PSYCHOLOGIES

The Origins of the Functional and Objective Psychologies. Psychologists at the beginning of this century were interested mainly in analyzing and classifying so-called states of consciousness. This group of psychologists, headed in America by E. B. Titchener, are commonly called *Structuralists*, and this school of psychology is called *Structuralism*. Other leading representatives of this school are M. I. Bentley and W. B. Pillsbury in America, and H. Ebbinghaus, O. Kulpe, and Narciss Ach in Europe. Early in this century there developed in America a feeling that this type of psychology was rather barren of both theoretical and practical value. There began to be an interest in mind as a factor in adaptation to environment, leading to the view that mind consisted of certain functions rather than of structures in a static sense. Among the founders of this movement were Angell, Judd, Dewey, Ladd, and J. M. Baldwin. The movement was given the name of *Functionalism*. For several years there was a lively controversy between the representatives of this school and the older *Structuralism*. Most of the psychologists to-day may be properly classified as Functionalists. Beginning in 1911, with the publication of Max F. Meyer's book, *The Fundamental Laws of Human Behavior*, and in 1914 with J. B. Watson's, *Behavior, An Introduction to Comparative Psychology*, the new school of *Behaviorism* came into existence. It can be thought of as the logical, though extreme,

continuation of the movement which created functionalism. The evangelist of this school has been Watson.
Much damage has been done to the furtherance of the
principles involved by the strong emotional attitude
adopted by many of its adherents and critics, while the
linking of the scientific movement with radical social
movements and with atheism has given it a bad reputa-
tion in many circles. The school is characterized by its
rejection of the older psychological concepts of consciousness and mind and its attempt to explain human life in
terms of behavior in a purely physical and chemical sense.

*Difference in Subject Matter and Method of Structural,
Functional, and Behavioristic Psychology.* When we contrast these three schools of psychology with respect to
the subject matter of the science, we find mainly a difference in emphasis with respect to the three fundamental
divisions of sensory processes, central processes, and motor
activity. These three divisions, which are fundamental
to the older psychology, represent three avenues of approach to the study of human action, and are based upon
three divisions of human anatomy. Human behavior
may be studied primarily with reference to the stimulating conditions. Approached from this point of view, *sense
organs* are all-important in determining action. This is
the point of view of structural psychology. The approach
to human action may be made from the standpoint of
central processes, that is, of mind itself, when we accept
the existence of such an entity. From the anatomical
point of view this approach is made through the study of
the *nervous system*, especially the central nervous system.
This approach, from the standpoint of central processes, is
essentially the attitude of the functional psychology. In
the third place, the subject matter of psychology may be
approached from the standpoint of *muscular and glandular*

activity. Behaviorists have asserted that this is the only proper procedure.

The structural psychology, which analyzes mind into sensory, imaginal, and feeling elements, and is not directly interested in action, finds the only acceptable psychological method to be *introspection*. The mind must look within itself to discover the mental elements, all of which are conditioned by the stimulation of sense organs, in the past or in the immediate present. Functionalism, which centers its interest on mind, likewise finds introspection to be the primary psychological method. Mind is, however, not an end in itself, but is an interesting object for investigation only because of its value as a factor in adaptation. This interest in adaptation makes a direct study of action desirable and necessary. Objective observation of behavior, therefore, has a legitimate place as a psychological method, although it remains secondary to introspection.

The behaviorists take *action* as their center of interest. They assert that the only means by which psychologists can understand the facts of sensory stimulation and the functioning of the central nervous system is through an observation of the resulting behavior. The whole process of stimulation of sense organs, activity of the nervous system, and muscular or glandular response can be studied only by the usually accepted procedures of the natural sciences. Since "mind" does not exist, introspection is ruled out. Verbal activity does exist as an important form of behavior, but the study of the facts of verbal behavior must not be confused with introspection, which the structural and functional psychologists believe to be the effort of mind to look within and study itself. When the chief reliance is placed upon introspection, the psychologist is forced to study mainly himself; when the objective method is used, the psychologist may study other people. The behaviorists have a profound distrust of self-study as a scientific procedure, although it is theoretically possible. Self-study, when used, is made as objective as the study of other people, and every effort is made to avoid the dangers of personal bias and prejudice in determining the results of the experiment.

The Subject Matter of Structural Psychology. Structuralism divides the field of psychology into three main divisions,—knowing, feeling, and willing. The primary task of psychologists is to take a complex mental state as it is found to exist in consciousness, analyze it into its elements, and discover how these elements are combined to make the complex state. Knowing, for example, refers to occurrence of such mental states as ideas and perceptions. The task of the psychologist is to analyze these ideas and perceptions into their elements. The structural psychologist invariably finds that the primary elements of ideas and percepts are images and sensations. The images are merely reinstatements of previous sensations, while the sensations are the most elementary forms of consciousness, which exist as the accompaniment of sensory stimulation. There is some controversy among structuralists concerning the presence or absence of a "thought" element, and concerning the number and kind of attributes of sensation. But there is no disagreement concerning the objectives of the science, which is taken to be the analysis of the more complex mental states into their elements and the discovery of the laws governing the combination of these elements into the complex states. The laws governing the combination of mental states are the laws of association (contiguity, similarity, and contrast), which, in their essentials, were formulated by Aristotle. With respect to feeling, the task of the structuralist is of a similar nature. He is concerned with discovering what are the elementary affects or feelings. Here again there is some disagreement. Many psychologists discover only two such elementary feelings,—pleasantness and unpleasantness; others find six,—agreeable and disagreeable, exciting and subduing, straining and relaxing. The structuralists are interested in the action side of mind only for the purpose of discovering what mental elements go to make it up. In their analysis of *willing*, they discover mainly kinesthetic sensations. In textbooks which have been written from the structural point of view, we find most space devoted to a discussion of the *cognitive* side of mind, that is, sensation, imagination, attention, perception, association, and the like. A small amount of space is devoted to feeling and willing. Primarily structuralists are interested in sensation and feeling, that is, in the stimulating conditions.

The Subject Matter of Functional Psychology. Functionalism takes as its starting point the principle that mind exists as a means of adaptation to environment. Man's adaptation to his environment is accomplished through the mediation of certain mental functions, one of which is sensation, and another feeling. There are, however, many other mental functions, such as attention, memory, learning, thinking, and perception. Some of these mental functions are more elementary than the others. The functional psychologist agrees with the structuralist in finding sensations, images, and feelings as the elementary mental processes. For the functional psychologist, however, these elementary mental processes are conceived as dynamic things, and are not static in the sense in which they are thought of by the structuralists. They are, for the functionalists, activities, whereas, for the structuralist, they are merely parts of a larger structure. These mental functions are conceived as ways of acting of the whole mind, and the certain result of any mental function is supposed to be bodily activity, that is, motor behavior, which is the external phase of adaptation. The mind, as a factor in adaptation, parallels or determines the central nervous processes, which come between stimulation and response.

On account of their dominating interest in the problems of adaptation to environment, the functionalists are deeply interested in *instinct*. They think of instinct as the original behavior equipment that man possesses to aid him in the work of adaptation. Their textbooks include lengthy discussions of instinct, which are not found in the earlier structural texts.

The Subject Matter of Behaviorism. In comparing functionalism with structuralism we find primarily a shift in emphasis from interest in sensory processes, that is, stimulating conditions, to interest in central processes, that is, the neurological conditions of behavior. In behaviorism we find a further shift in interest away from stimulating conditions and central processes to motor activity. Physical behavior is the thing of primary interest, and it is the belief of the behaviorists that it is the only thing about human beings which can be studied directly by psychologists. By observing human actions under various stimulating conditions, inferences concerning sensory activity or neurological events may be drawn. This information concerning sensory activity or nerve functioning is, however, merely a series of inferences which are drawn from the systematic observation of behavior.

Textbooks written by the behaviorists condense somewhat the elaborate discussion of sensory processes found in the structural and functional texts. Their discussion is presented in terms of stimulating conditions rather than in terms of mental elements. For the structuralist and functionalist sensations are mental elements; for the behaviorist, the sensory problems are concerned with the discovery of the differences in stimulation which will produce a differential response. For example, in the investigation of color vision, the behaviorist wishes to discover the wave lengths of light to which the individual can respond, the differences in wave length that will produce a differential response, and the character of the sense organs and nerves which make this difference in response possible.

Behaviorism at first accepted in its entirety the principles of instinctive and learned behavior as formulated by the functionalists, with the exception that the "mental" explanation was eliminated. In consequence of their interest in action they began to study instinctive behavior under controlled conditions and soon found it necessary profoundly to modify their views. Instincts were gradually discarded as explanatory principles; the importance of learned reactions was correspondingly increased, and new theories of learning began to appear.

The insistence that behavior should be explained in physiological and mechanical terms made necessary a familiarity on the part of the student with the more important facts of physiology and anatomy. The behavioristic texts began to include lengthy discussions of the physiology and anatomy of sense organs, nervous system, muscle, and glands. These discussions seemed necessary since students in psychology were ordinarily ignorant of such matters. More recently the tendency is to shorten such discussions and expect the student to get this information elsewhere before beginning his study of psychology.

Interest in the Application of Psychology Has Been a Cause for the Change in Psychological Theory. Structuralism, being concerned primarily with the analysis and classification of mental states, did not lend itself readily to practical applications in the conduct of human affairs. In America we feel that any science can justify itself only when it influences the every-day affairs of living. Psychologists such as Titchener believe that it will prove impossible to apply any psychological principles in a practical way for perhaps a century. Psychologists must concern themselves, for many years to come, with a careful analysis and classification of mental states, leaving to the distant future any attempt to use this material in a practical way. Early in the twentieth century, there grew up a mass of psychological data concerned with child study and the work of education in general. This psychological information did have practical value. There began to be increasing interest in the possibility of applying to practical affairs, especially to education, the discoveries of psychological investigations. The first result was the development of functional psychology; behaviorism is a later outgrowth of this attempt to be practical.

Developments in Psychology Are Similar to Developments in Biological Science. At the same time that this interest in the practical value of psychology was beginning to appear, there was occurring a shift in interest in the other biological sciences. For many years, botanists and zoölogists had been concerned with the making of classifications; toward the end of the nineteenth century interest had shifted to a study of the factors which enabled an animal or a plant to exist in its environment. This interest resulted in a study of the functioning of plant and animal organs, rather than in a mere classification of these organs. Following the lead of these biological sciences, psychologists became more and more interested in the functioning of mental structures as a means of adapting man to his environment, and began to lose interest in a mere classification of these mental structures. This interest in the study of mind as a factor in adapting man to his environment had much to do with the origin of functionalism in psychology. Behaviorism is a further outgrowth of this attempt to study man's adaptation to his environment.

Interest in the Study of Animals and Children Was an Important Factor in the Development of Behaviorism. Some psychologists developed an interest in the study of animal behavior. In studying animals it was impossible to make any direct study of so-called conscious mental states; study was necessarily confined to observable actions of the animals. Likewise the development of child study, which began to occur rather vigorously at the beginning of the twentieth century, emphasized the importance of behavior. It was impossible to get a small child to introspect and give any reliable information concerning his conscious states. Those who were interested in child study were forced to confine their interest largely to an observation of motor and verbal behavior. This study of child and animal activity led to the development of an objective technique, which seemed to have much value in the study of the behavior of adults. Those who had developed this technique for studying behavior began to believe that they could completely explain human actions without the assumption of anything beyond a natural sequence of physical events. They believed the assumption of the existence of a non-material mind or consciousness to be unnecessary. They therefore began to assert that mind or consciousness does not exist, since it is not needed as an explanatory factor in human behavior.

Objective Psychology. The name "Behaviorism," applied to this attitude, became attached to particular theories of learning and to the personality of J. B. Watson. On account of these restrictive connections it is widely felt that a new descriptive title should be used. The expression "Objective Psychology" is coming into use. This attitude in psychology is not committed to any one theory for the explanation of psychological data; it is committed only to a *method of investigation*, the method that is common to all natural science, and which is usually called "objective."

III. PURPOSIVE PSYCHOLOGY

Purposive Psychology Opposes Materialism and Mechanism. This school of psychology is characterized by its opposition to the mechanistic explanations of mental and bodily activity which have been developed by the structural, functional, and behavioristic psychologies. It insists that there are important mental driving forces in human nature which are effective in controlling and directing human affairs. The purposive psychologists insist that "Instinct," interpreted as force, purely mental, is just as natural as the physical forces of gravitation, inertia, etc. The leaders in this school of thought are William McDougall, Morton Prince, C. J. Herrick, and J. S. Jennings.

Inborn Desires Are the Sources of Human Activity. McDougall states: "We may say, then, that directly or indirectly the instincts are the prime movers of all human activity; by the impulsive force of some instinct (or some habit derived from an instinct), every train of thought, however cold and passionless it may seem, is borne along toward its end, and every bodily activity is initiated or sustained. . . . Take away these instinctive dispositions with their powerful impulses, the organism would become incapable of activity of any kind; it would lie inert and motionless like a wonderful clockwork whose mainspring had been removed, or a steam engine whose fires had been drawn." K. S. Lashley, while he has not definitely expressed himself as a purposive psychologist, has abandoned the current mechanistic explanations of learning. The most complete statements of the purposive, or hormic psychology have been given by Morton Prince and William McDougall.

McDougall thinks that recognition of purposive activity is widespread among present-day psychologists; only the crude behaviorists now ignore it completely. By "purposive psychology" he means a psychology which recognizes the goal-seeking nature of human and animal action and accepts it as a problem to be understood. Scientists of every kind have tried to avoid teleological explanations of the facts with which they deal. According to McDougall, this objection to a teleological (that is, purposive) explanation of natural phenomena probably had its origin in the conflict of science with religion. Theologians believe that all natural events are an expression of the divine will and purpose of the Creator. Scientists attempt to explain natural events as the effects of natural causes without supposing the interference of any supernatural force. The naturalistic explanations offered by scientists have been in terms of the antecedent events that lead up to a given event which is being explained. This has not *always* been true of natural science.

Spiritual Driving Forces Have Disappeared from Natural Science. Early in the development of physics and chemistry it was assumed that there were purposes running through all natural occurrences. For example, the early scientific attitude was that "nature" had an abhorrence of a vacuum, and stood ready to seize any available material to fill up a vacuum when there was danger of one being created. The first success in creating an approach to a vacuum, therefore, aroused intense interest among scientists. When Galileo learned that a suction pump would not draw water beyond a certain height, he was led to believe that the strength of nature's "horror of a vacuum" could be measured. It was generally believed by scientists of his time that everything in nature "knew" its place and "tried" to keep it. This tendency to interpret natural events in terms of purposes, desires, and strivings has gradually disappeared until it is now entirely lacking from the physical and chemical sciences.

Spiritual Driving Forces Are Needed to Explain Human Behavior. With the development of the biological sciences and psychology there has been a tendency to follow the lead of the physical scientists and discard all reference to purposes as an explanation of the course of animal and human behavior. McDougall believes that this tendency is an undesirable one. He believes that to desire, to strive, and to attain our goal is as natural as "falling off a log." In his view human beings do foresee particular events as possibilities. They do desire to see these possibilities realized; they do take action in accordance with their desires; they do seem to guide the course of events in such a way that the foreseen and desired events result. This teleological explanation is different from the explanation of the theologians who explain an event as occurring as a result of Divine will or purpose. The former type of explanation McDougall believes to be a purely natural one, even though it is teleological, since he believes desires, strivings, etc., to be natural to human animals. The purposive psychologists believe that ideas, purposes, and the like have an important effect upon human behavior just as much as physical causes.

Those people who are especially interested in artistic appreciation and creation as found in music, painting, dancing, and the like, are especially insistent that purposes and ideals are important causal factors. Such people invariably talk in terms of ideals, ideas, sensations, and find it extremely difficult to adopt the language of objective psychology. McDougall thinks that those of us who are especially interested in the psychical should boldly make the claim that we have found the creative and unpredictable element in nature.

Goal-seeking Behavior Furnishes the Basis for Purposive Psychology. The essence of the purposive psychology is indicated up by the question, "Why does an animal or man seek this or that goal?" The hormic psychologist answers, that man seeks a goal because it is his nature to do so. Animals of a given species or human beings seek and strive for a limited number of goals as, for example, food, shelter, and mates. For us human beings the kind of goals which are sought are definitely determined by the fact that we are human. It is our nature to seek certain goals because we inherit the tendencies of the human species to seek these goals. We have inborn tendencies, not merely to *act* in a certain way, but to *guide* our actions in such a way that certain ends will be accomplished. Some psychologists, as the behaviorists, reduce the number of these purposes to three, and call them the primary emotions or the prepotent reflexes of sex, fear, and rage. Other psychologists talk of *urges, unconditioned reflexes, congenital drives, motor sets, inherited tendencies,* and the like. Formerly these drives were called instincts, but the word "instinct" has gone out of fashion.

McDougall lists the following essential facts which demand a purposive approach to the problems of human action: (A) that the energy manifestation is guided into channels such that the organism approaches its goal; (B) that this guidance is effected through a cognitive activity, an awareness, however vague, of the present situation and of the goal; (C) that the activity, once initiated and set on its path through cognitive activity, tends to continue until the goal is attained; (D) that when the goal is attained, the activity terminates; (E) that progress toward and attainments of the goal are pleasurable experiences, and thwarting and failure are painful or disagreeable experiences.

Only the "Inborn" Impulses Are a Source of Power. The hormic theory is believed adequate to explain all forms of animal and human activity; the inborn impulses are thought to be the only sources of motive power. Purposive psychologists do not agree with the psycho-analysts, such as Drever, Freud, and Adler, and the dynamic psychologists, Woodworth and Moore, (discussed in section IV) who think that in addition to the instinctive driving forces there are also acquired motives depending upon individual experience. They think that the tendency to avoid painful actions and to perform pleasurable actions (which has been taken as a law of learning by other psychologists—the law of effect) merely helps to determine the *form* of the activity which takes place, but is not concerned with determining the *goal* of the activity. For example, when we are seeking a definite goal, such as food, and encounter painful stimulation, we may be turned aside from the pursuit of the goal completely, or we may change the form of our activity so as to avoid the painful stimulus. The pain, however, does not set up a new goal unless it is extreme. In this case a fear reaction may follow, but the fear reaction is itself an inborn tendency to seek a certain goal. After we have learned from our past experience that a certain method for obtaining food is pleasurable, we may continue to obtain food in that manner; but the pleasure refers only to the form that the activity takes, and does not help to determine the goal itself, which arises from our inborn tendency to seek food.

Woodworth believes that every habit which we have formed is not merely a capacity to perform an action in a relatively efficient manner, but is also in itself a source of energy, a possible driving force for the performance of the action. For example, when we have acquired the capacity to swim, we have also acquired a desire to swim. When we have acquired the capacity to read German, we have also acquired the tendency to read German.

This belief of Woodworth in the driving power of habits should be connected with Morrison's idea of *adaptation* as the special work of the elementary school. Morrison believes that the main function of elementary education is to set up certain primary adaptations, the reading adaptation, the writing adaptation, the number adaptation, and the social adaptation. Morrison believes that we should not merely acquire the technique of writing but also the desire to write, that we should acquire not merely the technique of reading but the desire to read, not merely the technique of handling numbers but the desire to use numbers in certain situations, not merely the technique of social intercourse but the desire for social contacts. He seems to imply that the desire for using the reading, writing, number, and social habits must be formed as something *in addition to the skill itself.* In this sense he does not agree with Woodworth.

McDougall objects to this view of Woodworth that habits can also be driving forces, and believes that it is merely the modern form of the old intellectualistic belief that ideas are forces. For the purposive psychologists, habits and ideas are merely so much inert machinery which may be set into operation whenever the impulses are present. These habits and ideas may remain latent and unused for years; they are brought back into action whenever environmental circumstances awaken one of the instinctive driving forces.

The psycho-analytic concept of "complex" is in harmony with Woodworth's belief in the driving power of habits and ideas, but McDougall believes that complexes have driving power only when they are motivated by an inborn tendency.

Alleged Advantages of the Purposive Psychology. (1) It enables us to understand the processes of organic evolution and to understand the evolution of body forms and mental functions in their relationship to one another. We cannot think of bodily organs as originating in an accidental fashion and remaining useless until some similar variation in instinctive tendency made them valuable; the purposive theory insists that the evolution of instinctive tendencies has always been the primary or the leading feature of each evolutionary advance. The first step in the development of a new form or function was the acquisition of a new instinctive purpose or drive. Given such a new instinctive driving force, natural selection may have brought about the development in the species of the particular bodily forms and functions best suited to meet the demands of the new instinctive tendency. (2) The purposive psychology can furnish a psychological basis for philosophy, which is properly concerned with values and with standards and scales of value. Purposive psychology finds the relative values of different forms of human conduct in the inborn desires and cravings of human nature; a mechanistic psychology can recognize no values, since it is purely descriptive of events as they occur; the latter can at best predict the direction in which events are tending, but can give no reasons why certain end results are more or less desirable than other end results.

Goal-seeking Behavior Is Explained by the Mechanists as a Result of Learning. The purposive or hormic psychology considers the fundamental fact of human nature to be the tendency to work toward certain natural goals. Activity stops only when the natural goal is attained. All habits and ideas are merely the means and material which are used by the natural driving forces in their attempt to gain the goals which are natural to the human race. The purposive psychologists do not recognize the possibility that what they have called purposes, desires, instinctive tendencies, and the like can be themselves explained on the basis of the course of development and experience of the person concerned. We are accustomed to accept the desire for food as being a tendency whose development needs no explanation, and for which no explanation is possible aside from the description of the physiological processes. Because such explanation seems impossible, McDougall lists this desire as being inborn and natural. The mechanist (objective psychologist) agrees that it is natural in the sense that it is the *normal* outcome of the development of a human being. He doubts, however, that a new-born infant has any *desire* or *craving* for food. It seems to him much more valuable to describe the hunger reactions of the new-born infant in terms of the type of physiological stimulation which exists and the kind of responses made. These responses contain in themselves nothing at all suggestive of *food-seeking* behavior. The infant merely wiggles and twists and squirms and cries. The activity of the specific organs concerned with getting food (the lips and throat) seems to be no more determined by the hunger stimulation than the blinking of the eyes and the wiggling of the toes, the moving of the arms and legs, which also occur as a result of the hunger stimulation. There seems to be merely a mass of miscellaneous activity. Anything in the nature of the desire for food seems to be an *interpretation* of this activity, based upon our adult understanding of the physiological need of the child for nutrition. The origin of true food-seeking behavior in response to hunger stimulation seems to be entirely a matter of habit formation, based upon accidental environmental stimulation and definite training on the part of the child's parents. It is a fact, too well known to need elaboration, that many children are under-nourished and literally starving, due to the fact that they have not formed proper food-getting habits. They are in the position of being desperately hungry with an abundance of food before them, and yet ignorant of what to do to relieve their hunger. Selection of food as opposed to worthless or even harmful objects, preparation of food, use of various foods in proper proportions—all these and many other basic feeding activities are the outcome of definite learning. In the same way, the behaviorist explains the other tendencies which McDougall has called inborn, such as those concerned with fear, anger, and sex. They are seemingly nothing more than a miscellaneous restless activity which may be generally of a positive or negative type; that is, the child is restless and active in such a manner that he either approaches or avoids a source of stimulation. Anything beyond this restlessness coupled with an approach or avoidance seems entirely the result of the type of training which the child has undergone.

IV. Psycho-analysis

Psycho-analysis as a Psychological Theory Grew Out of the Treatment of Nervous and Mental Disorders. At the same time that the structural and functional psychologies were developing there was growing up a mass of psychological material concerned with the treatment of nervous disorders. This school, which may be called "psycho-analysis," originated with the publication of the first work of Sigmund Freud in 1895. Other important leaders of this school are C. G. Jung, Alfred Adler, Morton Prince, Pierre Janet, and J. C. Flügel. The distinguishing feature of psycho-analysis seems to be the assumption of conflicting psychical forces as an explanation of character and, in particular, as an explanation of undesirable character traits.

Disturbance of Sex Instinct Was Made the Basis for Freudian Theory. Freud, as a practicing physician in Vienna treating nervous and mental disorders, arrived at the conclusion that almost all mental abnormalities could be explained as due to interference with the sex instinct. It will be worth while to point out that Freud thinks of sex instinct in a much broader sense than the word "sex" is ordinarily used. He makes it equivalent almost to the total life force of an individual. Freud further claims that mental abnormalities usually can be traced back to some occurrence in early childhood. These two ideas of Freud, that mental abnormality is due to the interference with the sex impulse and that this interference occurs ordinarily as early as two to five years of age, came as a great shock to most people; and it was just this shock to preconceived ideas which led to the great amount of publicity and the great popularity that greeted the Freudian theory. It had been the tradition that sex interests must not be discussed and must be covered up in every possible way. It had also been widely accepted, for centuries, that sex life does not begin until at least ten or twelve years of age. The work of Freud upset both of these opinions at the same time, thereby creating a great stir, both of interest and disapproval.

Environmental Factors Cause Suppression of Sex Impulses. Sex interests are supposed by Freud to begin their development with the beginning of life. During the first few years of childhood many things may occur to interfere with a normal and orderly course of development. Suppressions will take place which will be likely to cause trouble when maturity is reached and normal sex functioning should begin.

One of the commonest sources of abnormality is the *Œdipus Complex*, which grows out of a conflict between the early sexual attachment of a boy for his mother and the social situation that opposes this attachment. During the first three or four years of his life, the boy comes into close physical and mental contact with the mother; she feeds, bathes, coddles, and cares for him and guides his mental and moral development. Growing out of this close contact he develops a distinctly sexual interest in her. By the time he is four or five years of age he discovers that the father is also an object of sexual interest for the mother. He is forced to recognize that his own sexual attachment must be given up or profoundly modified. The manner in which he makes this adjustment, whether by a mere suppression of his desires into the unconscious, or by a satisfactory redirection of his sex interests, is of great importance for his mental well-being. Normal development demands not a mere suppression of sex interest in the mother without really overcoming it, but requires also a redirection of such interest to other persons. Such a crisis is inevitable in the life of every boy. Failure to make a satisfactory adjustment is common and furnishes the basis for much mental abnormality in later life. The later abnormality may take a form which, superficially, bears no resemblance to its earlier cause. It may appear as sex perversion, but also as criminality, bad personality traits, insanity, or even apparently physical disorders such as indigestion, headaches, or chronic illness of any kind.

In a similar manner girls may fail to make satisfactory redirection of infantile sex interest in mother or father with similar bad results.

Freud seeks to explain all mental abnormalities—and indeed all normal mental functioning—as the working out of sex impulses. Personality, character, criminality, sex perversions, interest in religion, music, and art, all these are merely manifestations of the driving power of sex as it is guided now in one direction and now in another.

Adler Believes that "Desire for Power" Is the Most Important Instinctive Driving Force. Adler began as an orthodox follower of the Freudian theory but very quickly arrived at the conclusion that although mental abnormalities were due to a conflict between an individual's interests and the interests of society, this conflict was not based on an interference with the sex instinct, but was due rather to an interference with desire for power. Adler points out that, at the beginning of life, the infant is utterly helpless and dependent upon the people around him for the gratification of all of his wishes and desires. He can do nothing whatever for himself: he cannot move from place to place, he cannot talk or make himself understood in any easy way, he cannot even feed himself; and this condition of helplessness persists for a great many years. The infant gradually comes to realize his complete helplessness, and as a result of this feeling of inferiority he develops a desire for power. His great aim in life becomes that of gaining power over the people and objects surrounding him.

Organ Inferiority Intensifies the Desire for Power. This feeling of inferiority and desire for power becomes intensified if the infant suffers from any organic defect. If he is undersized or weak or crippled in any fashion, he soon discovers that he cannot compete on equal terms with other children of the same age, and he may come to the conclusion that his attempt to gain superiority over other people around him is almost certain to fail. In the case of the normal child who does not show any organic inferiority, many things may happen which will cause discouragement and will lead the child to give up his struggle for superiority as hopeless. When this state of affairs occurs, the child, instead of completely giving up his desire for power, begins to look about him for easy ways to gain control over other members of his family or other people with whom he comes in contact. The more intelligent the child is the more likely he is to find these easy ways out of his difficulty, once he begins to search for them. These easy means for gaining superiority over other individuals are almost invariably anti-social in their nature, and therefore, undesirable. Because of their anti-social and purely individualistic character, these devices which a child adopts inevitably bring him into conflict with social customs and conventions. It is just this conflict that, sooner or later, causes nervous and mental disorders.

Some Environmental Sources of Mental Conflict. Adler proceeds to point out the occasions which are most likely to lead a child into these purely individual and anti-social habits. One of the most common situations of this character may be cited here. The first child of the family, for the first year or two of his life, is the center of attraction. His parents do everything possible to make life easy for him, to please him, and to grant his every wish. For him the problem of gaining superiority over his surroundings does not exist in an acute form, because he has such superiority freely granted to him. However, about the time he is two years old, it frequently happens that there is a new arrival in the family. The new baby now becomes the center of the stage and the two-year-old child is somewhat neglected. He has been forced out of his position as the ruler of the family in favor of his young brother or sister. He feels very keenly this loss of authority and power, and begins looking about him for a means to regain his former position. It is possible, and in fact highly probable unless he receives wise treatment from his parents, that he will develop such habits as frequent crying, refusal to eat, and temper tantrums. These bad habits are developed by him simply because he discovers that if he refuses to eat he again becomes the center of interest for his parents, or if he cries excessively he again receives a great deal of attention. Having once discovered the, to him, valuable result of crying, of refusal to eat, or of other bad habits, he continues them for the sake of their satisfactory results.

Now if it happens that the new baby in the family is a girl, the situation becomes intensified as years pass. Alder states that it is a matter of common knowledge that girls develop both physically and mentally more rapidly than boys. By the time the older boy is five years old, he discovers that his younger sister is beginning to catch up to him in both her mental and physical development, and by the time he is ten, she has become practically his equal in every respect. His attempt to maintain his superiority over his younger sister is hopeless and he is led to seek still further individual and anti-social activities as means for gaining power over the people around him.

Let us consider for a moment the situation of the younger sister. At first she, too, is the center of the family's interest. But by the time she is two or three years old she learns that in many important respects her older brother receives favors which are denied her. He is stronger than she is, and because of his strength he is able to dominate over her. She begins to be told that she is a girl and that some things which her brother can do ought not to be done by her. She begins to feel that this older brother of hers is one person whose authority she will never be able to escape, whom she will never be able to dominate. She, too, begins to hunt about for an easy way of securing power over her older brother and the other people in the family. If she has an older sister instead of an older brother, the situation is equally bad. Her older sister is set to watch over her, she is given the discarded clothing of her older sister, and is made in every way to feel that her older sister is superior in importance to herself.

If there are three or more children in the family, Adler discovers that the problem is likewise complicated for each one of the children. The situation is very bad for the oldest in the family for the reasons we have just pointed out. The middle child in the family does not have the prestige of the oldest child and does not receive the babying and the petting of the youngest. The youngest in the family receives the cast-off clothing of the older children, is always under their care, and always feels their dominance and authority. We are forced to believe, after reading Adler's writings, that it is a very dangerous thing to be a child at all. The general conclusion, which can be drawn from Adler's work, is that all throughout childhood many situations are certain to occur which will lead a child to become discouraged and give up his attempt to gain superiority in useful and social ways, unless he receives very wise treatment on the part of his elders.

Jung Makes Preservation of Individuality the Important Driving Force. C. G. Jung, another pupil of Freud, soon came to the conclusion that sex instinct was not the most important driving-force which could cause conflict in an individual's life. He points out that all of the instinctive tendencies are important, particularly the group which are concerned with self-preservation, and he interprets self-preservation as meaning particularly the attempt to preserve one's individuality against the interference of other people. This struggle to preserve a certain amount of individual freedom becomes acute very early in life, so that Jung, too, finds mental abnormalities having their origin in the events of the first two to five years.

Points of Similarity and of Difference in the Ideas of Jung, Freud, and Adler. If we compare the ideas of these three, Freud, Jung, and Adler, we find them in agreement upon two important points. They think that the first five years of an individual's lifetime are extremely important for the development of character and personality. In the second place, they agree that abnormalities of character are due to a conflict between the interests of the individual and the interests of society. This conflict results in abnormalities and anti-social activities or habits. These anti-social habits are entirely satisfactory if regarded purely from the standpoint of the individual concerned, but they are not satisfactory when it is remembered that the individual must take his place as a member of organized society. The disagreement between Freud, Jung, and Adler is a disagreement upon one point alone—they disagree concerning the nature of the driving force which is responsible for the conflict. Freud considers it to be the sex impulse, Adler the desire for power, and Jung a variety of forces but especially the desire for preservation of individuality.

The Nature of the Subconscious Mind. The discussion of this school of psychologists would be very incomplete if we did not point out a further characteristic of their theory, namely, their ideas concerning the subconscious. The psycho-analyst is first of all a dualist in his theories of the relationship between mind and body. He adheres to that particular variety of dualism which we have called interactionism; that is, he considers that mind does have a very important influence upon bodily activity, and that bodily activity does have very important influences upon mental activity. His ideas of the nature of mind are, however, rather different from those of other psychologists. He considers that mind must be subdivided into two or more parts. He thinks that there is a conscious mind and a subconscious mind. Some psycho-analysts add other divisions, such as the co-conscious and the unconscious. For the psycho-analysts each of these subdivisions is a well-organized entity. The subconscious mind, for example, has an organization all its own. Many important mental processes are carried on by it. In fact, the great majority of our ordinary activities are brought about through the activity of the subconscious mind. The conscious mind is concerned only with those activities which involve rational choice between different alternatives, and every rational choice is likely to be influenced in an important way by the workings of the subconscious.

The assumption of a subconscious mind makes possible a complete mental determinism. The gaps in conscious mental life are supposed to be filled in with subconscious mental activity, so that the causal series is complete. A consistent psycho-physical parallelism becomes possible, the psychical series showing no gaps but only conscious and subconscious parts.

"Complexes" Grow Out of Suppressed Ideas. The origin of the various divisions of mind is supposed to occur about in this fashion. At the beginning of life all mental activity is conscious and it remains conscious until conflicts arise between the individual's interests and the interests of society. Just as soon as these conflicts begin to appear (and we have pointed out that they occur as early as the second year of a child's life), some mental activities, because of this conflict, are suppressed. They are forced out of the conscious mind into the subconscious. The subconscious is thus gradually built up of those ideas which are found unfit for the conscious mind. By "unfit for the conscious mind" we mean that they run contrary to the demands of people around us. They are ideas which get us into difficulties and, because they get us into difficulties, we attempt to suppress them. Long before we have reached adult life we have, then, a large body of suppressed ideas, wishes, and the like which are stored away in the subconscious. They are not, however, lost, and they have lost none of their power. They have, rather, gained in power and strength because of their suppression. They represent so much bottled-up energy which is constantly seeking an opportunity to escape. Any group of suppressed ideas which has a strong emotional tone is called a "complex," for example, "Œdipus complex," "inferiority complex," "fear complex."

The "Censor" Holds Subconscious Tendencies in Check. In an attempt to explain the means by which these subconscious tendencies are kept in suppression, the psycho-analysts have supposed the existence of a "censor." This censor is supposed to have a real existence as a kind of metaphysical being which stands on guard between the conscious and the subconscious mind. He is a kind of guard who prevents ideas from the subconscious escaping and reaching the conscious mind, unless he feels certain that they will be satisfactory to the other ideas present in the conscious mind.

The Psycho-analytic Treatment of Nervous and Mental Disorders. This theory of the subconscious mind is a development from practical experience in the treatment of nervous and mental disorders. The method of treatment, therefore, deserves special attention. A patient, who may be of any age, complains of almost any type of disorder, ranging all the way from abnormal compulsions to steal or to commit murder, to sex perversions or chronic indigestion. The physician begins his treatment by attempting to discover what important occurrences in the patient's life have led to the suppression of one or another of the important instinctive driving forces. A strict follower of Freud will hunt for suppressed sex impulses, a follower of Jung will look for important interferences with the patient's freedom and individuality, a follower of Adler will hunt for some interference with the desire for power.

In the attempt to find this conflict the physician must very carefully analyze every detail of the patient's past mental life. He begins by asking the patient to tell him all of the intimate details of his previous life, especially those details that he would particularly like to cover up and not tell anyone. He makes much use of "free association," in which the patient sits in a kind of reverie speaking aloud every idea or thought which occurs to him however intimate and personal it may be. He continues his investigation by having the patient write down in detail all of his dreams, for the psycho-analysts consider that especially in dreams the subconscious ideas are finding means for evading the censor and escaping temporarily into the conscious mind. He takes particular note of slips of the tongue and of the pen as indications of subconscious tendencies which are trying to get past the censor. He continues this analysis of the patient's mental life until he has searched back through his entire history to earliest childhood. The whole procedure is one which requires months or years of patient, detailed work on the part of both physician and patient. The conclusion is ordinarily the discovery of a series of events which occurred during the first few years of life and led to important repressions.

When the physician has discovered the particular conflicts that are responsible for the nervous disorder, the method of treatment is comparatively simple. It consists, mainly, of recalling the earlier incident to the conscious mind of the patient, thinking about it rationally, and arriving at a rational and conscious conclusion concerning what would have been the proper method of action at the time of the earlier conflict. It is sometimes necessary to live through the conflict again, either in imagination or in reality, but in this second living-through of the conflict the attempt is made to reach a sensible solution of the difficulty. If this sensible solution can be reached, the nervous disorder which has caused the suppression may gradually disappear without further treatment. The positive treatment consists of guidance in working out a rational and healthful program of living.

During the process of analysis in the attempt to discover the suppression which is causing the difficulty, it is sometimes necessary to use hypnosis or milder forms of suggestion as an aid in recalling events which have been forgotten. Hypnotism is likewise sometimes used during the process of treatment, as an aid in making the correct adjustment. The use of hypnotism, particularly during the process of treatment, has come into disfavor because it is felt that it may lead to further undesirable suppressions. It may also be used merely as a device to cover up symptoms of the mental disorder without really removing the cause. In that event further mental disorder is quite likely to occur at a later date.

Summary of the Psycho-analytic Psychology. Psychoanalysis began as a method for the treatment of nervous and mental disorder. As a practical procedure it was found to be quite successful. Instead of turning to psychologists for an explanation of the manner in which the practical procedures did their work, Freud and his followers attempted to build up their own psychological theory. We should recall that the psychologies of the time were the structural psychology, the Herbartian psychology, and the faculty psychology. None of these psychological systems offered much which could be used in explaining the treatment of mental disorder. The result has been the development of psycho-analysis as a psychological theory which is independent of the main body of psychology. The psycho-analytic theory has never concerned itself with the problems which are of interest to psychology as a whole. It presents no systematic discussion of sensation or of the theory of learning. The psycho-analysts have concerned themselves exclusively with instinctive tendencies and their modification. If we may sum up the work of the psycho-analysts in the words of the modern objective psychology, we may say that they have concerned themselves with the conditions under which bad habits develop.

It seems highly desirable at the present time that there should be a real amalgamation of psycho-analytic theory with the main body of psychology. Up to the present the main body of psychology has attempted to take over a few of the concepts of psycho-analysis, such as the suppression of driving forces and the importance of early childhood, without really fitting them into a unified system. Psycho-analysis for its part has gone ahead with a large group of followers. They are to be found mainly among physicians, psychiatrists, and social workers. This is only to be expected, since psycho-analysis was developed in an attempt to solve the kind of problems in which these people are interested. It seems now that further developments in the treatment of nervous and mental disorder cannot take place until a more satisfactory theory is worked out. As an independent psychological theory, psycho-analysis seems to have gone as far as it can. All that we know about psychology as a whole must be brought to bear upon the problems of mental abnormality.

V. GESTALT PSYCHOLOGY

The Origin of Gestalt Psychology. The Gestalt psychology, as a distinct movement, began in Germany as a protest against the same type of psychology that we have called structuralism in America. The breaking away from this type of psychology in America began with appearance of functionalism at about 1903; in Germany structural psychology persisted for another decade.

The protest against the older psychology took definite form with the publication, in 1912, by Max Wertheimer, of an article on the perception of visual motion. The usual explanation of the perception of visual motion had been that the trail of after-images on the retina furnished the basis for the perception. Wertheimer showed to his observers two cards in rapid succession. These cards showed one line in two successive positions. By varying the time between exposures he was able to get a variety of illusions of motion. He found that if the time between exposures was exactly right the line seemed to fall from its first position into a second position. With varying intervals between exposures, four other possibilities of movement were found; *first*, each line may appear and disappear separately with no apparent movement between the two positions; *second*, each line may seem to move a little toward the other; *third*, one line may seem to move only a short distance; and *fourth*, both may seem to be present at the same time without motion. Wertheimer's explanation of this illusion of movement, which could not be based upon a trail of after-images, marks the beginning of the Gestalt psychology in its modern form.

It is true that since the beginning of modern psychology casual statements have appeared which can be taken as showing this same Gestalt viewpoint. At the present time the Gestalt movement has found many followers both in Europe and in America. Its chief representatives are Kurt Koffka, Wolfgang Köhler, and Max Wertheimer in Europe, and R. M. Ogden and R. H. Wheeler in America.

Gestalt Psychologists Object to the "Constancy Hypothesis." The essential feature of the Gestalt psychology seems to be a dissatisfaction with the belief of the structural psychologists that each separate stimulus will produce a definite and particular sensation, independently of other stimulating conditions that are present at the same time. Objection is likewise made to the view of the behaviorists, that each particular stimulus will produce a definite response that can be attributed to that stimulus alone, independently of other stimulating conditions present at the same moment. The neurological explanation of association, as given by the structural and functional psychologists, and the neurological description of learning of the conditioned reflex type, as given by the behaviorists, are especially objectionable. They point out that the assumption that learning or association consists of the establishment of definite nerve paths of low resistance is not literally true. The expression "Constancy Hypothesis" has been adopted for this theory, that to every stimulus there corresponds a definite sensation or a definite bit of behavior, and that the nerve impulse, in proceeding from the sense organ to the sensory area or to the muscular system, passes over a specific nerve path. Much of the work of the Gestalt psychologists is directed toward attack upon this constancy hypothesis.

It should be pointed out that these views, which have been attributed by the Gestalt psychologists to the structuralists and to the behaviorists, have never been literally subscribed to by leading representatives of either school. Both schools of psychology have definitely recognized that the effect obtained by the application of any given stimulus depends to a considerable extent upon other stimuli which are applied at the same time. Watson in his book, *Psychology from the Standpoint of a Behaviorist*, published in 1919, definitely points out that even reflexes are modified by other stimuli, in addition to the normal stimulus for the reflex. As an illustration, it is generally recognized that the knee-jerk reflex may be increased or decreased by other stimuli, such as the kinesthetic stimulation present when the hands are clenched. The Gestalt psychologists frequently misunderstand and misrepresent both the structural and behavioristic psychologies in their criticisms.

If we may evaluate the Gestalt psychology in a brief statement, we must say that it represents not so much the introduction of any new principle into psychology as an increased emphasis upon certain principles which have previously been generally accepted. This change in emphasis is concerned primarily with pointing out that behavior, at any given moment, depends upon the working together of all the stimuli present in the total situation in which we find ourselves, and that the attempt to ascribe each detail of behavior to some one detail of the situation does some violence to the facts.

Objection to a Mechanistic Explanation of Human Behavior. Köhler's criticism of objective psychology takes the form that human behavior should be called *dynamic* rather than mechanistic. He believes that the human being is best described as a dynamic system rather than as a machine. By a dynamic system he means something such as the solar system, in which the sun with the earth and other planets work together in an orderly fashion, but not in a way which can be called *mechanistic*. By a machine is meant an arrangement of parts such that any force applied to the machine can act in only one definite way, while in a system, as the solar system, the action of any part depends not upon a definitely prescribed *arrangement* of the other parts, but rather upon the interaction of all the various forces which go to make up the system. As another illustration of the meaning of system, Köhler makes reference to the surface tension as found in a soap bubble. This surface tension cannot be thought of, according to Köhler, in purely mechanical terms, but must be thought of in terms of dynamics. The distribution of a charge of electricity over the surface of an irregularly shaped conductor furnishes another illustration of a dynamic relationship, as opposed to a mechanistic one. Köhler thinks of human behavior as being dynamic in this sense.

Is There a Purely Spiritual Element in Gestalt Psychology? Some people have been inclined to accept the Gestalt psychology because they object to the view that human behavior is definitely determined and because they wish to make room for a spiritual force which is not subject to natural law. These people have objected to behavioristic psychology because it is mechanical and does not make room for the action of any such spiritual force. It is clear, however, that the Gestalt psychology has no more place for such a spiritual force than has behaviorism. The use of the word dynamic instead of mechanistic, when it is properly understood, will furnish no comfort to such people and will not be objected to at all by the behaviorists.

When we have read completely a book such as Köhler's *Gestalt Psychology*, or Koffka's *The Growth of the Mind*, we are, however, left with the impression that there is something of a mystical nature in the Gestalt psychology, something which does not depend upon either dynamics or mechanics for its action. The Gestalt psychologists will indignantly deny that this is true. A purely objective psychologist or a behaviorist, however, always finds such an element in the Gestalt psychology; the vitalist finds something of comfort in the Gestalt psychology. It is just this element of indeterminism which furnishes an important distinction between the Gestalt and the purely objective schools of psychology.

Meaning of the Word "Gestalt." The word "Gestalt," which has been taken as a name for this school of psychology, is rather difficult of explanation. It refers to the fundamental view that behavior depends upon the total situation present at the moment, rather than upon any of the parts of this situation, or even upon all of the parts of the situation regarded merely as a mosaic or arithmetical summation. Speaking in terms familiar to us in mathematics, the Gestalt psychologists inform us that in human behavior *the whole is almost never equal to the sum of its parts*, it is usually greater than the sum of its parts, although perhaps it might be less. Whenever the word "Gestalt" is used it refers to this general principle. English equivalents for the word which have been proposed are "configuration," "form," "shape," "pattern," "unitary structure," and "functional disposition," but none of these are very satisfactory. The growing practice at the present time is to retain the German word in the English context.

VI. Summary

Six viewpoints in psychology have been compared and criticized. Three schools of psychology—structural, functional, and objective—have been shown to be closely interrelated. Structural psychology dominated in America at the beginning of the twentieth century. It was concerned with analyzing and classifying mental states. Bodily activity was supposed to lie entirely outside the field of interest of psychologists. The structural psychology was without important influence upon the problems of everyday life. As a protest against this barrenness of practical value and in consequence of an increasing interest in bodily activity, the functional school originated during the first few years of the century. Functional psychology represents a shift of interest from pure science toward a science which can be applied. It represents, besides, a shift of interest from the purely "mental" toward an interest in bodily activity. It is concerned with an attempt to understand mind not as an isolated fact but as a factor of prime importance in adapting man to his environment.

The interest in bodily activity which resulted in functionalism continued to grow in importance. This interest was given an impetus by the desire of psychologists to investigate the "mental" life of animals and children. Psychological information concerning animals and children could be obtained only through a study of their bodily activity, that is, of their behavior. It was found difficult, in many cases, to interpret this behavior in terms of mind or consciousness. Growing out of this difficulty, there gradually arose the opinion that such interpretation was not needed in every case, and finally it was believed unnecessary to assume the existence of any purely mental events at all. Bodily activity became the center of interest, and mind was discarded as being irrelevant and even non-existent. This attitude toward psychology has been called behaviorism. The term "objective psychology" seems to be more appropriate.

Throughout the history of psychology, there have been certain people who have emphasized the importance of driving forces in human nature. These driving forces have had many names. They have been called instincts, emotions, desires, wishes, impulses, and the like. In contrast with the increasing tendency toward a mechanical explanation of human activity, these psychologists insist upon the importance of purpose and desire in human affairs. This attitude toward psychology can be called purposive or hormic. These psychologists believe that wishes and desires are just as natural for human beings as the laws of motion are for physical objects. They do not believe that these wishes and desires can ever be explained in mechanical terms.

Independently of the main body of psychology there has developed an important psychological movement growing out of the treatment of nervous and mental disorder. This school, "Psycho-analysis," originated with the work of Sigmund Freud. Within a short time, some of Freud's followers became dissatisfied with his belief that disorders of the sex instinct were the basis for every type of mental disorder, and that sex instinct furnished the driving force for all important life activities. Adler replaced sex instinct with the desire for power as the important motive force in human affairs. Jung proposed that the desire for self-preservation was the source of all human strivings. The school of psycho-analysis has introduced into psychological theory the concept of a subconscious mind which is the source of energy for all our mental life. The chief contribution to education of this school of psychology is its emphasis upon the extreme importance of early childhood in the development of character and personality.

In Germany the Gestalt psychology originated as a protest against the European counterpart of structural psychology. This movement began definitely in 1912 and has been introduced into America largely by the efforts of Wolfgang Köhler and Kurt Koffka. The distinguishing feature of the Gestalt psychology is its attack upon the "constancy hypothesis" of the structural, functional, and objective psychologies. The Gestalt psychologists insist that actions cannot be isolated into elements such as reflexes, that mental states cannot be thought of in terms of complications of elements, such as sensations, images, and feelings. They believe that such analysis does violence to the facts, and results in the omission of factors which are important for an understanding of mental activity. The Gestalt psychologists emphasize the unity of the human organism. They have chosen as their point of departure the principle that activities do not occur in isolation, but belong together with other activities in complete wholes. This view does not represent the introduction of a new principle into psychology, but does single out for increased emphasis certain principles which have previously been accepted.

In America, at the present time, the dominating school of psychology is functionalism; the structural psychology is fast disappearing; objective psychology is new and has many ardent supporters. The latter is in disrepute in many circles because it seemingly contradicts many theological beliefs. Many people believe that a mechanical explanation of human life will rob it of much that is worth while, particularly of an æsthetic nature. Psycho-analysis is popular among psychiatrists, social workers, and others who are interested in the treatment of mental abnormality and the development of character. This popularity has a sound basis in the practical results which have been obtained through the application of this viewpoint. The Gestalt psychology is important in combating an oversimplification of the facts of human activity. It has made an important contribution in pointing out the unitary character of complex activities. Hormic psychology represents the viewpoint of those who believe that there is more to human beings than matter and motion. It states that there is an important source of activity which can never be explained in material terms. The determination of the truth of this view must wait upon further scientific advance. It should be pointed out, however, that the elimination of any non-material force as an explanatory factor in human behavior would merely correspond to the earlier elimination of such forces as explanatory factors in the rest of the natural world. The modern tendency is to regard man as one important item in the natural world and not as an exception to natural law. Purposive or hormic psychology, therefore, contains a concept which is foreign to the general development of natural science.

CHAPTER IV

INSTINCT

I. Modern Views of Instinct

Instinct in the Structural Psychology. The term "instinct" has been used in both popular and technical language for many years, referring to supposedly inherited patterns of activity. The structural psychologists have little interest in action and make little use of the concept of instinct. Titchener in his *Beginner's Psychology*, published in 1915, devotes about one-seventh of his book to the question of action, while Ruckmick, who is one of the leading representatives of structural psychology to-day, in his book *The Mental Life*, published in 1928, devotes less than one-tenth of his book to questions of bodily activity. Titchener finds that instinct has two aspects; one, which he considers to be purely biological and physical, is concerned with the innate nervous tendencies to behavior; the other, which he considers to be psychological, is concerned with the innate tendencies which guide and form the stream of thought. It is only insofar as the touching off of an instinctive response is accompanied by mental processes, that is, sensation, feeling, and the complex mental states, that the psychologist has any legitimate interest in it.

The Biological Aspect of Instinct. Titchener describes very briefly what he considers to be the biological side of instinct. He recognizes several biological principles. *First,* the innate tendencies are rarely perfect; they are not completely ready for action at birth, but ripen as the organism develops. For example, a child does not really learn to walk, but the instinctive tendency for walking gradually develops as time passes. *Second*, each instinctive tendency has its own period of development. For example, interest in the opposite sex develops during adolescence; fear is not present at birth, but appears within a few days; bashfulness appears when a child is three or four years old, etc. *Third*, instinct is persistent. A boy, we say, goes through the collecting stage, but as a matter of fact grown men collect, too, if they have the time and money. *Fourth*, instincts are not harmonious among themselves. For example, the instinct to crouch and remain motionless conflicts with the instinct to run away from an object of fear. *Fifth*, instincts are not so definitely prescribed as is commonly supposed. The same response may be brought about by situations which resemble one another only in a very general way. For example, fighting may result from many kinds of stimuli. Likewise, situations which seem to be identical may bring about responses which are quite different from one another. A strange object, for example, may cause either the fear or the curiosity reaction. *Sixth*, instincts may be checked, turned aside, or inhibited by acquired nervous tendencies; that is, instincts are modifiable and are greatly changed by habit formation. We learn to use weapons for fighting; mothers learn new ways of caring for children. *Seventh*, instinctive responses become specialized. For example, a bird, having once built a nest in a particular place, may continue to go to the same location year after year. *Eighth*, the more complicated instinctive tendencies, especially in the case of man, may be broken up into partial tendencies, and these partial tendencies may then be combined in various ways with habits. The mating instinct functions only partially for months or years and only in conventional ways.

This statement of the biological aspect of instinct corresponds very closely to the discussion of instinct as usually found in textbooks of psychology written from the functional and behavioristic points of view, the difference being that, where Titchener devotes less than three pages of a 350-page textbook to this subject, the functional psychologists customarily devote several chapters to this discussion.

The Mental Aspect of Instinct. Of the mental accompaniments of instinct, Titchener states that we know practically nothing. He believes that some of the more definite instinctive responses, such as coughing, sneezing, and smiling have a characteristic mental correlate. Most of the more general instinctive tendencies, such as collecting, walking, fighting, etc., show themselves mentally in the volume and trend of the mental stream rather than in the addition of any new processes. They may involve specific body attitudes and arouse specific patterns of kinesthetic stimulation from breathing or from the muscular set of the trunk. We are familiar with such attitudes when we are on our guard against deception, or in cases of uncertainty, or when afraid of the dark. The kinesthetic sensations are usually supplemented by images. Feelings of all kinds, that is, agreeable and disagreeable, exciting and subduing, straining and relaxing, may appear in connection with instinctive responses.

From his discussion of the mental accompaniment of instinct, Titchener arrives at a new technical term, "determining tendency." He thinks that a determining tendency is not so much an affair of the mind as of the body. A determining tendency has no specific mental accompaniment apart from the usually recognized sensations and feelings.

Ruckmick devotes about one page of his textbook to

the subject of instinct, since he thinks of the instinctive act as being unconsciously performed.

Instinct in the Functional Psychology. The functional psychologists think of instinct as being one of the most important means by which man adapts himself to his environment. For them, the central problem of psychology is that of adaptation to environment. They therefore find instinct very important and discuss it at great length. They disagree somewhat among themselves concerning the proper classification of instinctive tendencies, but they all agree in making up long lists of instincts and in discussing each one quite fully, pointing out its value in the development of children and its importance as the basis for learning and educational procedures of all kinds. Their discussion of instinct falls in line with Titchener's discussion of its biological aspect.

Early Behavioristic Views of Instinct. Behaviorists at first took over in its entirety the attitude toward instinct which had been developed by the functionalists, leaving out, however, any points of the discussion which implied the existence or importance of consciousness or purely mental activity in connection with the instinctive tendency. Their classification and lists of instincts are identical with those of the functionalists. We may take Watson's definition of instinct as typical of the behaviorist position. He defines instinct as "an hereditary pattern reaction the separate elements of which are movements principally of the striped muscles," in contrast with emotion, which he defines as "an hereditary pattern reaction involving profound changes of the bodily mechanism as a whole, but particularly of the visceral and glandular systems."

Instinct Goes Out of Fashion among Objective Psychologists. Early in its development, behavioristic psychology began to discard many of the tendencies which had been called instinctive, and gradually there developed the attitude that the word "instinct" itself should be discarded because it was misleading. In the functional psychology, as an essential part of the concept of instinct, there had been the belief that there were spiritual driving forces which were of real importance in determining mental activity. In speaking of parental instinct, for example, it was assumed that there was a kind of mental force concerned with leading a mother on to desire children and to desire to care for them; in speaking of the fighting instinct, it was assumed that there was some kind of a spiritual urge leading an individual on to engage in the activities of fighting. Behavioristic psychology had completely discarded the view that there were spiritual or mental forces of any kind. It soon developed that this belief in the existence of mental and spiritual forces was such an important and inseparable part of the concept of instinct, that it was impossible to continue using the term, without at the same time implying the existence of spiritual forces as a part of the instinctive tendency. Watson in his recent discussions has, therefore, discarded the term "instinct." He gives the impression that he has also discarded the belief that there are inherited patterns of behavior. When we examine his writings closely, however, we find that he still retains the belief that many anatomical peculiarities are inherited and that these anatomical peculiarities form the basis for patterns of behavior. Suckling, for example, requires the use of lips, tongue, throat, etc., and the neurological reflex patterns concerned with their activity. Many people who continue to use the word "instinct" mean by it nothing more than just this fact, that behavior depends upon inherited anatomical characteristics—not excluding simple nerve patterns.

A few of the objective psychologists have taken another step in advance of Watson. They believe that nerve patterns are highly variable from the beginning of life, and that no nerve patterns exist at any time with a sufficient degree of fixity and definiteness to justify calling them inherited. They consider that behavior at any stage of an individual's development is simply the end result of his previous development. According to this view, nerve patterns change from day to day in accordance with the changing influences surrounding an individual. These nerve patterns are better called "acquired" since the word "acquired" definitely implies that important changes in nervous organization (and in behavior) have occurred within the individual's lifetime.

Instincts as Chains of Reflexes. Instinct has been considered as an inherited pattern reaction involving a definitely inherited anatomical arrangement of neurons, muscles, and sense organs. This is the view first proposed by the behaviorists. This view at first made the assumption that instincts were merely chains of reflexes. As soon as experimental work began to appear which involved detailed observation of instinctive responses, it was seen that instincts lacked the definiteness and invariability required by this theory.

Even such an apparently definite activity as nest-building by wasps was found to be highly variable. It was discovered that individual wasps built nests in their own individual way. Differences were found in the kind of material used and in the quality of the finished product. Some nests were so poorly constructed that they could not possibly fulfill their function in the hatching and development of a new generation of wasps; other nests were very finely built and perfectly adapted to the accomplishment of their object. The *behavior* of the individual wasps in building the nests was highly variable. One wasp would proceed like a highly skilled workman, while another would proceed in a very awkward and unskilled fashion.

Observations on the instinctive behavior of other animals showed results of a similar nature. The conclusion was reached that because of their lack of definiteness, instincts could not longer be thought of as chains of reflexes and this view has been very generally discarded. There still remains, however, the possibility that there are inherited anatomical arrangements within the nervous system and within our general bodily structure which have a very important influence upon behavior, without prescribing this behavior in a narrow and definite way. This latter view is essentially the present belief of functionalists.

Instinct Identified with Reflex. Some psychologists (L. L. Bernard) believe that only the simple reflex type of behavior may be considered to be inherited. They think that all the more complicated behavior patterns are built up during the individual's activity by processes of learning. Among these psychologists we sometimes find the word "instinct" used as the equivalent of "reflex."

Instinct as a Combination of Habit and Reflex. Most of the objective psychologists, or behaviorists, at the present time, believe that the activities which have in the past been called instinctive are in reality combinations of reflex and habit. Such an activity as fighting, for example, is considered to involve mainly habitual responses, together with a few reflex responses. Some of these psychologists prefer to discard the word instinct entirely and talk of these activities, such as fighting and collecting, as habits; others are willing to continue to use the term instinct, with the explicit understanding that these forms of behavior are not to be considered hereditary.

Instincts as Mental or Spiritual Forces. Instinct has been considered as a spiritual driving force. G. Stanley Hall may be taken as a typical representative of this view. He believes that just as an individual in his physical development shows traces of his earlier animal ancestry, so he does, in his spiritual development, show traces of the spiritual development of his earlier animal ancestors. Instincts are, for him, these traces of the spiritual development of the human race. This view, that there is a definite spiritual tendency present in all instinctive behavior, has not been entirely discarded from the discussions of instinct of the functional psychologists; it is particularly prominent in the purposive psychology and in psycho-analysis. It is this tendency which objective psychologists particularly oppose and which has led them to discard the word instinct.

Instinct in the Gestalt Psychology. Instincts as chains of reflexes or inherited neuro-muscular patterns are rejected by the Gestalt psychologists for much the same reasons that have been given by the behaviorists. They offer the general criticism that behavior can be inherited only to the extent that it is conditioned by organic structure: special organs and the nervous system controlling their use have developed as one organic whole. For example, the so-called instinct of a hen for brooding and hatching eggs requires the development of a unified system of special organs,—feathers, temperature-regulating organs, egg-producing organs and the nervous system— and sufficient insight in the use of these organs. In general, no behavior is determined by specific neuro-muscular patterns but only by the body as a whole. Too much stress should not be laid upon inheritance as an explanation of bodily traits, for the body is a product not only of nutrition but of environmental pressure patterns which help to determine the physical characteristics of the body. Standardized environment determines many of the traits which have been called hereditary.

Principles for Determining the Hereditary Nature of Behavior. Certain criteria of instinctiveness have been proposed. (1) It is usually stated that if a trait appears at birth or even a few days afterwards it should be classified as instinctive. This statement does not take into account the possibility of learning during pre-natal development, although it is entirely possible that such learning does take place. This statement also overlooks the attitude toward individual development which is presented later in this chapter. This later view of individual development assumes that the environment at all times enters actively into the physical changes which are taking place in the developing organism, so that the child at birth has already been influenced by all the environmental influences present during intra-uterine life. The uniform and predictable course of development before birth depends in large measure upon the standardized nature of pre-natal environment.

(2) It is usually assumed that if a trait appears after birth but with no opportunity for learning, it is properly called instinctive. At first sight this statement seems plausible, but it is not of much value in determining the things which are instinctive. We know so little about the course of development of human infants, and the kind of influences which change this development, that we are usually unable to determine definitely that opportunity for learning has not been present, even though the child is only a few days old.

(3) When a trait appears in every race of human beings, it is probably instinctive. This principle overlooks the fact that there are many features of the environment

which are highly standardized for all people, so that many traits, which are quite certainly learned, are universal. For example, stimuli at a distance from an individual (sounds, sights, odors) are effective among all races of people. The habit of walking doubtless depends in part upon the effectiveness of this class of stimuli. Likewise responses of feeding, fighting, running away from certain objects may easily develop in all races of men, because of certain similarities in their environment.

(4) If there is a true biological inheritance in the Mendelian ratio, which appears regardless of environment, the characteristic may be truly inherent. This principle assumes the point that is under discussion but adds no proof.

(5) When a trait can be definitely assigned to a particular structural or anatomical characteristic, it is to be considered instinctive. This principle seems plausible until we recall that every *habit* of whatever nature depends upon the existence of a particular anatomical structure which makes it possible. According to this principle every action of every kind would have to be called instinctive.

The Classification of Instincts. It is apparent, therefore, that great difficulty exists in determining which actions shall be called instinctive. When attempts are made to classify these actions we find a similar disagreement. Any classification is only a device which has been found useful in thinking about a certain group of events. The same group of events or facts may be classified in many different ways, according to the use which we expect to make of the classification. For example, a mixed group of men and women could be classified in many ways, among which the following are obvious: (1) According to sex. (2) According to height. (3) According to weight. (4) According to degree of pigmentation of the eyes. (5) According to intelligence. (6) According to economic status. (7) According to social status. Each of these classifications may prove useful under certain conditions.

In classifying instincts, three types of classifications have been widely used. The oldest type of classification is according to the utility of the instinctive tendency. When classified in this way, there are generally found to be three main divisions among instincts.

1. Those instincts which preserve the life and provide for the welfare of the individual.

2. Those instincts which are concerned with the perpetuation of the race.

3. Those instincts which are concerned with the tribe or social unit. Among the individual instincts are listed such actions as walking, cleanliness, fighting, and flight. Among the racial or family instincts are included those concerned with mating, reproduction, and care of the young. Among the social instincts are gregariousness, sympathy, and love of approbation.

A second type of classification which has been introduced largely by the behaviorists is based upon the type of bodily movement involved in the activity. It is possible to find a large number of activities to list in this classification, such as sneezing, hiccoughing, crying, eye movement, smiling, turning the head, holding up the head, grasping, arm movements, leg and foot movements, fighting, crawling, standing, walking, vocalization, etc. Some psychologists, as Arlitt, attempt to arrange these individual movements into groups or classes. Arlitt includes as her main headings the tendency to self-assertion, the tendency to do as others do, the tendency to become uncomfortable at the sight of suffering, play which includes manipulation, sex, and gregariousness.

A third method of classification is based upon the kinds of stimuli which will call forth the instinctive response. Jordan makes a classification of this kind:

1. Responses to organic stimuli, which involve the actions of food-getting and sex.

2. Responses to objects in the environment, which include the characteristic responses to sensory stimulation, vocalization, manipulation, and physical exploration.

3. Responses to others, which include mastery, rivalry, and fighting.

Max F. Meyer makes a classification which is based upon both the type of stimulus and the kind of movement. He lists the following forms of instinctive behavior:

1. Straight locomotion in response to lack of food.

2. Turning the body axis sidewise in response to an obstacle.

3. Positive localization, on the body surface or outward.

4. Negative localization.

5. Grasping (bending, action of the flexor muscles).

6. Adjustment of the sense organs.

7. Signaling.

8. Sleeping.

II. Developments in Genetics as Related to Attitudes toward Instinct

The Active Rôle of Environment in Individual Development. The early views of instinct were based upon theories in genetics which are being challenged at the present time. These early theories assumed that the potentialities of the germ cell worked themselves out actively and independently, with the environment playing only a passive or permissive part in their development. More recent genetic and biological theories (C. M. Child and H. S. Jennings) point out that in every stage in the development of the germ cell the environment enters actively into the development, and that this development cannot be thought of as a mere unfolding of germinal possibilities.

The Meaning of Heredity. To understand this active rôle of the environment it will be well to inquire into the meaning of the word heredity. A general definition is that given by Castle,—"organic resemblance based on descent." Stated in this very general fashion there can be no doubt of the meaning of the word. It refers to the commonly observed fact that children resemble their parents in many details of their physical structure and in their behavior. It is worth while remembering, however, that children also differ from their parents in many respects and that they resemble other people who are not their parents. Jennings points out that heredity means merely the dependence of the offspring upon the materials (genes) that it receives from its parents; this dependency may manifest itself in likeness but also in *unlikeness* between parent and child.

When we begin to examine into the details of inheritance the definition must be formulated in a much more restricted fashion. E. G. Conklin states that by inheritance he means the continuity from generation to generation of certain elements of germinal organization. Adult characteristics are the result of the interaction between germinal elements and environmental influences. According to this definition, "hereditary" (if we wish to exclude environmental influence) cannot be used in referring to any characteristic of an individual after the germ-cell stage of development has been passed. This is essentially the view of geneticists at the present time. Their discussions of heredity apply solely to effectiveness of the germ cell and its characteristics, in bringing about differences between individuals. They recognize very definitely that the characteristics which appear later in development are not a mere unfolding of these germinal characteristics, but are the product of development in an environment which is actively shaping the course of growth. Jennings explicitly adopts this view.

F. L. Wells, who wishes to retain the concept of instinct as inherited behavior, gives the following definition,— "Inherited means acquired in individual development as a result of germinal factors or determiners, plus normal environmental influences." It should be noted that in this definition Wells makes use of the word "acquired"; that is, for him inherited characteristics have been definitely acquired during the lifetime of the individual. It is the manner of their acquisition which sets them off as being different from habits. The word "normal" in Wells' definition is the all-important word for understanding his distinction between inherited behavior and learned behavior. So long as the child is developing in a *normal* environment all of its characteristics, according to Wells, will be inherited. It is only when the environment becomes abnormal that learning takes place. Learned actions are, therefore, always abnormal.

It is clear that Wells is not using the word "normal" in its usually accepted meaning. If by *normal* we mean that environment which is found in the majority of cases, then according to Wells' definition we should be forced to call the ability to add three plus four an inherited characteristic, because the environment in which such a habit develops is distinctly normal for children of to-day. But Wells states that "the environment of civilized man is largely abnormal from the biological point of view." He is apparently using the word *normal* in very much the same sense that we use it when we speak of a person as having *normal* health or *normal* lungs. We do not mean the kind of health or the kind of lungs possessed by the average individual, that is, health which is not particularly good and lungs that are more or less defective. We mean, rather, that kind of health and that kind of lungs which we call almost perfect, which are possessed by *very few* individuals. *Normal,* then, when used in connection with man's environment, means that type of environment which is almost never found but which would exist *if man had not lived and had not altered environmental conditions to suit his own needs.*

This view, that man's environment is largely abnormal when considered from a biological point of view, aside from its misuse of the word normal, is largely contrary to modern biological and philosophical views, which are based on the theory of evolution. According to the evolutionary theory, man is just as much a part of the natural world as any other animal or, as a matter of fact, as any feature of the physical world in which we live. Man is just as "natural" as a mountain or a tree or an elephant, and changes in the physical world which have been produced by man are just as much "natural" changes as those produced by wind or sun or an earthquake. If we adopt this broader conception of man's place in Nature, then Wells' definition of "inherited" completely loses its meaning.

Uniformity of Development Is Dependent upon Standardized Environment. If we look into the more recent biological work for an understanding of inheritance, we find the general conclusion that the constancy and uniformity of development in nature depends at least in part upon the fact that a certain degree of standardization has occurred as respects the range of accidents to which the developing individual is exposed. External factors are not eliminated; the range of variation is merely limited. For example, during the *pre-natal* development of the human being, the temperature conditions are highly uniform from day to day and are highly uniform if we compare the development of one embryo with that of another. Likewise the method of nutrition, the light and pressure stimulation are highly standardized. The same may be said with respect to most of the contacts which the embryo has with its environment. On account of this high degree of standardization in the environment of the *unborn* child, its development takes a highly uniform course.

When the child is born, its environment is greatly changed within the space of a few minutes. The child is at once subjected to a radically different and varying method of nutrition, to radical changes in temperature, light, sound, pressure, etc. From this time on its development is much less predictable on account of the variety of stimulation with which it comes in contact. There are, however, during the life history of any individual certain definite times at which fundamental changes occur in some of the relatively constant features of its environment. We have just pointed out that the time of birth is one of these turning points in individual development, due chiefly to the fact that great changes have occurred in the type of stimulation to which the individual is subjected. Other important turning points which are likewise due to radical changes in the type of stimulation are (1) the day of learning to walk, which at once opens up many possibilities of new contact with the surrounding world, (2) entrance into school, (3) changing from grade school to high school, (4) the maturity of the sex organs, (5) entrance into college, (6) marriage, (7) building the new house, (8) arrival of the first child, etc. It will be seen that in each of these cases certain factors of the environment which have been relatively constant up to that time are rapidly changed, and with this sudden change the individual enters upon an entirely new life and shows characteristics which previously have been almost totally lacking. Modern life is standardized in such a way that no individual can escape a certain number of these changes.

Effect of Environmental Change upon a Developing Individual. As an example of the effect of a fundamental environmental change upon the physical characteristics of a developing organism, we may refer to the experiment performed by Stockard, who found that the fish Fundulus developed a single median eye when the magnesium-chloride content of the sea-water in which its eggs hatched was increased above normal. Now if we may suppose for a moment, that, due to some great catastrophe in nature, the magnesium-chloride content of sea-water had been somewhat greater than it now is before this fish had been discovered and catalogued, we should then have found that all fish of this species had a single median eye. Stockard then, in his experiments, might conceivably have tried the effect of reducing the magnesium-chloride of the sea-water. He would have then discovered by his procedure that he could have developed an abnormal fish with two eyes instead of the one characteristic of the species. Apparently the determining factor in the development of one or two eyes in the case of the fish Fundulus is not merely the unfolding of germinal characteristics, but also the manner in which its environment is standardized with respect to the content of the magnesium-chloride.

Many similar illustrations can be drawn from experimental work in breeding plants and animals. Jennings states as his belief, even though final proof is lacking, that "Any kind of change of characteristics that can be induced by altering genes, can likewise be induced (if we know how) by altering conditions." This statement seems to mean that any characteristic which can be understood as being hereditary can likewise be understood as being due to environmental conditions.

The Meaning of Heredity When Applied to Behavior. If we turn to the psychological question of the existence of instinct, there are two principles which may guide us,— *first*, inheritance, as the term is used by biologists and geneticists, refers to anatomical, physiological, and neurological characteristics only, and the development of these characteristics in the usual way depends upon the existence of a highly standardized environment; *second*, the functioning of these physical structures, which constitutes the so-called instinctive behavior, is always the result of specific stimulation.

Inherited Physical Structure as a Determiner of Behavior. Physical structures are a necessary basis for any type of behavior, and the behavior varies directly with the nature of the physical structures. For example, it is relatively difficult to teach a rat to pull a string with its feet, while a cat learns to do this quite readily. It is rather difficult to teach a pig to walk on the edge of a board, while cats and monkeys learn to do so without any special provision for their teaching. Now, it is not necessary to suppose that pigs have some mysterious tendency, which we may call instinct, to avoid walking on the edge of a board, and it is not necessary to suppose that cats and monkeys have an instinct to walk on the edge of a board. We need only to refer to the differences in the physical structure of cats, monkeys, and pigs to understand the differences in their behavior. The differences in the feet, the legs, and the general flexibility of body may furnish an entirely satisfactory explanation of many of their differences in behavior.

There has been a tendency in recent psychology, both in discussion of instinct and of learning, to overlook the important part played by bodily structure other than nervous. These other bodily structures are relatively constant and, being constant, are usually disregarded. It is just as in an equation in algebra; since the parts of the equation which give us trouble are the variables, we tend to center all of our thinking about these variables. The most variable structure in its influence upon behavior is the nervous system. We have centered all of our thinking upon the nervous system, and have overlooked the very obvious fact that many of the classes of behavior which we have called instinctive represent nothing more than the normal working of our body in accordance with its mechanical possibilities. The term instinct, then, as it is frequently used, means nothing more than we have a body which has certain mechanical possibilities of behavior.

Whether there are special anatomical arrangements within our nervous system which we can think of as being inherited, in the sense that we inherit a special shape of nose or special size of hand, is a matter which has never been satisfactorily demonstrated. There has been a fair degree of success in the attempt to isolate some of the simpler reflex patterns. We know fairly well the course through the nervous system which is taken by the reflex arc concerned in the knee-jerk reflex or the pupillary reflex, but no one has ever attempted to work out a specific neuro-muscular pattern corresponding to the supposed instinct of fighting or collecting. It is clearly true that, at the time of birth, we do have a nervous system arranged in special patterns; but these patterns are so susceptible to change that we may question whether they are hereditary in the same sense that pigmentation of the eyes, or size of the hands, is called inherited.

Views of Instinct Based upon Comparative Psychology. One line of argument which has been commonly used in support of the view that human beings have many instincts is by reference to comparative psychology. Animals supposedly have many different instinctive tendencies. Then, according to this line of reasoning, human beings, who are biologically merely one species of animals, should also be expected to show many instinctive tendencies. The point is overlooked that the vague tendencies called instinct in human beings do not correspond, except perhaps in a very few cases which should properly be called reflexes, to the concrete reactions called instinct in animals.

Biological Attitudes toward Instinct and Habit. C. M. Child states that "all modifications of behavior in the individual are just as truly potentialities of the protoplasmic-action system, *i.e.,* just as truly hereditary, as the fixed behavior patterns." If we translate this statement of Child into simple language, he is saying that all habits are just as truly hereditary as all reflexes and instincts. We find that a number of psychologists at the present time have adopted the view that all reflexes and instincts are just as truly learned as all habits (J. B. Watson, Z. Y. Kuo). The difference between these psychologists and the biologists such as Child is merely one of terminology. They are all agreed that there is *only one class of behavior;* that behavior cannot logically be divided into classes, reflex and instinct on the one hand, and habit on the other. Jennings explicitly subscribes to this view. He believes that everything which can be called inherited can also be called the effect of environmental influence.

The Fallacious Belief in the Existence of Self-initiated Reactions. Another consideration which has led to confusion in popular thinking about instinct is the belief that there are self-initiated reactions, that is, reactions that do not require the presence of any physical stimulus. Such a view is entirely contrary to every kind of modern psychology. From the *objective* point of view at any given moment we are simply the end result of our accumulated organic history. We exist as a definite physical structure which is mechanically favorable to one type of response and unfavorable to another. All behavior is merely the "natural" consequence of the interaction of this physical structure (the human organism) and its present environment. If we had a physical structure which did not mechanically favor any special reaction, but which had an equal possibility of producing many different reactions, the behavior of a new-born infant would resemble nothing so much as an epileptic fit. Furthermore, learning so far as we understand it at the present time would be utterly impossible and we should never have the development of any special habits which could be used on special occasions. The number and kind of reaction systems which we find in any given animal or human being depend upon the number and kind of contacts which that animal or human being has with its surroundings,—(1) physical, (2) personal, (3) cultural and institutional, and the number and kind of contacts which an animal has with its surroundings depend upon the mechanical possibilities of that individual's physical structure.

From the *subjective* point of view (structuralism, functionalism, psycho-analysis, and purposive psychology) at any given moment our mental constitution is the end result of our previous mental history, just as our physical make-up is the consequence of our previous organic history. All behavior, both mental and physical, is merely the natural outcome of interaction between our psychophysical structure and its present environment.

III. Practical Consequences of Acceptance or Rejection of Instinct

Education Based upon Instinct. If we could be certain that instincts exist; if we could show that they are present in all children; if we could isolate and classify them; and finally if we could develop techniques for controlling them for educational purposes, many educational problems would be greatly simplified.

(1) Knowing the universal characteristics of man we could develop a course of study and methods of teaching which would be universally applicable. Final solutions for educational problems could be found.

(2) Based upon a knowledge of the age at which each instinctive tendency appears, we could adapt the methods and materials of instruction to the stage of development of the child.

(3) Instincts could be used for motivating forces.

(4) The modification of instinctive tendencies—*i.e.*, habit formation—could be undertaken intelligently.

Classification of Behavior According to Probability of Occurrence. The important question for the parent or the teacher is not whether a given kind of behavior is inherited and therefore instinctive, but rather what is the probability that a certain kind of behavior will take place. It is much more important for a first-grade teacher to know the probability of the occurrence of such behavior as a fist-fight between two of her pupils than it is to know that such behavior should be labeled instinct or habit.

When we approach the question of instinct from the standpoint of the probability of the occurrence of a given action, we arrive at results which are much more useful than when we attempt merely to group behavior into two distinct classes. For example, in 1903, Miss Burke made a study of children's play. She found that at the time of her study about 90% of the children investigated were actively engaged in making some kind of collection. This is a fact which must have been of considerable importance to teachers and parents who were concerned with directing the learning of children. On the basis of her findings, collecting was classified as instinctive. This classification entirely disregards the interests of the 10% of children who were not making collections and is, in this respect, contrary to the modern tendency to take into consideration individual differences. In 1926–27, Lehman and Witty made an extensive study of children's play. They found that at the time of their study about 11% only of the children were actively making collections. They have recently repeated their investigation with a different technique and find a much larger percentage of children thus engaged. They conclude that the making of collections is a function of sex, age, locality, and season. In other words, collecting seems to be an activity in which children can be interested rather easily if proper environmental conditions are provided. Whether parents and teachers should make an effort to establish collecting as a habit depends not upon the "native" character of this activity, but upon its educational and social usefulness. Wherever a child is found already to have this interest it can and ought to be utilized to further his education.

"Instinct" Psychology Is a "Finished" Psychology. When we classify any activity as an instinct we are likely

to look upon the classification as being final and complete. We are likely to think that here is a kind of behavior which is characteristic of *all* children and which will *continue* to be characteristic of all children. An *instinct* psychology represents a *finished* psychology, finished in the sense that no further investigation is necessary. We assume that we have discovered certain facts about human nature which will change only as centuries pass and further evolutionary development takes place. When we approach such tendencies as collecting from the point of view that they occur only when environment is standardized in a certain particular way, it is necessary to be always on the lookout for a change in these tendencies due to some change in the standardization of the surrounding world. It may be rather difficult to point out just what feature of the environment has changed between 1903 and 1927 which has produced a difference in the percentage of children who are interested in collecting and hoarding, but it is important to parents and teachers to know that such a change has taken place.

Human Nature Does Change. Collecting has been discussed in some detail merely as an illustration of the fact that it is likely to prove misleading to label any activity as instinctive. Many other illustrations could be found. Hunting, for example, is certainly disappearing very rapidly. It is comparatively easy to point out the change in environmental conditions which is responsible for the disappearance of the tendency to hunt. This change is doubtless due to the fact that all the waste places of the world are becoming well populated. What we have called the fighting instinct seems also to be rapidly disappearing. We may not change our habits quickly enough to prevent the occurrence of another great war or several wars; but

living conditions have sufficiently changed, due primarily
to scientific and economic developments together with
the consequent increase in transportation facilities, that
we may expect war to disappear entirely in the comparatively near future. Likewise, what we have called
parental instinct and mating instinct are changing very
rapidly. The causes of the great changes in this respect
are again undoubtedly the radical changes in modern
living conditions which are brought about by the great
increase in population of the past century.

Instead of continuing the common assumption that
human nature has not changed for thousands of years and
will change only very slowly, it is clear that we would
do well to recognize the fact that human nature has
changed in many important respects and at the present
time is changing very rapidly. Human nature is, after
all, only the product of the development of the fertilized
germ cell in an environment standardized in a particular
fashion. As the standardization of the environment becomes different, human nature becomes different. At the
present time we seem to be in a stage in which environment is being rapidly standardized in a new way, with
many consequent changes in the fundamentals of human
nature. The important thing, then, for the teacher and
parent as well as for the economist, political-scientist,
and sociologist is to attempt to work out a classification
of human behavior based upon the probability that a
certain action will take place and to recognize in doing
so that this probability may be increased or decreased
within the space of a few years. Studies in human nature
can never be finished; they must be repeated from time
to time as living conditions change.

IV. SUMMARY

The structural psychologists have little use for any study of instinct. They consider instinct to be primarily the concern of the physiologists and biologists. The functionalists are very much interested in instinct and devote a great deal of time to its discussion. They consider instinct to be a truly inherited form of behavior. They discuss it sometimes from a purely mental standpoint and definitely imply that there are mental driving forces or urges of an inborn nature. They also discuss instinct in terms of behavior and in terms of the underlying nervous and physical structures. The behaviorists have completely discarded the concept of instinct as a *mental force;* some of them have discarded the term entirely and believe that the activities which have been called instinctive are merely habits. The psycho-analysts base their entire psychological system upon the assumption of strong mental driving forces which they call instincts. Their explanation of all forms of mental abnormality and indeed of normal mental activity of all kinds is based upon the assumptions that these instinctive tendencies exist and come into conflict with one another and with social conventions. Their position corresponds very closely to that of McDougall when he states that if we were to remove the strong instinctive dispositions from human nature, the human machine would remain inert and motionless and totally incapable of any action. The Gestalt psychologists have discarded instinct in consequence of their belief that no behavior is determined by the functioning of specific neuro-muscular patterns.

Geneticists are inclined to emphasize the importance of the hereditary factor in all behavior, not excluding even learned actions. Nevertheless, biologists generally have come to recognize the active rôle of the environment in all individual development, and restrict the concept of inheritance to the effect of germinal organization as one factor in development. The conclusion seems to be that it is impossible to separate behavior into two distinct classes, inherited and acquired; these two words are purely relative when applied to behavior.

For the practical uses of parents and teachers it seems best to classify behavior according to probability of occurrence rather than to separate it into two distinct divisions, inherited and learned. Studies in human nature can never be finished, because human nature changes as the environment becomes standardized in new ways. Those who are concerned with directing and controlling the actions of boys and girls, men and women, must be constantly on the lookout for such changes in the fundamentals of human nature.

CHAPTER V

EMOTION

I. THE NATURE OF EMOTION

Central vs. Somatic Theories of Emotion. There are two classes of theory which seek to explain emotion. On the one hand are the theories which assert that emotion is a mental phenomenon, correlated with activity of the cerebral cortex; this central activity is primary and all the bodily signs of emotion are subsequent to it and are properly called "expressions" of the emotion. On the other hand, there are the theories which assert that the bodily activities are primary, coming first in the causal series; all central activity, whether cortical or mental, is the result of the somatic disturbance. All the early psychologists and many modern ones take the first-named view—that the central processes are primary. The James-Lange theory emphasizes the importance of the somatic changes as antecedents of the mental state of emotion; the behavioristic theories omit the mental aspect of emotion entirely and place full reliance upon the bodily activity.

Emotion as a Mental Disturbance. Emotions have been regarded traditionally as vague, confused states of mind or consciousness, almost totally resistant to scientific analysis. Some emotions which have a high social value have been regarded as essentially spiritual, while other emotions of less moral value have been called base physical passions. The scientific treatment of emotions has been largely confined to their classification.

113

This is essentially the attitude of the structural psychology. Titchener thinks that in emotion there are no new mental elements; there is merely the presence of a confusion of sensations and feelings. Emotion is, then, from the descriptive standpoint, a *temporal* experience; it begins with the perception of the exciting stimulus and lasts through and beyond a whole series of bodily activities and their parallel mental states. The last traces of the emotion may not disappear for days. It usually begins quite *suddenly*, although it disappears very gradually. It is highly *complex;* its stimulus is not a simple object, but a total situation, including especially a great confusion of *organic* stimulation. It always involves much *feeling;* the emotive response is always definitely pleasant or unpleasant. It is a *predetermined* experience, since it issues from determining tendencies of an instinctive or habitual nature.

The functional psychologists likewise agree that on the mental side emotion is characterized chiefly by its confusion. They are inclined, however, to be deeply interested in the physiological accompaniments—the "expressions" of the emotions. Psycho-analysis and purposive psychology emphasize the importance of emotions as driving forces.

Emotion the Cause of Bodily Accompaniments? Emotions are frequently called motives. Just as hunger impels us to seek food, in the belief of some psychologists, so fear causes us to flee from danger and anger causes us to fight. In general, the stronger emotions produce greater changes in bodily activity than the weaker ones.

Many observations and experiments have been made to determine the exact nature of the bodily expressions of the emotions. The classical study is that of Darwin, who published in 1872 his *Expressions of the Emotions in Man and Animals.* His work furnished the basis for

James and Lange, whose new theory emphasized the importance of the bodily changes and stimulated many later researches to determine the exact nature of the physiological mechanisms involved.

The James-Lange Theory. This theory takes its name from Carl Georg Lange, a Danish physician, and William James, an American psychologist who, in 1884, independently arrived at the same general conclusion concerning the nature of emotion. The popular theory had been that the sequence of events during emotional excitement is: *first,* the occurrence of the exciting stimulus (noise, presence of a wild animal, painful stimulation, etc.); *second,* the psychological changes, characterized chiefly by their confusion; and *third,* the occurrence of the bodily changes, the expression of the emotion. The James-Lange theory states that the *sequence* of events is different from that just described. *First,* there is the exciting event; *second,* the bodily changes occur as reflex or instinctive responses to the situation; and *third,* the confused mental state, the emotion, follows. The emotion proper consists of the perception of the confused and vigorous bodily changes. The visceral and skeletal activities, which are directly caused by the exciting stimulus, furnish in their turn the stimuli for organic and kinesthetic sense organs. The confused mass of sensations and feeling following upon this stimulation makes up the mental state of emotion.

Modification of the James-Lange Theory. The James-Lange theory gained much publicity and wide acceptance, in part because it was in such striking contrast to the views previously held, and in part because it fitted in with the growing tendency to emphasize the importance of the physiological factors in human behavior. Most psychologists who preserve a dualism between mind and body now accept the theory of James and Lange, at least in part. They believe that although the bodily changes may not furnish the complete explanation of emotion, they are nevertheless important in adding to it. Perhaps in the beginning the emotional state consists of a confusion of mental elements accompanying cerebral activity which is produced directly by the exciting stimulus. The bodily changes are secondary. They, however, have the effect of adding to the mental confusion, because they contribute a great mass of organic and kinesthetic sensation and a variety of feelings of pleasantness, unpleasantness, strain, etc.

Emotion Involves Much Bodily Activity. Strong emotions such as fear and anger have been found to have as their physical signs a great variety of external and internal bodily activities. The following classification includes the symptoms commonly mentioned and shows their contradictory nature as well as their variety.

1. Expression of the Face:
   (a) Brows contracted, brows raised, or brows level.
   (b) Eyes narrowed, eyes wide and glaring, or eyes fixed with glance cold and steady.
   (c) Mouth closed with lips thin and jaws set, mouth open, mouth open slightly with lips curled or twisted.
   (d) Nostrils distended.
   (e) Face flushed, pale or of blotchy appearance.
   (f) Perspiration on forehead and upper lip.
2. Vocal-motor Reactions:
   (a) Nasal and gutteral sounds, cries, screaming.
   (b) Cursing, sarcasm, insults, words of distress, etc.
   (c) Voice loud, hoarse, husky, low.
3. Cardio-respiratory, and Vaso-motor Reactions:
   (a) Very marked chest movements, deep and rapid breathing, catching of the breath.
   (b) Increased strength and rate of heart beat.
   (c) Blood vessels of face, neck, and arms distended, face flushed or pale.

4. Skeletal Posture and Movement:

   (a) Body erect and rigid, slightly crouched and bent forward (anger) or withdrawing (fear), trembling, erection of hair, running toward object (anger) or away from object (fear).

   (b) Hands clenched or claw-like, emphatic gestures of attack or avoidance, kicking, etc.

5. Internal Changes:

   Checking of digestion, increased rate of heartbeat, higher blood pressure, increased secretion of adrenalin, increased secretion of blood sugar, increase in clotting qualities of the blood, increased sensitivity of muscles to nerve impulses.

The bodily changes during a state of joy differ only slightly from those outlined above, the chief points of difference being in the external appearance and skeletal activity.

Grief and sorrow are states of depressed rather than increased physical activity; skeletal muscles are generally relaxed. Such movement as occurs is weak and slow. The relaxation of facial muscles permits the corners of the mouth and the eyelids to droop. Organic activities during grief and sorrow have not been extensively studied, but it seems probable that digestion is impaired, blood pressure is lowered and the energy-regulating mechanisms generally are working at a low level. Max F. Meyer has characterized grief and sorrow as "a wasted sleeping reflex"—a person shows much of the behavior useful in sleeping in a situation where such behavior does not serve its true function and is therefore "wasted."

Examination of this list of bodily changes during emotion shows a coöperation between visceral and skeletal systems. The visceral changes are of such a nature as either to increase (anger, fear, joy) or decrease (grief, sorrow) the energy output of the body. The strong emotions represent relatively great changes in energy output while the mild emotions represent relatively slight changes of this nature. Skeletal activity is vigorous or weak according to the amount of energy output permitted by the visceral activity; its specific form is determined by the inherited or learned reaction patterns of the individual. It can be classified as being generally of a positive (approach) or negative (avoidance) type.

Experimental Tests of the James-Lange Theory. The James-Lange theory asserts that the physical changes noted during emotional states precede and give rise to the emotions proper. Considerable experimentation has been done in the attempt to establish or to disprove this theory. (1) If the sensations from the viscera are surgically removed emotion ought not to occur. Such operations have been performed upon dogs and cats. Emotional expressions continued to occur in the parts of the body which remained capable of reacting. Since these animals cannot give us any report of their consciousness, the experiments are not convincing to all, for they do not test what the James-Lange theory considers the emotion proper: they are all concerned with the initial stage. There is nothing in the James-Lange theory which would lead us to expect that those parts of the body unaffected by the operation would not show the emotional responses, since these responses are supposed to be of a reflex and instinctive character caused by the exciting stimulus directly and not by the emotion. (2) The case of a woman is reported,—a woman who, as a result of a fracture of the neck suffered complete paralysis of the skeletal muscles of the trunk, arms, and legs together with complete loss of cutaneous and deep sensitivity from the neck down. There was also no possibility of emotional discharge of sympathetic impulses. She experienced no loss of emotional consciousness. (3) If emotions are the consequences of visceral changes, we should expect them to occur no matter how the visceral changes are produced. The visceral changes characteristic of emotion can be produced by the injection of certain drugs, but they do not give rise to emotional experience. Such visceral changes are likewise produced by violent physical exercise without resulting emotion. (4) The visceral activities are too uniform to offer a satisfactory means for distinguishing between the different emotions. (5) "Acting" the emotion by putting the skeletal muscles in the attitudes of joy, fear, anger, etc., does not bring real emotion. (6) Pathological laughing and crying frequently occur when the patient does not feel joyful or sad. A pathological mask-like expression does not indicate lack of emotional experience.

The Diencephalon as the Basis for Emotion. Dana and Cannon have each proposed the theory that emotion requires the interaction of the diencephalon and the cerebral cortex. Emotional consciousness is supposed to accompany action of the cerebral cortex. The activity of the cerebral cortex, however, is caused by the discharge of afferent impulses from the diencephalon. The reaction to an emotional situation is supposed to occur in about this fashion: (1) There is the occurrence of the exciting event (noise, presence of a wild animal, painful stimulation, etc.). (2) The resulting nerve impulses reach the diencephalon (directly from the incoming sensory fibers and indirectly by way of the cerebral cortex). At this point they are redistributed in such a fashion that the neural mechanisms responsible for the bodily signs of emotional behavior (visceral and skeletal) are thrown into activity; at the same time the diencephalon discharges into afferent paths leading to the cortex of the cerebrum.

(3) Thus it happens that the *expressions* of the emotion (bodily) and the emotion itself (mental) occur at about the same time. They may, however, occur independently as they are observed to do in pathological cases.

This theory seems to fit the experimental facts quoted in the discussion of the James-Lange theory. Cannon states the theory in these words, "The peculiar quality of the emotion is added to simple sensation when the thalamic processes are involved."

Emotion in the Objective Psychology. It should be pointed out that the traditional theory of emotions, the James-Lange theory, and the theory of the thalamic origin of emotion all make two important assumptions. (1) Mental events occur only when the cortex of the cerebrum is active; and (2) Mental events are separate and distinct from physical or neural events. The first assumption has been challenged by Langfeld (Presidential Address, American Psychological Association, 1930) and others. The effect of this challenge upon theory of emotion is problematical. The second assumption has been challenged by the behaviorists with far-reaching effects; from the standpoint of the objective psychology, the three theories of emotion previously mentioned must all be discarded.

For the objective psychologist emotion is usually identified with the occurrence of rather widespread visceral and glandular disturbances. If the motor neurons leading to the visceral and glandular systems have not been destroyed, emotion should be expected to occur upon appropriate stimulation. If there is partial destruction of such motor neurons, emotion should be reduced in amount but those reactions whose nerve supply is unimpaired should continue to take place. To the extent that emotional stimuli have become tied up with verbal responses by conditioning, emotional "consciousness"—*i.e.*, verbal

statements that emotion is experienced—should continue
to be found in those pathological cases previously described where there was extensive destruction of nerve
connections between the cerebrum and the viscera. The
thalamic theory of Cannon and Dana becomes a merely
interesting statement of the normal course of distribution
of nerve impulses during states of emotional excitement.
The behavioristic theory likewise embraces all the observed facts except for those who insist upon the reality
of the "fact" of conscious or mental occurrences.

*Recent Modifications in the Behavioristic Theory of Emo-
tion.* It has been pointed out by Cannon that all the visceral and glandular changes which are considered to be
characteristic of emotion are present on many occasions
when we do not speak of an emotion as being present.
During any vigorous physical activity, however unemotional it may be, there are changes in blood pressure, increased secretion of adrenalin, stopping of digestive activity, and all the other visceral and glandular changes
which have been supposed to characterize emotion. The
truth of the matter, then, seems to be that during emotional states there is widespread visceral disturbance
which usually takes the form of preparation for an increased energy-output by the body as a whole. This
same thing, however, occurs on many occasions which
are clearly not of an emotional nature. We need some
additional means for distinguishing between emotional
behavior and behavior of other kinds.

The distinction which has been proposed has long been
recognized by psychologists. In its application to behavioristic theory it has been recognized first by Max F.
Meyer and recently by H. A. Carr. Emotion should be
contrasted with skilled behavior. The characteristic feature of emotion seems to be a lack of coördination, a con-

fusion of activity, an inappropriateness of response, that is, a kind of awkwardness, while the characteristic thing about unemotional behavior seems to be a coördination of the body activities, so that an end result is accomplished in an efficient manner. The person who is angry may dominate because he frightens the other person or by reason of his strength, but he cannot fight with his own best skill when angry. The trained boxer or soldier "keeps his head" and does a skillful job of fighting.

The exciting emotions are wasteful of energy; the depressing emotions conserve energy without appropriate cause; during unemotional behavior the energy-output is nicely regulated to suit the demands of the organism and is efficiently used. During fear and anger, for example, the energy output usually exceeds the demands of the organism; during grief or sorrow, on the other hand, the energy output is so low that the necessary work of the day is not well done—the person is listless and inactive; when working at a familiar task under normal conditions the energy output is well suited to the demands of the situation. The contrast is between emotion on the one hand and skill on the other. Emotion, then, should be classified as unskilled behavior or awkward behavior, which is at the same time unnecessarily vigorous and forceful or inappropriately weak and listless.

As opposed to skilled behavior, which is well-coördinated and adapted to the situation, there remains a kind of awkwardness which is not emotional, due primarily to the fact that it does not involve much change in the energy-regulating mechanism of the body. This is the kind of awkwardness shown by beginners in learning a new performance.

Emotion in the Gestalt Psychology. Emotions are essentially "inner behavior." As mental experiences they are primarily affective. They occur when the activity of the body as a whole is vigorously directed toward some goal or source of stimulation. Wheeler defines emotion as "A response of the organism-as-a-whole, the outstanding criterion of which is an intra-organic and muscular stimulation that depends upon the functioning of the autonomic nervous system and its related organs. At the same time, emotive behavior involves insight." During emotive behavior the person is perceiving a goal and acting with reference to it; the reactions are quicker and more vigorous than other behavior because of the greater stress under which they begin. The vigor of the activity can be understood when we think of the function of the autonomic nervous system in quickly releasing stored energy. Behavior is not controlled *by* emotion; the behavior *is* the emotion and is controlled by goals and by intra-organic stimulation. Except for the concept of "insight" and "goals" and the retention of "experience" as something in addition to bodily activity, the view of the Gestalt psychologists is similar to that of the objective psychologists.

II. CLASSIFICATIONS OF EMOTIONS

Early Classifications of the Emotions. Emotions have been classified in many ways. An early classification placed them in two groups according to their social value: (1) the base physical passions such as fear, anger, and lust, and (2) the spiritual emotions such as pity, sympathy, and love. Another classification was based upon the order of their appearance: (1) the primary emotions such as fear, anger, grief, and lust and (2) the derived emotions such as pity, gratitude, and sympathy. Another classification was based upon the object of the emotion: (1) the subjective emotions such as shame, embarrassment, and pride and (2) the objective emotions such as fear, anger, and love. None of these classifications have proved to have much value and have been generally abandoned.

Titchener's Classification of Emotions. An attempt to classify emotions in such a way as to relate them to the structural psychology of feeling has been made by Titchener. He groups them to fit the tri-dimensional theory of feeling. (1) Agreeable-disagreeable group such as joy and fear. (2) Straining-relaxing group such as hope and relief. (3) Exciting-subduing group such as anger and grief. Titchener's classification, in common with much of the structural psychology, is rather barren of practical value.

McDougall's Classification to Parallel Instinct. McDougall has worked out in detail a theory which has been popular among many psychologists since the time of Descartes. He assumes that emotion is a specific mental process that is associated with instinct, which is a specific physical response. For every instinct there is a corresponding and accompanying emotion. We will include only a partial list of these instinctive and emotional activities.

Instinct	Accompanying Emotion
1. Instinct of escape, self-preservation, etc.	Fear, terror, fright
2. Instinct of combat	Anger, rage, fury
3. Parental	Tender emotion, love
4. Pairing, mating	Lust, sexual emotion
5. Assertion, self-display	Elation, feeling of superiority
6. Laughter	Amusement, jollity

Critics of McDougall's theory believe that he has frequently over-extended himself in his effort to find an emotion to place in relation to every instinct. He has also not explained which is cause and which is effect. In calling them aspects of the same thing he has provided no information about the thing of which the two are different aspects. His classification is losing favor in consequence of the recent attacks upon the instinct theory and the recent studies of the physiological basis for emotion.

Watson's Behavioristic Classification of Emotions. Objective psychology identifies emotion with the occurrence of rather widespread bodily activity, especially with disturbances of the visceral and glandular systems. Watson at first defined emotion as: "an hereditary 'pattern-reaction' involving profound changes of the bodily mechanism as a whole, but particularly of the visceral and glandular systems." He gives us a genetic classification of emotion corresponding to the ancient classification into *primary* and *derived* emotions but based upon the observation of a number of infants during the first few months of life. The *primary* emotions, those belonging to the original and fundamental nature of man, are *fear, rage,* and *love* (using *love* in approximately the same sense that Freud uses *sex*). All other emotions are developed from these three by a process of conditioning—*i.e.,* by learning; in some specific cases there is the possibility of maturation.

The stimuli which are originally capable of bringing out these emotional reactions are: for *fear,* removal of support, a slight shake, and loud sounds; for *rage,* hampering of the infant's movements; for *love,* stroking or manipulation of some erogenous zone, tickling, shaking, gentle rocking, patting and turning upon the stomach across the attendant's knee.

The responses are: for *fear,* sudden catching of the breath, clutching with the hands, sudden closing of the eyelids, puckering of the lips, crying, possibly flight and hiding; for *rage,* crying, screaming, stiffening of the body, slashing and striking with hands and arms, foot and leg movements, holding the breath and flushing of the face; for *love*, smiling, gurgling, cooing, extension of the arms, and cessation of crying.

It is noteworthy that Watson's description of emotion is largely in terms of external activity although his definition emphasizes visceral and glandular activity. His classification of emotion has been almost universally adopted, and his belief that all other emotions are developments from these three as a result of training has had great influence upon education, especially during infancy.

Watson thinks of emotional responses as being rather definite and well-organized. We believe that much of this definiteness and organization is read into the child's behavior, because Watson, as a psychologist, is looking for a definite organization. His three types of emotional response seem to be nothing more than (1) in the case of *fear*, a miscellaneous set of *avoiding* reactions, (2) in the case of *anger*, a group of merely violent activities which later become more specialized as *approach* reactions, and (3) in the case of *love*, a merely *passive* attitude or *mild approach* toward the source of stimulation. If we were to make a logical classification of the behavior of any human being, we might easily adopt these three classes, even though there were no definitely organized neuro-muscular patterns specifically and separately concerned with producing each of the three. In other words, anger seems to be merely a *class name* for a large group of separate and individual responses concerned with violent reactions, especially when they result in approaching the source of stimulation, while fear and love are similarly merely *class names* for a large number of separate and distinct reactions of the kind that have been described.

III. The Influence of Education upon Emotion

Conditioned Emotional Behavior. Watson carried on a series of experiments to determine to what extent learning might take place in emotional reactions in infants. He found that it was possible so to condition emotional responses that they came to be made to other stimuli than those which originally called them out.

If a loud noise is produced close behind an infant by striking an iron bar, a fear response occurs. If a rabbit is brought near to the child so that it can be seen, the child may reach out its hands to pat and stroke the rabbit and show every sign of enjoying the presence of the animal. If, now, the iron bar is struck, making a loud noise at the same time that the child is stretching out its arms for the rabbit, both the fear reaction and the playing with the rabbit are inhibited to some extent. The child will cease reaching for the rabbit and appear somewhat startled. When this same kind of stimulation, that is, the presentation of the rabbit and the production of the loud noise, is presented on several different days, the fear reaction gradually comes to predominate. When the fear reaction has become well established with the two kinds of stimulation present at the same time, it is found that the presence of the rabbit alone is sufficient to produce the fear reaction; the noise is no longer needed.

Watson carried on a number of experiments of this general character and came to the conclusion that the great variety of fears which we find in older children and adults are built up by such a process of conditioning from the original fear responses to loud noises and loss of equilibrium.

If we follow Watson's line of reasoning we come to the conclusion that fear of snakes, for example, might be built up in some such way as follows. A child living in the country may see a snake while playing in the yard. The only responses it should be expected to make would be to approach the snake, perhaps pick it up, and play with it. When a child is quite young, however, it is not ordinarily left alone for any great length of time. Its mother or an older brother or sister, seeing the child and the snake, will perhaps scream, rush toward the child, seize it, and violently pull it away from the neighborhood of the snake. In this situation there are introduced both of the original stimuli for the production of fear responses,— the *loud noise* is produced by the scream of the older relative, and the *disturbance of equilibrium* is produced when the child is seized and roughly pulled away from the neighborhood of the snake. It should not require many repetitions of this situation to build up in the child a well-established fear of snakes. Of course, through the medium of language we can build up other fears without the direct presence of the objective situation.

The Place of Emotion in the Development of Personality and Character. The psycho-analysts have pointed out the great importance of emotion in shaping the attitudes of men and women toward all the problems of life. They have especially shown that these attitudes become fixed early in life and continue to be of prime importance during maturity because of the strong motive forces underlying them. They have been especially concerned with the abnormal and anti-social tendencies which are based upon emotional conflicts that force these strong driving forces to seek unusual and undesirable outlets. Some of the well-recognized undesirable attitudes which may develop as a result of suppression or wrong direction of emotional forces are *compensation, introversion, day-dreaming*, suffering-hero or conquering-hero types of *identification, ration-*

alization, sour grapes mechanism, and *regression.* On the other hand, by a process of *sublimation,* the emotions may be made to furnish the driving power for many highly ethical and valuable tasks and vocations. These attitudes will be discussed in a later chapter.

The Place of Emotion in Training for Appreciation of Art, Literature, etc. Emotion is commonly supposed to have an important place in the appreciation of art. When we analyze the appreciation of art, we find that it has two important phases; on the one hand there is the appreciation of *form* and *technique;* on the other there is the appreciation of *content,* the understanding of what the particular example of art *means.*

We may first choose an illustration that is not usually thought of in connection with artistic appreciation, but which seems to involve the same kind of attitudes and reactions. When we watch a football game, we can appreciate it only as we know the rules of the game and are familiar with the skills which are involved in good playing. This understanding of rules and skills depends definitely upon a course of education in football. The greater the amount of training, the greater the amount of appreciation. On the other hand, the appreciation of a football game involves a considerable amount of emotional activity which may be based upon a gross understanding of the results of the game. Little or no training is needed with respect to the form of emotional responses; almost any kind of behavior is acceptable at a football game. There are a very few things a spectator may do that will interfere with the other spectators' appreciation of the game. In appreciating a painting, the situation is similar in part. Appreciation of color, form, use of the brush, etc., depends upon a definite education in these matters. The subject of the painting is likely to arouse emotional responses in the observer, the type of the emotional responses depending upon the past experiences of the observer with that kind of subject. These emotional responses, however, must fit into certain conventional patterns; there are many kinds of emotional responses which are *not permissible* in an art museum or in a home where a picture is hung on the wall. The kind and variety of emotional responses in this situation are much restricted when compared with the responses that are permissible at a football game. A considerable amount of training in conventional form of response is therefore necessary in connection with the emotional reactions to paintings.

The same general situation exists with respect to music. Appreciation of the technique of the performer demands a special training in the understanding of musical skills. Appreciation of content depends upon the past experiences of the listener. Such appreciation is frequently emotional, but the emotional responses must conform to conventional standards. Appreciation of dancing requires some understanding of the various bodily skills found in this activity. Emotional responses are of considerable importance, but must conform to conventional standards.

From the standpoint of emotion, then, appreciation of art consists of the making of emotional responses according to conventional patterns and requirements. From the standpoint of a dualistic psychology, appreciation of art involves the occurrence of an emotion which is a purely mental affair, but whose expression is confined to conventional physical behavior. From the standpoint of objective psychology, the physical behavior in which a person engages during appreciation of an example of art constitutes the emotion. This physical behavior we have found to have two main characteristics. It consists of a change (increase or decrease) in the energy output of the body and of wasted or inappropriate behavior. Appreciation of art from this point of view may be thought to be merely a *socially acceptable way of wasting energy or behavior*. Training in appreciation of art from the standpoint of emotion consists, therefore, of an attempt to preserve the infantile reactions in certain situations, together with the building up of a greater or less amount of skilled response concerned with confining these infantile reactions within conventional limits.

The Place of Emotion in Creative Work in Art. The place which emotion has in creative work in art is complicated by the fact that there is both an artist and an audience. For the sake of clarity it is necessary to think of emotion from the standpoint of the artist, temporarily disregarding the audience.

It has frequently been stated that the artist when engaged in productive work is *expressing* an emotion. Whenever we make this statement we are assuming a dualism between mind and body. We believe that emotion is a purely mental thing which can be expressed in bodily activity. Recently we have begun to apply the language of the psycho-analysts, saying that artistic production is a *sublimation* of emotional responses. That is, painting a picture or engaging in a dance has been assumed to be an expression of an emotion which is socially more desirable than the expression which might ordinarily be expected to occur. When, for example, a financial reverse is suffered, we may give way to an emotion of sorrow. A socially more desirable type of response, which the artist is capable of making, is painting a picture or composing a musical selection or some other creative effort of an artistic type. If we find that some friend has forsaken us, we may become angry or we may *sub-*

limate the anger, that is, express our anger in the form of dancing, playing the piano, or some other creative effort which is socially more useful than the infantile anger reaction. From this point of view, the emotion as a mental state is present just as fully as if it were not sublimated. The sublimation refers to the expression which the emotion receives.

Langfeld, in his discussion of emotion in the Wittenburg Symposium, thinks that while the work of artistic production is actually taking place, emotion must be wholly lacking. He believes that emotional response may precede the creative effort but cannot accompany it. The emotional response is not to be thought of as the cause for the creative activity. Some untoward event, such as a financial or social difficulty, may produce an emotional response. This emotional response may in turn be followed by creative effort in art. On the other hand, the disturbing event may directly produce creative effort. The emotional response and the creative effort may both be caused by the original social or other difficulty, without the emotion being considered as the direct cause of the artistic work. We have previously pointed out that there seems to be an opposition between any kind of skilled activity and emotion. Langfeld believes that this is true in artistic production. From the standpoint of the psychologist, therefore, artistic production is not merely a special means for *expressing* an emotion, but is rather a *substitute* for an emotion. When a stimulating situation produces artistic effort, emotion either does not occur at all or disappears when effective creative work begins.

From the standpoint of the audience, an effort which is highly skilled and wholly unemotional on the part of the performer may result in strong emotional response. However, we recognize that some musicians or dancers have excellent technique but seem to lack in feeling or expression. This statement depends upon a confusion between the behavior of the musician on the one hand and the audience on the other. By this statement is usually meant that the musician or dancer fails to arouse emotional responses in the audience despite the fact that his musical or dancing technique is excellent. The question involved here is concerned with the *best means for arousing an emotion in an audience*.

A public speaker, for example, may have an excellent delivery, his enunciation of words may be well-nigh perfect, his choice of words may be good, he may be guilty of no grammatical or rhetorical errors, yet his audience may show no emotional response. It may be that the production of an emotional response in an audience demands an enunciation which is not too perfect, a choice of words which is not entirely suitable to the subject, the making of some grammatical or rhetorical errors and other indications that the speaker is himself emotionally disturbed. Likewise, in piano playing and dancing, it may be necessary for the performer to preserve just the right balance between skill and emotion for the sake of producing a sufficient emotional reaction in the audience.

The technique of the artist must, of course, be directed toward portraying some event or situation. This content may on its own account arouse emotional responses in the audience. To insure such emotional response, artists ordinarily choose subjects which form a part of the common experience of large numbers of people. Such subjects as family life, fighting, children, landscapes are chosen because of their universal appeal.

The course of development of creative ability in art may be somewhat as follows: in the beginning the reactions are largely emotional and unskilled; the artist is unable to create any worth-while piece of work because he lacks technique. Besides gaining technical skill he must also gain a wide personal experience with events and situations which commonly arouse emotional responses; this experience furnishes the basis for his choice of subjects. During the course of training the skilled element becomes more and more important, until in the finished artist it is the predominating factor. The emotional element must not, however, be completely lost and subjects chosen must have general appeal, or the artist will exhibit a high degree of skill and good technique but nothing more; that is, he will be unable to produce emotional responses in the audience. Training in artistic production, therefore, demands a wide experience with emotional situations and a partial preservation of the infantile unskilled reactions to these situations, together with the building up of a greater or lesser amount of skilled response or technique. There is, then, a reason for the amount of temperament which we usually find among artists. It is necessary that they have had emotional experience and that they preserve a readiness for emotional response if their work is to possess a certain degree of feeling and not become too technical.

Training in the Bodily Aspects of Emotion. Training the emotions seems to have four important aspects. (1) Emotion is almost synonymous with awkwardness. When thought of in this way, training the emotions consists simply in increasing the skill which a person exhibits in any situation until the point has been reached where action is reasonably efficient and effective. When this point has been reached we ordinarily think of the emotion as having disappeared. (2) In some special types of skill, especially in art, it is desirable to preserve a certain amount of emotional response and not let skill, in the sense of efficiency, be developed to too high a point. (3) There is a kind of training of emotions which is concerned with the ability to prevent the occurrence of more than a minimum amount of emotional activity. This kind of training consists very largely in developing an attitude which is unfavorable to impulsive and vigorous response. If we can learn that on meeting a new situation for which we have no well-developed system of habits, we must preserve for a time the existing state of activity, we have gone far toward establishing emotional control.

(4) There is one aspect of emotion which makes this emotional control the more difficult. The energy-regulating mechanisms of the body, whose level of output is altered during emotional reactions, tend to persist in their activity for some time. The action of smooth muscles and glands changes rather slowly, so that when the energy-output of the body has been increased or decreased it is likely to remain at a high or low level for a considerable time. After the situation which has brought about this changed energy expenditure has disappeared, we are still under the necessity of adjusting our actions to the persisting visceral conditions. An important phase of emotional training consists in developing habits concerned with the use of energy which has been left over from an exciting emotional situation and habits concerned with adjustment to low levels of energy output left over from states of depression.

When children have been on the playground engaged in some athletic game there arise great changes in the energy-regulating mechanism of the body, due both to the vigor of the activity and to its emotional elements. These children come into the classroom and are required to engage in activities such as reading or writing which make very small demands upon bodily energy. Unless play has brought extreme fatigue, the result is that in addition to the desirable study which is expected by the teacher, much additional physical activity is certain to occur. The teacher is confronted with the problem of controlling and using this excess activity in some useful way. She should recognize that for the period of a half-hour or longer after the play period some provision of this sort is absolutely essential.

We have all had the experience of having difficulty in getting to sleep at night after an exciting and interesting evening at a party or a dance. Likewise it is commonly recognized by parents that for a half-hour or an hour preceding bedtime children should be kept more or less quiet and not permitted to play too violently. This is true because sleep is a condition in which we are preoccupied with remaining quiet and preserving a bodily attitude which is favorable to rest. If the energy output of the body is high it is impossible to assume and maintain this attitude at once.

When a person has experienced some great grief or disappointment, his energy level is likely to remain low for many days. It is desirable to give training which provides adjustment to this situation. Ways must be discovered and made habitual for restoring the normal level of activity as soon as possible. The difficulties are increased by the fact that the situation producing the grief or disappointment usually cannot be removed; hence the depression cannot be fully overcome until a new adjustment to this situation has been worked out.

Status of Research in Emotional Behavior. Our knowledge of emotion is in a confused and unsatisfactory state. The amount of research which has been carried on is comparatively small. This is doubtless due to two facts.

(1) In the past the interest of psychologists has centered about the so-called intellectual processes. The emotions were believed to be a lower order of mental events and not worthy of the same serious consideration. They were considered to be disturbing factors in mental life rather than matters of immediate and direct importance. (2) During recent years attempts to carry on researches in emotional reactions have encountered difficulties of technique as well as difficulties due to prejudice and lack of opportunity. When it was recognized that changes in the energy-regulating mechanism of the body were important during emotional responses, attempts were made, notably by Cannon, to discover the nature of those changes. The technique concerned with discovering the nature of visceral and glandular change is a difficult one, but has been rather satisfactorily worked out. We know now a great deal concerning the changes in digestive activities, blood pressure, heart rate, adrenal secretion, etc. This technique has, however, been applied mainly to animals.

Researches on emotional reactions in human beings have proved difficult, both because of obstacles in the way of observing the visceral and glandular changes and because of the difficulty of producing emotional reactions in a laboratory. It is not easy to frighten a person in a laboratory when he knows that he is to be made the subject of an experiment. If he were successfully frightened his reactions would likely be so vigorous that it would be impossible to make use of the delicate apparatus needed to record the internal changes. The same observation may be made with respect to the emotion of anger. Love reactions might be more easily observed under laboratory conditions, but because of the connection between love reactions and the taboos of sex they have not been extensively investigated. Since the first work of Watson it has been assumed that only three fundamental types of emotion exist, namely, fear, rage, and love. Because of the difficulty of investigating any of these three, little progress has been made.

Persons could easily be found who are passing through emotional reactions of sorrow and a technique could be worked out for observing the kind of visceral and glandular change which takes place. That this has not been done is probably due to the fact that sorrow does not fit into either of the three types of emotional response as proposed by Watson. We have pointed out earlier that Watson's three classes of emotion probably represent nothing more fundamental than a classification of unskilled behavior into rather vigorous approach reactions in the case of anger, avoiding reactions in the case of fear, and relatively passive behavior in the case of love. It is unfortunate that this classification has led to the neglect of opportunities for studying behavior during states of depression.

When we approach emotion from the standpoint that it consists of relatively unskilled behavior, it is clear that every study of learning may be a study of emotion. This hypothesis, that there is an opposition between skill and emotion, needs to be tested out by studying and comparing the physiological reactions which take place at different stages in the development of skill. Studies, for example, should be made of changes in energy metabolism which correspond to increasing degrees of skill; likewise, corresponding changes in blood pressure, breathing, digestive activity, etc., should be observed.

The emotional reactions of artists and audiences need further investigation. Some valuable studies have been made of the effect of music upon visceral activity. These studies need to be extended to include both visceral and skeletal responses to other forms of art and to include the artist as well as the audience.

IV. SUMMARY

Emotion has long been regarded as a vague, confused state of mind. Until the presentation of the James-Lange theory, the bodily signs of the emotion were supposed to be secondary and properly called "expressions" of the emotion. In 1884 James and Lange proposed that the bodily changes were primary, preceding the emotion proper. After much experimental work designed to test the James-Lange theory, there is still difference of opinion concerning the rôle of bodily activity in emotional states. Dana and Cannon have proposed that emotion requires interaction between the diencephalon and the cerebral cortex; the bodily changes are incidental and not of primary importance.

Behavioristic psychology has discarded the mental aspect of emotion and has identified it with the bodily changes. It has been found impossible, however, to distinguish clearly between the different so-called emotions on the basis of difference in physical and physiological reaction. It has been proposed that emotion involves change in the energy regulating mechanisms of the body and lack of coördination or skill in adjusting to the external situation. The Gestalt psychology retains the mental concept of emotion as a part of the reaction of the organism as a whole. The physical changes are an integral part of the emotion, not merely correlates or expressions.

Many classifications of emotion have been proposed. Their close relationship to instinct has been recognized. The most popular classification at present divides them into two groups: the primary emotions of fear, rage, and love; the derived emotions of pity, sympathy, etc.

It has been shown that emotional reactions may be conditioned to new stimuli. The emotional life of adults is supposed to depend upon a previous process of conditioning of the primary emotions. The psycho-analysts have shown the importance of habitual emotional attitudes in determining personality and character. Emotional reaction habits are of great importance in the production and appreciation of art, but the kind of training needed for their best development is not well understood. The development of emotional control seems to depend upon the development of skill in general and the development of an attitude unfavorable to impulsive action in new situations.

Research in emotion has been scanty because of the absorption of the interest of psychologists in the so-called intellectual processes and because of the inherent difficulties of investigation. During recent years the technique for studying bodily changes has been developed, but such studies have been confined largely to animals. States of excitement, such as fear and anger, have been extensively investigated, but states of depression, such as grief and sorrow, have been neglected. Emotional behavior offers a fertile field for careful investigation.

CHAPTER VI

MENTAL INHERITANCE

I. The Importance and Nature of the Problem

The Problem of Mental Inheritance Has Great Social and Educational Importance. There are many social, economic, and political problems concerning the relationship of different races upon which a measurement of the average (native) intelligence of the races could throw much light. There are likewise customs and laws concerning the relationship of the two sexes which are based upon the belief in the native superiority of one of the sexes. Democracy as a political system rests ultimately upon the facts of the nature and distribution of degrees of mental, social, and moral traits among the population. Universal education such as has been attempted in America demands an understanding of the possibilities and limitations of development of every part of the population.

Changing Attitudes toward Mental Inheritance among Educators and Psychologists. For may centuries education was conducted on the theory that any child could learn anything. Failure was accounted for by lack of application, stubbornness, disobedience, and the like. Following the development of biological science, educators and psychologists adopted the biological attitude toward the all-importance of hereditary factors in determining the course of individual development.

The development of mental tests and their widespread administration during and following the great war further emphasized this fatalistic attitude. It was believed by many to be possible to determine for any individual the limitations which had been placed upon him by the constitution of his germ plasm. We were told that each person should be content to fill his predestined niche in life, whether high or low; the administration of a psychological test was all that was needed to discover this predetermined place in society.

At the same time that this fatalistic attitude was developing, there was a vigorous psychological movement which was proclaiming the all-importance of environmental factors in the development of sane social and moral attitudes toward life. Psycho-analysis, from the time of its origin during the closing years of the past century, has emphasized environmental determination of the course of individual development. Concerned at first with mental abnormalities, it denied the importance of hereditary constitution as a factor in mental disease. Recently its findings have been extended to include normal mental life.

The functional psychologists recognized the importance of a biological basis for psychology. Out of this recognition came an uncritical—even enthusiastic—reception of the belief in the importance of heredity in mental affairs. The behaviorists seemed even more interested in human biology than the functionalists; but the discovery by Pavlov of the conditioned reflex fundamentally changed their attitude toward the relative importance of heredity and environment in determining human behavior. Based upon the great complexity of the human organism, especially the nervous system, it seemed possible by proper control of conditioning factors—i.e., environment—to develop any desired behavior in any individual. If this assumption could be shown to be true, there would be no limit to the possibilities of education in securing individual development. The limitations laid down in the genes of the germ plasm could determine only the starting point of development; the limit of development could be determined only by the ingenuity of parents and teachers in providing conditioning stimuli.

In order to resolve this difference of opinion concerning the place of genetic constitution in determining development, it is necessary to examine in some detail the theoretical and factual basis of mental inheritance.

The Physical Basis of Mental Inheritance. Mental inheritance has been commonly supposed to be of two kinds,—the inheritance of general mental abilities, such as general intelligence, and the inheritance of special abilities, such as ability in mathematics or music. Mental inheritance of any kind seems to depend upon the inheritance of favorable anatomical characteristics. When we consider the anatomical possibilities there seem to be only two means by which general intelligence can be inherited. (1) There is the possibility that the individual having a larger quantity of nervous material will be especially favored. (2) There is the possibility of the inheritance of a different *quality* of nervous material; it may have a greater or lesser susceptibility to change. The inheritance of special ability must clearly depend upon the inheritance of some special detail of anatomical structure (nervous or somatic) which is favorable to some special task or vocation.

The Phrenologists Attempted to Correlate Mental and Nervous Characteristics. In the attempt to determine whether the anatomical characteristics of the brain can be used in estimating intelligence, many measurements have been made. More than one hundred years ago the phrenologists worked on the problem unsuccessfully.

They assumed that the mind consists of a large number of independent faculties, each of which has its particular place in the brain. It was assumed that if a person possessed a high degree of a particular mental faculty, such as combativeness, determination, or the like, some particular part of his brain would be especially well-developed, and this special development could be detected by careful measurement.

Correlations of Brain Size with Intelligence. After the failure of phrenology, the problem of the relation between brain characteristics and intelligence assumed the simpler form of the attempt to estimate in animals and persons their general intelligence by their brain weight. A large number of brains of men and women have been measured. It has been found that the average male brain is somewhat heavier than that of the female. The average brain weight for males is in the neighborhood of 1450 grams and that for females 1225 grams. It is likewise known, as the result of such measures, that the average brain weight is different for different races. The Chinese, for example, have a larger brain size than the Japanese. So little, however, is known concerning the difference of intelligence between races that it is impossible to state whether this difference in brain size has any relation to intelligence, unless the importance of brain weight as a determining factor in intelligence can be determined in some other way.

Correlations between brain size and intelligence which have been found by investigators dealing with measurements of different members of the same race are positive but very small. These correlations are so small that they have no practical value in predicting the intelligence of an individual. We know that an individual with a small brain may be highly intelligent or stupid, while an individual with a large brain may likewise be intelligent or stupid. About the only statement that we can make with any degree of certainty is that a brain which is extremely abnormal, either extremely small or extremely large, is undesirable. Any size of brain within the normal range may show a high or low degree of intelligence.

Relationship between Size of Brain and Size of Body. Some investigators have thought that more important than absolute brain weight is the relationship between brain size and body size. That is, the amount of nervous material in its relation to the volume of the body as a whole is thought to be more important than the single fact of brain volume. When brain size alone is considered, males are found to be superior to females. When the relationship between brain size and body size is taken as the criterion, women are found to be superior to men. It is interesting to note that the superiority in brain weight of men has been taken to indicate that men are natively superior in intelligence to women, while no one has taken into consideration the fact that women are favored when the ratio between brain weight and body size is taken.

The development of psychology during the past thirty years has brought into prominence the view that the nervous system exists primarily as a set of connections between sense organs and muscles. The view that the brain is the seat of some mysterious governing power which controls life has been largely discarded. It has further been recognized that the sense organs which are most important for intelligence are distributed near the surface of the body. Max F. Meyer concludes that a relationship between brain and body which is also important in determining the intelligence of a person or an animal is the ratio between the amount of nervous material and the amount of surface of the body. When this ratio is taken it is found that men are slightly superior to women. The superiority, however, is far less than that indicated by the figures for absolute brain size. However, the amount of surface of the body alone no more than the volume of the body alone determines how much nervous tissue is needed to serve the whole animal well. Considering the volume of the body in relation to brain size, women are slightly favored. Considering the surface of the body alone in relation to brain size, men are slightly favored. The truth of the matter probably lies between these two sets of figures. That is, there is probably no important advantage to either sex in amount of nervous material.

Relationship between Brain Growth and Temperament. Porteus, in his comparison of the mental characteristics of different races, came to the conclusion that brain size is not an important factor in determining intelligence, but that there is some relationship between the post-pubescent growth of the brain and temperamental traits. The growth of the female brain is ordinarily completed earlier than that of the male. That is, there is little further increase in brain size in women after about fourteen years of age, while the male brain continues to develop until about eighteen. Porteus associates this later period of development of the male brain with the development of the male temperamental characteristics. He takes for granted the traditional temperamental differences between men and women and assumes that they are native, that is, that men are more aggressive, while women are docile, men are more self-assertive, while women are submissive, etc.

Porteus finds that the difference in brain development of the Japanese and Chinese corresponds to the difference between brain development of men and women. That is, the Chinese brain continues to grow in size only slightly after about fourteen years, while the Japanese brain continues to grow in size until about eighteen. The curve of development of the brains of Japanese men corresponds very much to that of American men, while the curve of brain development for Chinese men corresponds very much to that of American women. In his investigation of temperamental characteristics, Porteus finds that Chinese men possess essentially the feminine characteristics, that is, they show the docility and submission of women, while the Japanese men show distinctly male characteristics of aggressiveness and self-assertiveness.

When we adopt the point of view suggested by Meyer that the important relationship is that between body surface (and volume) and brain size, this greater development of the male brain after puberty can be understood as being necessary, because the male reaches a later maturity in physical size than the female. That is, the general body growth of women is completed a few years earlier than the general body growth of men. With continued increase in physical size in the case of men, there must be a continued increase in size of brain if the brain is to continue to serve the body well, while upon the completion of general physical growth in the case of women, the brain does not need to continue further growth. This seems to be a more probable explanation than that offered by Porteus, who has simply taken for granted the traditional opinion concerning temperamental differences between men and women.

Inherited Difference in Susceptibility to Changes in the Nervous System. A second possibility of a general anatomical factor in intelligence is found in the susceptibility of nervous material to change. It may be that some individuals have a nervous system which is more easily modified and changed than the nervous system of other individuals. That is, some individuals who learn easily may do so because their nervous system is easily changed. We have pointed out previously that we believe learning of all kinds involves definite changes within the nerve system. While general observation of behavior and learning makes it seem probable that this condition of greater or lesser susceptibility to change exists, no one has ever demonstrated it by any direct observation of nerve cells.

The Inheritance of Special Ability. There are many possibilities for the inheritance of special abilities. Some of these possibilities are very obvious. A person cannot become a great singer unless he has a vocal apparatus and mouth cavity of just the right kind; relatively long and flexible fingers are essential to a good pianist; a big bony frame and big muscles are essential to certain kinds of work requiring physical strength. Recent study of the endocrine glands has shown that the over-activity or under-activity of some gland, such as the thyroid, may cause radical differences in disposition and character. It is likewise possible that some individuals have an especially good set of nerves leading from the eyes to the fingers or from the ears to the vocal organs, etc. Such special anatomical arrangements of the nervous system might easily prove highly favorable to certain special kinds of work. When we speak of any of these characteristics as being inherited we must do so in the light of recent advances in biology which we have pointed out earlier. We must remember that the course of development taken by the body cells depends upon the active participation of the environment. Special characteristics will develop or fail to develop according to the interaction between the two forces, the germ cell and the environment. In the present stage of knowledge the existence of special aptitudes can be better determined by observation of behavior than by observation of anatomical peculiarities. The claims of the physiognomists are largely false in spite of their wide popular acceptance.

Observation of Behavior Is the Best Means for Judging Intelligence and Special Aptitude. We may conclude by saying that differences in intelligence which are essentially nothing but differences in forms of behavior cannot yet be estimated better (or even as well) from a study of the nervous system or other anatomical characteristics than they can be estimated by a direct observation of behavior. In fact, the best way to estimate intelligence or to predict future development seems to be to observe carefully and systematically the actions of a person. While his actions, without doubt, depend upon his anatomical features, these anatomical features can function in so many ways, and, especially in the case of the nervous system, anatomical differences are so obscure and difficult to determine that they cannot yet be made the basis for any important conclusions concerning difference in intelligence or differences in more specialized mental characteristics.

II. The Science of Genetics

The Scientific Study of Heredity Is an Affair Largely of the Twentieth Century. The first important work in inheritance, it is true, was done some thirty-five years earlier. In 1865 Mendel published experiments which had far-reaching importance. The biological world as a whole was not ready for his conclusions and they lay neglected until 1900. At this time several biologists, working independently, re-discovered Mendel's laws. His work, which had been forgotten, was re-published and his priority recognized.

Mendel's Law Is a Statistical Statement of Facts of Heredity. Mendel worked with garden peas. He crossed a kind of pea whose plants were tall with one whose plants were short. He found that the result of the cross was a kind of pea whose plants were all tall. This hybrid generation of tall plants was allowed to reproduce again. In this second generation there were some tall and some short plants. The number of tall plants exceeded the short ones by a ratio of 3 to 1. When these short plants were allowed to reproduce they continued to reproduce short plants only. When the tall plants were allowed to reproduce, one-third of them continued to reproduce tall plants only; the remainder of the tall plants reproduced both tall and short in the ratio of three tall plants to one short one. The tall plants all looked alike but some of them were capable of reproducing only tall descendants, while others were capable of reproducing both tall and short. Mendel found that precisely the same thing happened if he used a variety of peas which had a green pod and another which had a yellow pod. The green and yellow pods were reproduced in exactly the same ratio as the tall and the short vines.

Descriptive Words Used by Geneticists; Unit Character, Dominant, Recessive, Linkage, Blend. Mendel called this difference between the two plants *the unit character,* that is, *tallness* is a unit character or the *green pod* is a unit character. He called the character which appeared in the first generation the *dominant* character, and the character which did not appear in the first generation but which reappeared in the second he called the *recessive.*

Mendel found that each unit character was inherited independently of any other unit character. For example, a variety of pea has a tall plant and a purple blossom, another variety has a short plant and a white blossom. In crossing these two varieties of pea, plants can be developed which are tall with white blossoms or short with purple blossoms. Each unit character is inherited independently of the other.

Later experiments show that all unit characters are not inherited in this independent fashion. Some characters are *linked* to other characters. One of the commonest kinds of *linkage* is with sex. In human beings it seems that color-blindness is a masculine characteristic, appearing among about 3% of men but very rarely among women.

Experimentation has also shown a phenomenon called *blending*. That is, the first generation may not show either the dominant or the recessive unit character but may be a compromise between the two. A common example of this in humans is the crossing of two races of different colors. Whites and Negroes when crossed produce descendants who are neither so white as the one parent or so black as the other. Many examples of this blending have been found in studies of heredity. Such blending can be satisfactorily explained upon the basis of unit characters, if it is assumed that the characteristic consists not of one but of several unit characters. If the black pigment in the skin of the Negro depends not upon the presence of a single unit character but upon the presence of several, it is at once possible that the mating between a white and a Negro will result in an offspring which has some but not all of the unit characters responsible for producing the black pigmentation. The result will be a child not so black as the Negro parent nor so white as the other parent.

The Explanation of Mendel's Law Has Been Furnished by Geneticists during the Present Century. It is well known that the only possible basis for heredity is the germ cell. This slender bridge furnishes the only possible hereditary connection between parent and offspring. It was discovered that when the germ cells were stained, certain parts of the cell absorbed more of the stain or coloring matter than others. Nothing was at first known of the function or principle of these parts of the cell, but because they became colored they were called *chromosomes*. It was soon discovered that any species of plant or animal had a definite number of these chromosomes. The number was not accidental, apparently, but had some significance. It was next discovered that these chromosomes behaved in a peculiar manner while the germ cell was maturing or becoming ready to unite with the germ cell of the opposite sex, for the formation of a new individual. In this ripening process, the chromosomes which had originally been distributed in a sort of chromatin net-work became segregated into a definite number of pairs of rod-shaped bodies. In the human being, for example, there are twenty-four such pairs of chromosomes. During the maturation of the germ cell, by a complicated process which we will not attempt to describe here, the number of chromosomes in the mature germ cell is reduced to one-half the original number. The mature germ cell of the human being has twenty-four such chromosomes instead of the original twenty-four pairs, or forty-eight. The new individual, formed by the union of two such mature germ cells, therefore has the original number which is characteristic of his species. One-half of his chromosomes have come from one parent and one-half from the other.

When we apply this information about the germ cell to Mendel's observations concerning inheritance, we are furnished with a fair explanation of his findings. If we assume that the germ cell of the tall pea contains a chromosome which has within it the determiner for tallness and that the germ cell from the short pea does not have in its chromosome the determiner for tallness, then the offspring will be tall because of the presence of this determiner for tallness, which is dominant. The germ cells of this offspring, however, will contain a pair of chromosomes, one of which contains this determiner for tallness while the other is without this determiner. During the process of maturation of this germ cell, there will be an even chance that the mature germ cell will or will not contain that member of the pair which has the determiner for tallness. If the matured germ cell does not contain this determiner for tallness, the descendants will be short. If we assume a cross fertilization between such hybrids, the result will be the ratios which Mendel found, three tall plants to one short one.

The phenomenon of linkage, which has been discovered since the work of Mendel, can likewise be explained by the chromosome theory, if we assume that each chromosome contains within it many determiners or *genes*, but that each chromosome tends to maintain its unity. For example, in the human being where an individual has forty-eight chromosomes, he has received twenty-four of these chromosomes from his mother and twenty-four from his father. During the process of maturation these forty-eight chromosomes are reduced to twenty-four. Which ones of these forty-eight will remain is apparently a matter of chance. That is, in any mature germ cell it is possible that ten chromosomes originally received from one parent will be present and fourteen of the chromosomes from the other parent, or it may be that sixteen from the one parent will be present and only eight from the other, etc. Each chromosome is inherited independently of each other chromosome. The individual chromosomes, however, tend to maintain their unity. The whole chromosome is inherited in most cases or none of it. When two characters are linked together it is assumed that they are represented by genes which exist within the same chromosome.

It is true that there is a certain amount of crossing over. That is, characters which are linked do not always remain linked, although they tend to do so. This crossing over is assumed to depend upon a partial splitting up of the chromosome under certain conditions. It is assumed that if two separate genes which determine the development of two separate unit characters lie far apart on the chromosome, the chances for their crossing over are relatively high, while if they lie close together on the chromosome the chances that they will continue to be linked are very high.

A Gene May Affect More than One Unit Character. For a time there was a tendency to assume that each unit character is produced by a single identifiable unit in the germ cell—a simple gene. It has been clearly shown, however, that a simple gene may, and usually does, affect more than one of the hereditary characters of an individual. It is true that the absence of a particular gene may completely prevent the development of a given unit character, but if that gene is present the development of the character is altered by the action of many other genes. Many single genes produce substances which permeate the entire body, affecting all its parts, while other genes are more limited in their action, affecting mainly certain specific body organs.

Can Mendel's Law Be Applied to the Inheritance of Human Traits? Some unit characters have been definitely established, for example, color of hair, color of the eyes, color-blindness, night blindness, hæmophilia (bleeding) and brachydactylis (short fingers). This law undoubtedly applies to many other human traits.

Attempts have been made to apply it to mental characteristics as well as physical traits. Goddard, in his studies of feeble-mindedness, came to the conclusion that feeble-mindedness is hereditary according to the Mendelian laws. If we assume that *intelligence* depends upon the presence of many unit characters rather than only one, so that we may allow for many different degrees of intelligence in the offspring, the way is theoretically open to the assumption that intelligence is hereditary according to Mendelian principles. Proof that such is the case will then depend upon the accumulation of a sufficient number of observations to enable us to reach a conclusion which is based on fact. Goddard has made many such observations. His observations are, however, open to question. His investigators were apparently too ready to classify a person as feeble-minded upon insufficient evidence. Recent developments in psychology have emphasized the great importance of the earliest years of childhood for the development of intelligence. A better understanding of these early years may well reduce the number of individuals who are classified as feeble-minded and may upset the ratios which have previously been worked out.

Attempts have been made to study the inheritance of special abilities of many kinds as well as the inheritance of genius. These studies show that special abilities and generally high intelligence run in families. They remain unconvincing because of the fact that there is such large opportunity for environmental factors to influence the development of the individuals concerned. That is, the children of genius may have the advantage not only because they have inherited special ability, but because they are given exceptional opportunity for development. The children of defectives may be defective not merely because of their bad heredity but also because of their bad environmental opportunities. Convincing proof of the inheritance either of intelligence or special mental ability of any kind still remains for the future. Studies of the inheritance of insanity are likewise unconvincing, although there seems to be a tendency for certain types of insanity to reappear in families.

Comparison of Galton's Law and Mendel's Law. Galton made many statistical studies of inheritance. His studies of the inheritance of genius in human beings are especially interesting. He came to the conclusion that a child inherited half its characteristics from its immediate parents (that is one-fourth from each parent), one-fourth of its characteristics from its four grandparents (that is, one-sixteenth from each grandparent), one-eighth of its characteristics from the great-grandparents, etc. When we compare Galton's law with Mendel's law we find a certain discrepancy. Mendel's tall peas, for example, resembled one of the parents and not the other. In the second generation three-fourths of the plants resembled one of the grandparents and one-fourth of them resembled the other grandparent. When we consider that Galton's law is applied to individuals who are not pure strains but are themselves mixtures, and that his law is based upon a statistical treatment of large numbers of people rather than an analysis of the heredity of individuals, it is clear that his law agrees with that of Mendel. When we consider the descendence through several generations and take averages, we will find the number of individuals showing each trait to correspond roughly to Galton's law. We may summarize the relative values of Mendel's law and Galton's law by saying that for the purpose of understanding the hereditary characteristics of large numbers of people Galton's law is adequate, but for the purpose of understanding the heredity of any individual, Galton's law is of no great value, while Mendel's law is satisfactory.

III. MENTAL INHERITANCE AND EDUCATION

Geneticists and Educators Have Different Points of View. For the geneticist, the study of inheritance is concerned with the adult body structure for the purpose of inferring germ-cell structure. Genetics is concerned with germinal characteristics rather than with somatic characteristics. Heredity is the continuity from generation to generation of elements of germinal organization. The geneticist wishes to maintain environmental influences in a highly standardized condition so that somatic development will occur in a highly standardized fashion generation after generation. It is only by maintaining these standardized conditions of nurture that the geneticist is able to make inferences from somatic development to germinal characteristics. When he finds that a bodily characteristic develops in the same way in succeeding generations under standardized environmental conditions, he assumes that it is laid down in the germ plasm.

On the other hand, educators are interested primarily in matters of growth and development as they can be influenced by varying the environmental circumstances. Educators do not wish to maintain a standardized environment. They wish to introduce variety into human behavior rather than universality. They seek to do this by introducing varied conditions of nurture. The interest of the educator is not so much in the germ cells as in the somatic characteristics of successive generations. The educator wishes to know to what extent the somatic characteristics of the child or the adult resemble the somatic characteristics of his parents, but he is more interested in knowing to what extent changes in environmental circumstances can change the somatic characteristics of a developing individual. The continuity of germinal characteristics may limit the variations in somatic characteristics which the educator can produce, but it does not eliminate such variations.

The method by which the educator attacks his main problem requires the use of controlled environmental changes in the attempt to produce variability of somatic development. He calls a characteristic hereditary when he can find no means for changing its course of development through environmental pressures. There is no reason why the educator should feel it necessary to adopt the point of view and the technique of the geneticist. The educator has problems of his own which are just as real and just as important as those of the geneticist. He should assert his ends and should feel entirely free to use methods which are best adapted to the solution of his own problems, which are essentially the problems of modifying development by means of environmental change.

Approaching the problems of heredity from these two points of view, it is conceivable that the geneticist will find many characteristics to be hereditary which the educator will find are not hereditary. That is, the geneticist will find many characteristics which continue to develop generation after generation in a standardized environment while the educator will find that the same characteristics will not develop generation after generation when the environment is modified.

Mental Traits Are Not Discontinuous. The geneticist differentiates between his characters in a qualitative fashion. That is, he deals with such things as color, or the presence or absence of a trait; he does not allow for overlapping. Whenever he finds traits which are not discontinuous, he discards them as being unsuitable for genetic study. The educator, who is dealing with mental traits, cannot do this. Mental traits have not been successfully classified into a discontinuous series. That is, mental traits do overlap to a considerable extent. The differences in mental characteristics which exist between individuals are quantitative rather than qualitative. In dealing with mental traits we are concerned with the question of a greater or lesser amount of some mental characteristic, such as intelligence, musical ability, mathematical ability, and the like, and not with the presence or absence of this trait. Psychologists have not as yet been able to discover a single mental trait which is positively known to be distinct and separate from other mental traits in the same sense that one color is distinct and separate from another color in the wings of a fruit fly. Studies of mental inheritance cannot, therefore, proceed in the same fashion in which the geneticist has studied inheritance of a particular kind of biological characteristic.

It is true that the geneticist has developed a theory for explaining the blending of characteristics and the presence of characteristics in different degrees, which is the outstanding feature of mental traits. Whether this hypothesis can be applied to the inheritance of mental characteristics is as yet undetermined. It needs to be carefully tested by direct study and observation of mental characteristics of succeeding generations. Such study of the mental characteristics of successive generations requires the development and use of tests of mentality for a mixed adult population, together with the development of some scheme for making allowance for differences in opportunity and environmental circumstances. This procedure is so difficult that it has not been successfully carried through up to the present, and we frankly do not know how it can be done. However, until some scheme of this kind is devised for testing hypotheses concerned with mental inheritance, it would seem unwise to accept as proven for mental inheritance the hypotheses that have been developed by the geneticists in their studies of the fruit fly, peas, and the like.

The Mendelian Hypothesis Has Been "Applied" to Mental Traits—Not Developed from Their Study. Goddard's attempt to explain feeble-mindedness as being a recessive unit character which is inherited according to the Mendelian ratio is an example of this attempt to fit the facts to an hypothesis without sufficient reason. Every person who is familiar with tests of intelligence knows that feeble-mindedness is not a single trait, which can be differentiated from normal intelligence. If feeble-mindedness is to be explained by the Mendelian theory, it must be assumed to be not a single unit trait, but a composite of several of such unit traits.

Freeman, Holzinger, and Mitchell studied 26 children, both of whose parents were rated feeble-minded. According to the Mendelian law, all of these children should have been feeble-minded if feeble-mindedness is a unit character. It was found, however, that only four had an I.Q. below 70. The average I.Q. for these 26 children was 81, which is higher than would be expected according to the Mendelian law. That is, the children of feeble-minded parents tend to have higher intelligence than the parents.

Porteus, in his studies of racial differences in intelligence, points out that any portion of a race quickly develops the whole range of social and intellectual differences which are characteristic of the race as a whole. The immigration of Chinese to this country took place from the lower social and intellectual groups, but within a comparatively short time the succeeding generations of Chinese in this country show the normal characteristics of the entire Chinese group. The upper intellectual groups appear within the second and third generations where the ancestors have been chosen entirely from the lower intellectual and social groups. Jennings affirms his belief that this change in a group of low intellectual status can occur.

There can be no doubt that the mental traits of children are more similar to those of their parents than to people in general, but the present state of our knowledge of mental inheritance does not justify the assumption that it occurs according to a dominant or recessive pattern. We could summarize this discussion by saying that Mendelian theories of inheritance are neither in conflict with data concerning mental inheritance nor do they throw any light upon the problems of mental inheritance. Educators need to continue their researches in mental inheritance independently and develop their own theories as they are needed.

Studies of Mental Development of Twins. Pearson found a correlation of .52 for the resemblance of siblings in eye color, hair color, and cephalic index. Thorndike found a correlation of .60 for the resemblance of siblings (16 years old) in intelligence. He assumes that this difference between .52 and .60 represents the influence of their common environment upon intelligence, on the assumption that environmental factors have not influenced the resemblance of siblings in eye color, hair color, and cephalic index, but have caused them to become more alike mentally. On the basis of Thorndike's and Pearson's figures, T. L. Kelley concludes that factors in environment common to both siblings introduce change (increased resemblance) in intelligence to the amount of about 9%. Kelley thinks that other factors of the environment which are not common to both siblings are probably equal to the common factors in their influence upon intelligence. He therefore concludes that the figures quoted show that an individual child's intelligence has been influenced about 20% by the environment of the first sixteen years of life. Kelley thinks that the correlations as found by Thorndike are too low, due to the selective nature of Thorndike's samples. He believes that the correlation of intelligence between siblings should be nearer .70 than .60. If this is true, of the total development in intelligence, about 44% is due to environmental factors. Whether of the total development in intelligence 20% or 44% is due to environmental factors, the amount is certainly great enough to emphasize the extreme importance of these external influences, and to emphasize the view that the problem of the inheritance of mental characteristics must be approached with a different technique than the problem of the inheritance of characteristics commonly studied by the geneticists.

Studies of the correlation between mental traits of identical twins as compared with fraternal twins show that identical twins resemble one another in characteristics more than fraternal twins or siblings. This has properly been taken as proof of the importance of hereditary factors in mental development. These studies have usually assumed that it is possible to separate twins into two distinct and discontinuous groupings, identical twins on the one hand and fraternal twins on the other. Kelley points out that it is a justifiable assumption that twins differ in closeness of their inherited similarity in a graded manner, from most similar to the similarity of unlike siblings and not in a sharply bi-modal manner. Kelley quotes a study by Freeman of three pairs of twins classified as identical, the members of the pairs having been reared apart from infancy. Two pairs showed very similar intelligence quotients, but the third pair had intelligence quotients which were distinctly different. The occurrence of a considerable difference in *one* such pair is sufficient to nullify a belief in the *all-importance* of heredity in the development of intelligence.

It Seems Impossible to Reach an Abstract Statement of the Relative Importance of Nature and Nurture in Mental Development. The relative importance of either the environmental or hereditary factor depends upon the amount of variability which exists in the one or the other factor. When we are comparing the mental characteristics of two children who have grown up in an environment which is highly standardized and similar, the environmental factor seems to be of little importance in explaining the differences between them, and can be disregarded, especially if there are pronounced differences in the genetic structure of the parents. On the other hand, when we are comparing the mental development of two children whose parents have similar genetic structures, the genetic factor seems of little importance in understanding the differences between them, particularly if the children have grown up under widely different environmental circumstances. In other words, the factors in mental development which seem important are always the *variables*, while the constants seem of little consequence. It is just as in a mathematical problem, the constants give us little difficulty; we usually center our thinking about the variables and consider them to be the important factors of an algebraic equation. When environment is highly standardized (and the environment of modern civilized man is highly standardized in many important respects), heredity seems to be more important than environment in determining variations in mental development. On the other hand, when considerable variety is introduced into environment the importance of environmental circumstances is emphasized.

From this point of view we can understand the results of May and Hartshorne, who found that deceit is inherited fully as much as "intelligence." Their study simply means that environmental circumstances are sufficiently standardized with respect to the development of the mental characteristic of deceit, that they are of relatively little importance in determining individual variations in this character. If environmental characteristics concerned with moral training were less highly standardized, we should expect to find them of relatively more importance and heredity of less importance.

It seems, then, that in determining mental development it is not environment and inheritance in an absolute sense, but *difference* in environment and *difference* in inheritance which are significant. As we pointed out in Chapter III, the concept of heredity as used by the geneticists is possible only when we assume development in a *highly standardized environment*. The educator is interested in directing development by introducing *variations into the environment*. To this extent the concept of heredity as used by the geneticist is not applicable to his work.

What Are the Causes of Differences between Individuals? From the standpoint of the educator and the psychologist, the problem of mental inheritance reduces to the problem of the probable causes of observed differences between individuals. Jennings points out the fallacy of the belief that a characteristic which has been proven to be due to genetic factors in one case must be due to genetic factors in all cases. This is a fallacy to which the biologists are

especially addicted. It is equally fallacious to assume that
a characteristic which has been proven to be due to environmental factors in one case must be due to environmental factors in all cases. Psychologists and educators
are especially inclined toward this fallacy. The extreme
statements of the Behaviorists and Psycho-analysts concerning the all-importance of environment in determining behavior are based upon this fallacy. It seems fair to
read into Jennings' statements the view that the same
observed difference in intelligence, in special aptitude,
in morality, in personality, or in any other characteristic
whatever, may be due in some cases to genetic factors,
in other cases to environmental factors, or to a combination of the two. It is impossible to make a single generalization which will cover all cases. It may be that certain
differences are *more commonly* due to genetic factors and
other differences *more commonly* due to environmental
factors, but there will be important exceptions.

The matter can best be summarized in the words of
Jennings:

"1. All characteristics of organisms may be altered by
changing the genes, provided we can learn how to change
the proper genes.

"2. All characteristics may be altered by changing the
environmental conditions under which the organism develops, provided that we learn what conditions to change
and how to change them.

"3. Any kind of change of characteristics that can be
induced by altering genes can likewise be induced (if we
know how) by altering conditions. (This statement is
open to more doubt than the other two, but it is likely
eventually to be found correct.)"

IV. SUMMARY

The development of genetics caused many educators to abandon the tradition that any child could learn anything if he only applied himself. The fatalistic attitude was adopted that individual development was fully determined by the constitution of the germ plasm. The contrary belief in the all-importance of environmental factors in determining individual mental development was emphasized by the psycho-analysts and the behaviorists.

It seems impossible to think of mental inheritance independently of inherited anatomical characteristics. The possible physical bases for mental inheritance seem to be: (1) brain size, (2) susceptibility of the nervous system to change, and (3) special anatomical characteristics, bodily or nervous. Investigations have shown a low positive correlation between brain size and intelligence, but the mental qualities of individuals cannot satisfactorily be estimated from their brain size. Susceptibility of nervous material to change may be an inherited characteristic, but it can be studied only by observing changes in mental characteristics or behavior. Special anatomical characteristics doubtless do have an important influence upon mental traits and behavior, but the more important peculiarities (nervous) cannot be studied directly. We deduce their existence only by studying mental or behavior traits. Mental traits are very susceptible to environmental modification. Mental inheritance must, therefore, be studied directly and independently of bodily inheritance.

During the twentieth century genetics has furnished an excellent account of the inheritance of many physical characteristics. Educators, however, have a point of view of their own which prohibits the uncritical application of genetic principles to mental development. Psychologists and educators must develop laws of heredity from their own observations rather than merely apply laws developed by geneticists working with physical characters.

It seems impossible to reach a general statement of the relative importance of nature and nurture in development which will apply to all individuals and all traits. The development of the same trait may be due primarily to hereditary factors in one individual and primarily to environmental factors in another. Development is always the *product* of genetic and environmental factors, never a mere *summation;* in different individuals one factor or the other may be large or small, even though the product is similar.

CHAPTER VII

LEARNING

I. Learning as Association

The Laws of Association. Formerly learning was discussed under the heading of association. The *laws* of association,—contiguity, succession, similarity, and contrast —date back to Aristotle. These laws were re-defined and clarified, but not essentially changed, up to the time of the recent work of the objective psychologists upon the psychology of learning. Association in the commonly accepted view is the tendency of two mental states, having once occurred together, to occur together again. When one of them reappears it recalls the other one also. A variation of this traditional view, which is perhaps an improvement upon it, is Sir William Hamilton's theory of redintegration—"If two ideas have formed a part of the same experience, when one of them occurs it will reinstate the whole." This principle of Sir William Hamilton is very similar to the views recently expressed by the Gestalt psychologists.

The traditional statement of association is typical of the structural and functional psychology. The behaviorists and objective psychologists have, for the most part, been content merely to translate into objective terms these earlier laws of association. The concept of reflex as it is found in the functional and objective psychology is merely a statement of association in motor terms. The laws of learning as formulated by a study of conditioned reflexes represent only a further objective statement of the older laws of association.

Learning and the Structural Psychology. Titchener, whom we may take as typical of the structural psychology, considers that association refers to the re-occurrence of mental events in their previous connection. An association is a group of ideas found uniformly together. The explanation of the fact that the ideas belong together must be sought in the nervous system. We must not, however, be misled into believing that the nerve processes cement the ideas together; the nerve processes are merely the accompaniments of the ideas. Structuralists usually reduce the four laws of association to one—temporal contiguity. Titchener summarizes this law in the following words: "Whenever a sensory or imaginal process occurs in consciousness there are likely to appear with it (of course in imaginal terms) all those sensory and imaginal processes which occurred together with it in any earlier conscious process." The structuralists explain meaning in terms of association, since meaning is always context. One idea furnishes the meaning of another idea, one sensation the meaning of another sensation.

Learning and the Functional Psychology. The functionalists have adopted essentially the same view of association as that held by the structuralists. They believe that association is a matter of establishing specific nerve pathways leading from one brain center to another. Nerve pathways are supposed to lead ordinarily from sensory centers to motor centers. They seldom lead from sensory to sensory centers. Judd describes association as "the tendency for a pathway to be established between any two brain centers that are active at the same time." This process of association is an important fact in adaptation, which is the central fact of all function. The functionalists are inclined to give more thought to the *value* of association than do the structuralists. They look upon association as a means of adjustment to environment. Associations are almost universally of such a nature that stimulation is connected with appropriate response.

The stimulus-response psychology has grown out of functionalism. According to this psychology the building up of human activity consists of a process of associating stimuli with responses. The normal outcome of every stimulus is supposed to be a nerve process which leads inevitably to a motor outlet. Sensory and motor areas in the brain, which are believed by the structuralists to be essentially centers for conscious processes of a particular sensory or motor character, tend to become in the functional psychology merely inlets and outlets for the cerebrum. The really important work of the cerebrum is done by the association centers. Consciousness is believed by the functionalists to be the point in mind at which adaptation is going on most actively. This process of adaptation is an associative process and is primarily a function of the associative centers of the brain.

Learning and the Objective Psychology. John Dewey pointed out many years ago that the reflex arc is association in motor terms. In the reflex arc there is a stimulus which is linked by a nerve pathway to a muscular or glandular activity. This connection of sense organ and muscle or gland is the typical fact of association. In the writings of behaviorists such as Watson, the *conditioned* reflex is equivalent to association. Association has come to mean the connection of a stimulus with a motor or glandular response which was not originally connected with that stimulus.

From the behavioristic point of view, the conditioned reflex is typical of all learning; there is nothing to any kind of learning in addition to the mere process of conditioning. The facts of conditioning of responses may, of course, become quite complex. Two reflexes may become associated in such a fashion that the stimulus for one calls forth the response for the other. When this first conditioned reflex has been set up, it may in turn become associated with another reflex or with another similarly conditioned reflex, and a secondary exchange of stimulus and response may occur. The learning of an adult individual is supposed to consist primarily of this exchange between stimuli and responses that did not in most cases belong together as a part of the person's original equipment of reflexes. These stimuli and responses have themselves become joined together by an earlier process of conditioning, and may be removed many times from the original reflex equipment of the infant.

From the practical point of view, habit formation depends upon the simultaneous occurrence of two stimuli, each of which calls forth its own response; that is, learning always requires *double stimulation*. If two stimuli which call forth separate and distinct responses are presented at the same time or in close succession, with sufficient frequency, it is supposed that an exchange will occur; the one stimulus will become connected with the response which formerly took place when the other stimulus was presented. The thing that determines which of the two original responses will persist has not always been clearly stated by the behaviorists. Presumably one response is prepotent, that is, it is somehow stronger. The nerve impulse which brings it about is somehow more intense so that it comes to predominate as opposed to the other. The law of effect is an attempt to explain this selection of one of the two responses. Many behaviorists, however, prefer to reject it because of its original statement in the subjective language of pleasure and pain.

Learning as the Fortuitous Joining of Discrete Atoms.
All three of these schools, the structuralists, functionalists, and behaviorists, have the view that the stimulus
is a kind of "atom," which is joined together with a mental process or a motor activity merely because it has
occurred together with one of these processes at some
time. All organization of mental life on the one hand, or
behavior on the other, is believed to take place by this
associative process.

Subjective psychologists tell us that the visual appearance of a mathematical symbol is joined to the idea of
the symbol by association and that one idea is similarly
joined to another. Thinking is originated by some sensory stimulus which is joined to an idea, it is continued
because ideas are joined in chains and patterns. The solution of the most complex problem depends upon the fact
that the proper ideas have previously been joined together by association—*i.e.*, they were originally separate
and discrete, but because they were found together in
some earlier conscious process, they became artificially
joined and continued together thereafter. Ideas carry
over into actions because they have been joined by
association to the proper bodily movements. Teaching
consists of providing occasions for the occurrence of sensory stimuli, ideas, and actions in their proper order and
connection.

Objective psychologists assert that a stimulus which
originally produced one response may, by a process of
conditioning, become joined to another—a response that
did not at first belong to that stimulus. Each response
because of its movement aspect furnishes new kinesthetic
stimulation, that becomes in its turn the starting point
for a new one. Ideas, thoughts, and the like are merely
types of response in which the movement phase is *im-*

plicit—*i.e.*, not detectable by ordinary means of observation. Learning consists entirely of a process of exchange between stimulus-response systems. All activity—even the complex processes of thinking as found in mathematics, science, and philosophy—depends for its order and sequence upon the fact that the person has built up, through conditioning, complex systems and patterns of response.

The basis for all mental activity or all behavior is supposed to be the existence of nerve paths of low resistance which either existed in the beginning in the form of reflex or instinct, or were built up by experience in the form of associations between ideas or conditioned reflexes. While it can be stated that all three of these schools consider stimuli, ideas, behavior, etc., as atoms which are artificially joined together by a process of association or conditioning, it must be pointed out that there is some recognition of the fact that every response or mental activity involves the entire organism. It is recognized that what is important is occurring in the entire nervous system and is not merely the specific activity in the specific nerve path.

Learning and the Purposive Psychology. The purposive psychologists take as their starting point the belief that certain desires or cravings are natural to human beings. The motivation of all learning depends upon the functioning of these inborn tendencies. The thing which is learned may depend upon the accidental circumstances of stimulation and response; but a description of learning in terms of stimulus and response will always be superficial. The fact that learning occurs depends not upon the accidental occurrence at the same time of two sets of stimuli and responses, but rather upon the fact that the child is already active, is already striving to attain a certain goal. This goal is set up for the child not by the circumstances which it happens to meet, but by its own inborn nature. Environmental circumstances may cause the child temporarily to abandon its goal or to seek new ways to attain this goal, but the goals themselves which are fundamental to learning are not environmentally determined. Pleasure or pain, for example, may lead a child to continue or to avoid a particular manner for attaining a desired end, but they are mere incidents in the child's progress toward its goal. They arise out of the child's activity, which began independently of them.

School learning, therefore, depends upon the child's inherent goal-seeking behavior. The child has certain desires, wishes, and purposes; arithmetic, reading, history, etc., must be presented as means for their attainment. Until the child sees the relationship of school studies to his own strivings, the right kind of learning cannot take place. The purposive psychologist, then, is interested in the motivation of learning rather than in the mechanics of attaining skill.

Learning and the Psycho-analytic Psychology. The psycho-analysts have had little or no interest in the nature of the neurological activity underlying learning. They have concerned themselves rather with the environmental conditions which are responsible for the establishment of anti-social habits. They have contributed nothing toward an explanation of the mechanism of learning. They are quite content to leave to other psychologists the determination of the theoretical problems involved.

If we may be permitted to approach their investigations from the standpoint of the functional or objective psychology, we can see that they attempt to determine the arrangement of stimulating conditions which will result in the development of social or anti-social behavior. They are not interested in the routine tasks of teaching as found in spelling, arithmetic, or reading. They are concerned, rather, with lying, stealing, sex perversions, unsocial attitudes, over-agressiveness, etc. They begin by classifying behavior on the basis of its value to society. Those activities that contribute to the attainment of goals which are purely individual, which have no social value and are ordinarily socially harmful, are the activities whose development has been most studied by this group of psychologists. The psycho-analysts take it for granted that certain situations will call forth certain types of activity. While the functionalists and behaviorists think of this original linking of situation and response in terms of reflex and instinct as nuerological mechanisms, the psycho-analysts are likely to think of it in terms of *goal-seeking* behavior. It is true that they call this goal-seeking behavior instinctive, but it is of such a general nature that it is rather difficult to think of it in terms of specific neuro-muscular patterns, such as are required for the understanding of conditioned responses. The psycho-analysts like to introduce purely mental or spiritual driving forces to explain original activities. They believe that a purely physical and physiological description in terms of nerve connections between sense organ and muscle or gland is inadequate to explain the original behavior of a child. Learning for the psycho-analysts consists of a change in direction of original mental driving forces rather than of a mere exchange of stimuli and responses in a purely physical organism.

Learning and the Gestalt Psychology. The Gestalt psychologists abandon the fundamental assumption of the functional and behavioristic psychologists. They deny that learning is a matter of eliminating errors and fixing responses which are already present; they deny that learning is a matter of establishing specific nerve pathways of low resistance leading from sense organ to muscle or gland. They insist that the total activity of the entire body influences every specific action. The Gestalt psychologists insist that we do not learn by experience; we learn instead by insight. Experience merely gives the opportunity for insight. When we have an experience but lack sufficient insight to profit by it, we do not learn. The measure of progress is the degree of insight into an experience which we possess.

When a child meets a situation for the first time, he responds according to goals of his own rather than according to the goal which has been fixed by the experimenter. His actions must not be thought of as *errors* but rather as being merely *irrelevant* to the situation when judged from the standpoint of the experimenter. Just as soon as the child perceives and begins acting in accordance with the goal which the experimenter has set up, his behavior becomes relevant and the learning process is finished. *Repetition* of the relevant action is wholly unnecessary to fix it. The learner eliminates the so-called errors or wasteful movements merely because he adopts new and different goals. The successful movement is repeated for just the same reason that it was made in the first place. When the learner has gained an insight into the situation, that is, when he has discovered and adopted the goal which the experimenter has set up, his actions begin to conform to that goal and his previous actions, which were directed toward other goals, disappear. Fluctuations in efficiency in any performance depend upon chance variations in stimulating conditions which are not under control of the experimenter or the learner.

Learning Is a Process of Maturation (Gestalt Psychology). The appropriate response in a new situation is not established by use. It is established rather by stimulation which produces a continuous maturation of the learner. This maturation shows itself externally in the adoption of new goals, internally this maturation is a process of development in the learner's nervous organization.

Maturation may be thought of as a growth process taking place within the child's nervous system. Such growth processes may go on both before and after the nervous system has reached its limit of size and weight. We know that every structure, whether animate or inanimate, undergoes a change with the passage of time. There are qualitative changes going on in the earth and in every physical object. Fruits, for example, ripen and then decay. Muscles harden and eventually lose their flexibility. The water content of the nervous system decreases during senescence, and metabolism in general becomes more sluggish. We may think of maturation as being the reverse of the process of decay. Maturation may be thought of as a process of differentiation of energy patterns or systems of stresses within the nervous system. These nerve patterns are organized during the process of maturation. Exactly what this organization consists of we do not know. It may be a process of change in the organic composition of the nervous system, a change similar to changes in patterns of electric potential, a growth of inter-cellular connections, or probably the growth of previously undeveloped nerve cells which were present since early in life. Maturation may be a process of formation of physiological gradients, that is, it may be a matter of changes in irritability or in metabolic rate of living tissues particularly in the nervous system; we know that there is a difference in physiological gradient or metabolic rate in different tissues in various parts of the body.

Maturation is probably caused by stimulation. We know that in many ways growth is a function of stimulation. Callouses on the hands or feet may be produced by rubbing. Germ cells may develop into monstrosities instead of into normal animals when the medium in which the embryos are developing is changed. Cancer is believed to be due sometimes to irritation. In general, any kind of stimulation which affects the physiological processes going on within the nervous system can be thought of as a condition of maturation, for example, food and oxygen supply, temperature, the presence of toxic substances. Maturation is clearly the outcome of an interaction between the organism and its environment. We do not know why an organism responds to environmental stimulation by growing at one time and disintegrating at another, neither do we understand the kind of growth which will be determined by different types of stimulation; we are, therefore, unable to predict the course which will be taken by evolution or by individual development. Out of the combination of environmental circumstances and the existing organism there emerges a new type of organism and a new type of behavior; it is this *emergence of something new* which is learning.

Repetition Does Not Cause Learning (Gestalt Psychology). Repetition has the same place in learning that time has in growth. Time does not explain growth; it merely furnishes the opportunity for the occurrence of growth. Repetition likewise does not explain learning; it merely gives opportunity for learning to take place. A repetition is merely a cross-section of the learning process; to complete the description of learning it is necessary to permit the occurrence of additional repetitions. Repetition should be taken for granted as a constant factor in learning, just as time is taken for granted as a constant factor in growth. For the explanation of the learning which takes place, we must look to the level of maturation which has been reached. The factors which really explain learning are such things as the character of the goal, the time interval between repetitions, the learner's own level of insight, incentives, distractions, rhythm, method of procedure, etc. Learning must be explained in terms of these other factors which are present as repetition continues.

According to Wheeler, the learning process is "a form of intelligent behavior that inevitably takes place when the organism finds problem situations repeated at intervals of time. It is a function of (a) maturation, (b) the repetition of stimuli, (c) the time intervals between repetitions of stimuli, (d) the relation of the problem to the learner's level of maturation, (e) the completeness with which the stimulus pattern is repeated, and (f) the degree of tension under which the learner is behaving."

In learning to solve an algebraic equation, for example, the learner must first adopt the correct goal, he must know what is to be accomplished. His success depends, in the second place, upon his level of insight; by insight is meant his understanding of algebraic symbols and his ability to relate them to the goal. He will fail if his "insight" has not yet reached a high enough level. Once he has succeeded, further increase in skill—*i.e.*, speed, accuracy in detail, etc.—depends upon maturation. The speed with which maturation takes place is a function of the factors mentioned in the preceding paragraphs.

II. THE NATURE OF LEARNED ACTION

Common Attitudes toward Learned Actions. When we begin the study of learned actions—*i.e.*, habits—we find that there are several attitudes which need to be understood. These attitudes may be best stated as questions. (1) How do we name habits? (2) What is the physical basis for habit? (3) What is the place of the physical stimulus in habitual action? (4) Is there an internal drive in habit? (5) What are the advantages and disadvantages of habit?

Habits Are Named Objectively. We customarily think about and name habits and learned activities in terms of movement or result accomplished by mental activity or bodily movement. In other words, we tend to be objective in the names which we give to learned activities. Such names are walking, riding, throwing a ball, playing golf, adding numbers, reading, thinking, etc. In our popular thinking we frequently go no further into the question of learning than the mere assigning of names of this character.

Is the Nerve Path of Low Resistance the Basis for Habit? Just as soon as we begin a study of psychology, we discover that learning must be thought of in terms of nervous organization. The traditional view of the nature of this organization is the nerve path of low resistance. It is assumed that in the beginning the nervous system is so organized that some pathways (for example, reflexes), have low resistance, while other nerve pathways have much higher resistance. Learning is thought to be a matter of reducing the original resistance of these nerve pathways. Two theories have been advanced to explain the manner in which this reduction of resistance takes place.

The most widely accepted theory assumes that the original resistance to the passage of a nerve impulse along a nerve pathway occurs at the synapse. The nerve impulse is supposed to find passage throughout the length of a single neuron without resistance at all. If the neuron discharges, it is believed to discharge completely. However, when the nerve impulse reaches the end of the neuron (the end brush), it does not readily cross over to

the dendrites of the next neuron. It may find its passage
from end brush to dendrite completely blocked or it may
be merely retarded. Learning is thought to be a matter
of reducing this resistance to the passage of the nerve
impulse from one neuron to the next. If the nerve impulse succeeds in crossing from one neuron to another, it
does not again encounter resistance until it reaches the
next synapse. At this point its passage will again be interfered with, depending upon the degree of resistance
offered at this next junction between two neurons.

The second view of the nature of resistance to the passage of the nerve impulse assumes that this resistance is
an affair of the entire neuron. As the nerve impulse
proceeds through the cell body and the axon, it is supposed to encounter resistance. Reduction of resistance
is thought to be a matter of rearrangement of molecules
or some other change in the material which goes to make
up the nerve cell. The resistance at the synapse is not
believed to change permanently; sometimes temporary
changes may occur in the synapse resulting in the phenomenon of pre-occupation or absent-mindedness. The
changes in resistance at the synapse are supposed to be
merely temporary; the permanent changes which are
called learning take place as a result of changes occurring
throughout the entire length of the nerve cell. This theory
has the advantage, that it furnishes an explanation of
the phenomenon of pre-occupation, but it seems to be
opposed to the all-or-none law which is widely accepted
among physiologists. Both of these theories assume that
learning is a matter of reducing resistance along specific
nerve pathways.

The Gestalt psychologists have recently upset our confidence in this neurological theory. Experiments have
been performed which show that our earlier views must

be modified, if not entirely discarded. It is found, for example, that a chicken may be taught to take food from a background which is colored red and reject food placed on a background which is colored green. The training may be carried on with the right eye only open, the left eye being temporarily covered. After the habit has been well established for the right eye, this eye may be covered and the left eye opened, but the habit continues to function just as well as before. This means that the habit when it was first set up did not consist merely of a specific nerve path of low resistance leading from the right eye to the muscles concerned in the production of the movement. This experiment is all the more convincing in the case of the chicken, since there is no partial crossing of the optic nerves as is found in the case of human beings, so that a nerve path leading from the left eye to the muscles concerned with the activity of taking or rejecting food must be different to a considerable extent from the nerve path involved when the right eye is used.

Norman Cameron, in experiments upon the effects of cerebral lesion on the maze learning of rats, found that destruction of parts of the cerebrum by operation did not completely destroy maze habits but did impair their efficiency. He found also that such operations did not prevent the formation of new maze habits, but did prevent such maze habits from being perfectly formed. If the maze habit depended upon the establishment of specific nerve paths of low resistance, the habit should have been completely destroyed by the operation, or else not affected at all. In the same way, if the learning had consisted of the establishment of specific nerve paths of low resistance, the operated rats should have been able either to form new maze habits perfectly or be totally unable to form such habits at all.

So far as the exact nature of the neurological patterns is concerned, we must admit at the present time that we know very little about learning. We are, however, fairly well convinced that learning does depend upon the occurrence of definite nerve changes of some kind.

Habitual Actions Are Not Self-initiated. A third attidude toward learning which we adopt as soon as we begin to study psychology is that habits or learned acts never occur unless there is some immediately present stimulation. By this we mean that some physical force, such as light, sound, pressure, temperature change, etc., must be acting upon a sense organ immediately preceding the occurrence of the habitual response. Habits never initiate themselves, there is no self-activity in the sense of activity without an adequate physical stimulus. We must bear in mind, however, that some sense organs are located internally and may be stimulated by internal physiological changes.

Is There an Internal "Drive" in Habit? There are seeming exceptions to this view that a response requires a sensory stimulus. These seeming exceptions have led to the development in popular thinking of another attitude toward habits. It is commonly assumed that there is an element of *drive* contained in many habits, such as, for example, drug habits. It is thought that in the absence of any stimulus a person possessing a habit, as smoking, may want to smoke, and engage in activity concerned with hunting the materials for smoking. The thing which is overlooked is that *wanting* or *hunting a cigarette* is itself a learned response which has its own stimulus.

Such a habit as smoking may be built up in about this fashion. At first the beginner will smoke only when some other person is present and offers him a cigarette. In this case there is no question of an internal drive which leads to smoking. In addition to the stimulus of the presence of the other person and the offering of the cigarette, there are present certain other incidental stimuli. If any one of these additional stimuli is regularly present it will, in the words of the older psychology, become associated with the act of smoking; or in the words of the objective psychology, it will become a conditioned stimulus leading to the performance of the act of smoking. One such additional stimulus which is commonly present is the organic stimulation proceeding from a full stomach; that is, a very common occasion for smoking is the finishing of a meal. When people are sitting about a dinner table, or are engaging in a conversation following a meal, smoking very commonly takes place. For the beginner the first stimulus, as we have pointed out, is the offer of the cigarette by someone else who smokes. After a time, the mere presence of food in the stomach becomes a sufficient stimulus to lead that person to look for a cigarette and light it. We may continue in this fashion and explain how the act of smoking gradually comes to be connected up with a large part of our daily routine. The person who is a confirmed smoker is a person who has connected up as a stimulus for smoking almost every act of his daily routine.

If such a person wishes to break the habit of smoking, his best procedure in the beginning would seem to be to change as far as possible his regular manner of living. This will, however, be only a temporary measure, for as soon as his manner of living returns to normal all the old stimuli will be present and the act may again be expected to take place.

There are many other common illustrations of the fact that habitual acts do not take place unless the customary stimulus is present. If a person has lived in a small community for many years and has traveled very little, we commonly recognize that we cannot predict his behavior if he goes alone to a new locality. His behavior in his home community, for example his moral behavior, has become tied up definitely with stimulating conditions of which the presence of friends and relatives is an important part. When he is now placed in a situation from which his friends and relatives have been removed, his behavior becomes unpredictable. This same fact may be illustrated by an anecdote. A man of rather wide experience engaged in conversation with the cashier of his bank. The cashier stated with much pride that he had never in his entire lifetime been tempted to steal money. The man of more experience at once transferred his account to a new bank. The transfer was justified when a year or two later the cashier found himself in personal financial difficulties and misappropriated funds from the bank. A habit of honesty works only in the situations which have been definitely connected up with that habit. Until habitual methods of response have been developed for a particular stimulus a man's action is wholly unpredictable when that situation occurs.

Drive, then, seems to refer merely to the fact that if we build up within our nervous systems the particular set of nerve structures which are concerned with the performance of any given act, that act can be expected to occur invariably when the proper stimulus is supplied. When this stimulus is rather obscure and easily overlooked we are misled into the belief that the action is occurring without stimulation; then we talk of wants, desires, and cravings as if they were sources of action, needing no stimulation.

Advantages and Disadvantages of Habituation. Another attitude which we take toward habits is that they are sometimes valuable and sometimes harmful. This view represents a social evaluation (1) of the act itself, or (2) of the nature of habit in general. One of the features of habit which contributes to its social value is its predictability. Much of our educational effort is directed toward making habitual acts highly certain and predictable; for example, the processes of addition, subtraction, etc., in arithmetic. Here we wish to make quite certain that when a child is presented with the stimulus, 3 + 4, he will make only the response 7, and not something else, such as 6 or 8. Likewise, in moral training, we wish to make the responses to certain stimuli highly predictable and invariable. Many of our responses in social and political situations are of this nature.

So long as habitual responses fit quite well with the commonly accepted social conventions they are valuable to the individual who possesses them. If, however, the social or political situation changes in some respect so that a new type of response is demanded, the old established response may lead into difficulties; it then becomes harmful. This harmful aspect of habit formation we ordinarily sum up in such words as "conservative," "old-fashioned," "set in his ways," "narrow-minded."

III. THE CHARACTERISTICS OF LEARNING

Theoretical Problems to Be Solved. Three theoretical questions involved in learning have commonly been distinguished. (1) Motivation. Why do we engage in the activity which results in learning? (2) How are errors eliminated? (3) How does the correct response become fixed?

All psychological systems at the present time are concerned with the first problem, the problem of motivation. The next two problems, the problem of the elimination of

errors and the fixation of the correct responses, assume
a particular theory of learning which is acceptable to the
structural, the functional, and the behavioristic psychology, but is not acceptable to the Gestalt psychology.
It seems better to discuss these last two problems before
the problem of motivation.

*Learning as the Fixation of Correct Responses and the
Elimination of Errors.* This theory assumes that in the
beginning there exist a large number of so-called random
responses. Out of this chaos of random activities there
are gradually selected just those actions which are most
appropriate to the given situation. All other responses
are to be considered as errors which must be gradually
eliminated.

One of the early experiments which has had much to
do with the development of this theory is that of Bair.
He gave his learners the task of learning to move the
ear by contracting the retrahens muscle. He assumed
that at the beginning of the learning process this muscle
could not be contracted at all. He observed that at first
the learners made a great many movements of other
muscles of the head and face. In connection with the
movement of these other muscles the retrahens muscle
was stimulated, apparently by accident. Gradually,
however, the contraction of the retrahens muscle became
more pronounced and the contraction of the other head
and face muscles gradually disappeared. Bair does not
report any observations on movements of other parts of
the body, for example, the toes. There is little doubt,
however, that if he had watched them he would have
found a contraction of muscles all throughout the body
at the beginning of the learning.

In one respect Bair disagrees with the psychological
theory that we have just outlined. He assumes that at the

beginning of practice the retrahens muscle could *not be contracted at all*, while the more recent psychological theory assumes that if some contraction of this ear muscle had not been possible from the beginning, *it could never have been learned*. The attitude of the functional and behavioristic psychology toward Bair's experiment is essentially this: at the beginning of practice a great many movements were made; most of them would be classified as errors, but the one correct movement of the retrahens muscle did occur sometimes. The process of learning consisted in selecting and fixing this one correct movement and eliminating all the others. This process of selection, according to the usual theory, depended upon the lowering of resistance of the nerve path concerned with contracting the retrahens muscle of the ear. The stimulus in this case was simply the verbal directions of the experimenter to engage in the attempt to make the movement.

Among the other investigations of learning which involve the elimination of errors and the fixation of correct responses, we may refer to the many experiments upon maze learning. A rat on being first put into the maze makes many errors, that is, it goes into many blind alleys. It does, however, eventually get through the maze, that is, it does, besides entering the blind alleys, also move along the correct pathway. The learning of the maze is supposed to consist of the elimination of the entrance into the blind alleys and the fixation of the movement along the correct pathway. This learning is believed to result in the building up of a specific nerve pathway concerned with the correct traversing of the maze.

Such observations tend to overlook the fact that even if the rat has become able to go through the correct pathway without entering any blind alley, it may do so in a very different way at different times. Its speed may be different on different runs, it may cut the corners shorter, it may make many other slight variations in its behavior as it proceeds through the maze. While the elimination of errors is still occurring the rat may behave very differently on different runs. Maze learning is only apparently a matter of fixing responses that are *wholly correct* and eliminating others which are *wholly wrong*. Movements may be partially right or partially wrong and there may be many alternative right movements.

Learning as Progressive Variation of Response. Maze learning has furnished us much valuable information, but it has also tended to fix one type of error in our theories of learning, because when we consider only the maze itself there is very obviously a correct pathway and many incorrect pathways. We are led to the view that in the behavior of the animal that learns the maze there must be a correspondingly correct and an incorrect mode of behavior. When we observe the behavior itself our faith in this view is much weakened. Learning apparently does not consist of the selection of a correct mode of response from a large number of previously existing responses, many of which are incorrect; it consists rather of the discovery of better and better ways of running the maze, which may be entirely different from the actions that preceded them.

In the activity of juggling two balls in one hand as reported by Swift, improvement very clearly consists in completely changing the movement cycle of the hand and arm. It does not apparently consist in repeating any one set of movement elements over and over until they become definitely fixed to the exclusion of other possible movement elements which can be classified as errors.

The writer has studied this activity exhaustively by means of slow motion pictures of learners in differing degrees of skill, and has made the following observations. When we compare *two different people* who are learning to juggle balls we find that they behave very differently. The height to which they throw the balls may be quite different, requiring a totally different strength of muscular contraction and a totally different timing of the entire movement. Their manner of throwing and catching may vary. One of them may make the movement as primarily a shoulder and wrist movement, the elbows moving very little. Another may make the movement primarily an elbow and wrist movement, the shoulder remaining relatively fixed. When we observe the *same individual* in different stages of his progress we find the same situation to be true. It is utterly impossible to analyze his movement early in the development of this skill and discover in it any of the specific elements which are found later when the movement is well learned. The learning seems to be more a matter of progressive variation of response than a fixation of response, that is, responses seem to vary not merely from day to day but from trial to trial, in such a manner that it is almost impossible to find any two responses which are identical as a whole or contain identical elements.

This variation of response seems to take place in a definite direction. If we think of these variations as approaching a limit in the mathematical sense, we have a fairly true picture of what takes place. However, when an individual has developed this skill to the point that he can make a thousand or more successful catches in succession, we still find that each throw is different from the preceding one,—the ball is thrown to a different height, the movement from the wrist, elbow, or shoulder is different, and in every respect the movement seems to be different from time to time. The theoretical concept that learning consists of the fixation of a single mode of response seems not to apply at all to this kind of activity.

That verbal and symbolical learning consists of such progressive variation of response is not so readily apparent. In learning a date in history, for example, it seems that there is *only one* right response, while there are many other responses that are clearly *all of them* wrong. But if we examine even briefly into the verbal and symbolical activity of a person memorizing, or trying to recall, an historical date, we find that now one procedure is utilized and now another. Related events which make up the setting of the date in question are passed in review until finally the correct date is recalled. The activity which leads up to the recall of the date may be vastly different on one occasion than on another—and yet it is correct each time if the final result is achieved. There is a tendency during learning to decrease the range of variation, but it is wholly unnecessary, if not impossible, to reach a final, fixed, stereotyped procedure.

Learning as the Discovery of New Configurations. We have pointed out that the Gestalt psychologists look upon learning as a maturation process in which new configurations of stimulation and response are developed. These new configurations—learned responses—are not a mere summation of correct responses which were present in an original chaos of behavior. Wheeler states that the original behavior is all "correct" when judged from the standpoint of the learner and is all "error" when judged from the standpoint of the experimenter (teacher). The learner merely has a "goal" of his own which does not correspond to that of the experimenter (teacher). When he has adopted the correct goal he may still have to wait for "maturation" to take place before his behavior will be entirely appropriate. In effect, Wheeler states that learning is a gradual process in which the learner approaches an appropriate way of acting, but not by a process of eliminating errors and combining correct response elements. Learning is always the development of something new.

Motivation Has Been Based on Appeal to Instinct and Emotion. The problem of motivation has traditionally been tied up with the problem of instinct and emotion. Those psychologists of the functional and psycho-analytic schools who emphasize the reality and importance of instinct believe that it furnishes the starting point and the driving force for all habit formation and learning. Gates has a special section in the first edition of his book on educational psychology devoted to "The Dynamic Rôle of Instinct in Habit Formation." It has been commonly assumed that all learned activities consist of modifications of instinct, emotion, and reflex. The original behavior of a child is assumed to be entirely of an inherited kind. As the child gains in experience the original tendencies are modified, suppressed, or given a specialized expression, but they always remain as the driving force back of the habitual response. If a teacher wishes to interest a child in any activity it is assumed that it is necessary to appeal to some instinctive or emotional tendency. It is therefore important for the teacher to be familiar with the whole list of instincts so that she may use them in modifying the doing of school work.

Some psychologists, as Woodworth, specifically recognize the dynamic power of already established habit. Habit, once established, may be used in modifying later learning.

When we examine carefully into the meaning of the

word "motive" as it is used by these psychologists, we find that they may mean two things. In the first place motive can be thought of as a kind of mental driving force; it may be a spiritual force which is assumed to accompany instinctive and emotional behavior. Woodworth thinks of motive in more purely mechanical terms. He thinks of instinct, emotion, and habit as being mechanisms which, once set in action, may furnish the drive for other mechanisms. Used in this sense, motive means merely the antecedent of any action and does not imply the existence of any special force which sets off the activity.

A Motive May Be Merely the Antecedent (Stimulus) of an Action. To an increasingly large number of psychologists this appeal to instinct and emotion as the basis for motivation has no meaning, since instinct and emotion have been discarded as psychological terms. To them, all behavior is directly dependent upon the type of physical and psychological structure which any individual possesses from moment to moment, and the kind of stimulation which is immediately present. From this point of view motive means, first of all, merely the stimulus applied to a sense organ which is effective in producing an action. The problem of the teacher who wishes to interest a child in a given activity is simply the problem of so arranging stimulating conditions which act upon the physical and mental organization of the child that the desired responses will follow. If the teacher is only wise enough this type of motivation is always possible. A teacher needs to have as much familiarity as possible with the physical and mental make-up of each individual child so that she may use good judgment in selecting the proper stimuli for securing the desired learning activity.

Motivation Must Be Based upon the Nature of the Learner. Under schoolroom conditions the range of stimuli which can be applied to a child is rather limited. When this is true the most variable factor in the situation is the make-up of each individual child. The immediate problem of the teacher, therefore, is not so much the selection of the proper stimuli, since she has only a limited range of stimuli available, but is rather the understanding of the children as a group and as individuals. In practice, therefore, the problem of motivation frequently reduces to the problem of understanding child nature. It is this aspect of motivation which is referred to when psychologists speak of appealing to instinct and emotion. Motivation, then, seems to have two legitimate meanings. It may refer, first, to proper technique in using occasions for securing a desired action, and second, it may refer to the proper use of knowledge of physical and mental make-up of learners.

Motivation Depends upon Initial Failure. The practical problem in which parents and teachers are interested is that of the technique of motivation. The fundamental problem in the technique of motivation is simply—how can a child be induced to engage in a desired new action? The general answer to this question seems to be rather clear—new activity occurs when the external situation is so arranged that already established habits fail to accomplish some specific end result which is needed to meet the situation. By meeting the situation we do not mean merely the occurrence of a subjective sense of satisfaction resulting from the behavior; we mean, rather, that a situation which produces activity is satisfactorily terminated when the activity results in a radical change in the situation itself. When the result of the action is the removal of the stimulus, the situation has been satisfactorily met. Or, if the stimulus is considerably changed in any fashion, the situation has been successfully met. If, however, the habitual responses which are first made permit the situation to remain relatively unchanged or merely result in intensifying it, then we say that these habitual responses have failed. It is just such situations which are the starting point for learning. The primary technique of motivation, therefore, consists in arranging situations in which the child will fail because his already established habits are inadequate.

If we wish to interest a child in learning to add, we must place him in such a situation that, because he cannot add, he fails to do something that he is already trying to do. He must himself see clearly that his lack of knowledge of addition is responsible for his failure. If we wish to motivate a child to use *he is not* as a language form instead of *he ain't*, we must place him in such a position that usage of the incorrect form leads to failure in an action which he already has under way. If, however, the action already under way is too weakly stimulated, failure in it leads merely to its abandonment. One reason why motivation of school work is often difficult is that the activities available for motivation are too weakly stimulated.

Motivation Requires a Goal. Having secured this initial failure, the teacher is responsible for so directing the child's activity that learning will not be a purely trial-and-error process. The first step in directing learning seems to be the setting of a goal. That is, the child must be given some directions concerning the degree of skill which is expected of him in meeting the new situation. In order to maintain effort while progress is being made toward the goal, it is usually desirable to have some means for measuring improvement. One of the most important functions of standardized tests in school work is of this kind. They furnish objective measures of the child's improvement so that he can see how much he has accomplished and how far he has yet to go before he attains the goal which has been set for him. It is commonly stated that the degree of difficulty of the activity must be adapted to the stage of progress of the learner if proper motivation is to be secured. By this statement we simply mean that the amount of variation in activity which is possible is only slight, progress is by short steps, the goal must not be too remote. A child can do things to which it has been accustomed or things which are very similar to them. A teacher or parent must not expect to introduce much new activity at any one time. That is, the progressive variation in activity, which we call learning, takes place slowly.

Motivation Refers to "Direction" of Activity. Discussions of motivation which proceed in terms of appeal to instinct and emotion frequently assume that it is necessary to stir the child up to activity. We are never inactive until we are dead. A child is always doing something. The teacher's problem is not to make the child active but to *direct* his activity, and the problem of motivation is fundamentally a problem of direction. The first question the teacher needs to ask concerning children in her care is—"What activities will these children engage in if I do not attempt to direct them?" Upon the answer to that question depends the teacher's whole procedure in securing motivation and directing learning. This is the type of question which we pointed out as being important in our discussion of instinct.

Motivation as the Conditioning of Responses. When we think of learning from the standpoint of the conditioned reflex, there is no special problem of motivation. The teacher must, first of all, secure the desired *response* by using whatever stimulus proves to be most effective for that purpose. Until she finds *some means* for securing the desired response, the next step in learning is wholly impossible. The next step consists in providing the *stimulus* which she wishes to connect with the desired response. It must be provided at the same time that the child is making this response as a result of other stimulation. When this situation (double stimulation and response) has been repeated for a number of times, the new stimulus in which the teacher is interested will become sufficient to produce the new response when presented alone. This means, for example, that in teaching a child to multiply 7×9, it is necessary first of all to secure the response 63, in some manner. Almost any stimulus which can secure the response 63 is entirely satisfactory. It may be the visual, auditory, or kinesthetic (writing presentation) of 63. Then when the response 63 has been secured, the stimulus 7×9 is applied. When this procedure has been repeated a sufficient number of times the new stimulus will secure the desired response.

If we wish to teach a child the breast stroke in swimming, it is necessary, first of all, to provide some stimulus, it matters not what, which will secure the desired arm and leg movements. Until we find some stimulus which is effective in producing these desired arm and leg movements progress is impossible. Having once produced these movements, it is only necessary to see that they are repeated a number of times in the special situation with which we wish to connect them. This special situation is ordinarily the stimulation produced by the presence of the body in the water.

The only additional meaning which motive could have from the standpoint of the conditioned reflex is that of why we are willing to put ourselves in the situation in which learning can take place, that is, in the schoolroom or in the water. This question, if we examine into it, reduces into a further problem of conditioning. When reward and punishment are used to induce children to put themselves in the learning situation, they may be effective for the specific problem, but they represent additional sources of stimulation which may be undesirable in the finished activity. They may become a necessary part of the stimulus for the finished activity so that it will not occur without them. They are, to this extent, undesirable. From the standpoint of the conditioned reflex, therefore, there is no special problem of motivation aside from the general problem of learning.

The Gestalt View of Motivation. Motivation is a matter of "insight." Just as soon as the child adopts the "goal" which has been set up by the teacher his activity begins to be appropriate. Increase in efficiency is secured by providing opportunity for maturation. The goal must not be set too far ahead of the learner, for fear he will not have sufficient insight to grasp it. At any stage in our development we are capable of insight into problems of a given degree of difficulty. If the problems are beyond our level of insight, *trial-and-error* behavior results and progress is slow; if the problems are adapted to our level of insight we progress steadily, making *no errors at all*.

IV. THEORIES WHICH SEEK TO EXPLAIN LEARNING

The Law of Use. Based upon the assumption that learning consists of the selection and fixation of the correct elements out of an original chaos of random activity, certain so-called laws of learning have been developed. The *law of use* has commonly been considered as basic. Some psychologists have attempted to explain learning entirely in terms of this law. Watson believed that the maze learning of rats could be explained entirely in terms of frequency. He tried to point out that based upon

chance alone a rat would take the correct turn at any
critical point in the maze oftener than the incorrect turn.
In a simple T-maze the turn to the left may be the
correct one. The rat on reaching the turn the first time
has an even chance of turning to the right or to the left.
Let us suppose that the rat turns to the right, which is
incorrect. On reaching the end of the blind it must turn
around and come back to the crossing. This time it may
continue ahead, going in the correct direction. According to Watson the rat on this occasion has made the incorrect turn once and the correct turn once. If the rat
on first coming to the critical point takes the correct
turn to the left, it does not make the incorrect turn at
all. As a matter of chance then, the rat will sometimes
take the correct turn without making the incorrect one,
but if it makes the incorrect turn it is forced eventually
to make the correct turn. It, therefore, makes the correct
turn oftener than the incorrect one and so it eventually
learns the maze on the basis of frequency alone. Watson
overlooks the fact that coming from the blind alley and
going straight ahead down the correct pathway is different
from coming up the correct pathway and turning to the
left, and cannot be counted as its equivalent.

When we observe the behavior of a cat in a problem box
the difficulty of explaining learning entirely on the basis
of the law of use becomes even more obvious. Let us
suppose that there is a loose bar in the cage in which the
cat is confined. The cat will be observed to go to this
bar and shake it many times, during the early stages of
learning. The cat will also extend its paw through between the bars many times. The correct movement is
the pulling of a loop or the pushing of a button, which occurs *only once* each time the cat is confined in the box,
since it is always followed by the opening of the door and

the reaching of food. By actual count extending the paw through the bars and shaking the loose bar occur many times to each one time the correct movement of pulling the loop occurs. The cat learns to perform an activity which it has repeated much less often than certain of the other activities which are eliminated.

The Law of Disuse. The corollary of the law of use is the *law of disuse.* According to this law an activity which is not repeated for a time tends to be forgotten and, therefore, eliminated. While this seems to be true in general there is no evidence that the forgetting takes place quickly enough to account for the elimination of errors during the process of learning. We know that activities which have occurred only a few times may reappear after a lapse of many years. It is at least open to question whether forgetting, due solely to lack of exercise of a nerve path, can ever occur except over a very long period of time.

The Law of Effect as a Supplement to the Law of Use. In the attempt to explain why some repetitions are much more valuable for learning than others—why the law of use doesn't always work—Thorndike has formulated his *law of effect.* This law is essentially that when modifiable connections between stimulus and response are used, these connections are strengthened if the response is satisfying, and are weakened if the response is annoying. Thorndike further states that by a satisfying state of affairs he means a situation which the animal or child does nothing to avoid, often doing things which maintain or renew it. By an annoying state of affairs is meant one which the animal or child does nothing to preserve, but often tends to avoid and not to repeat.

Let us recall, however, that by the laws of learning we are seeking to explain how it happens that out of the chaos of random activities certain ones are picked out to be fixed and repeated and perpetuated. If we state that some one of these acts is picked out to be fixed and repeated because of its satisfying nature, we are saying, in effect, that a particular act is picked out and repeated because there is a tendency to repeat it. That is, the Law of Effect as stated by Thorndike furnishes no real explanation at all, but merely furnishes a second way of saying that somehow action is learned.

As a guide in teaching, this statement of the Law of Effect may, however, have some value. We have grown accustomed to using the word "satisfying" with reference to certain classes of situations. If we inform a teacher or parent that by making a response satisfying he will lead a child to learn it, the parent or teacher will probably know what to do even though our directions mean nothing more, when examined carefully, than the mere statement that certain kinds of stimulation accompanying or following an action favor the perpetuation of that action, while certain other stimuli favor its elimination. "Satisfying" and "annoying" remain subjective descriptions of learning situations, even after Thorndike's attempt to make them objective.

Recently the Law of Effect Has Been Restated in Terms of the Principle of Double Stimulation. Gates uses as an illustration of the working of this law the behavior of a cat which has learned to come in response to the call "Kitty, kitty." When the experimenter calls, the cat comes running. If the experimenter then throws cold water on the cat, the cat runs away. If, however, the experimenter gives the cat food, the cat eats it. If the series of stimulation (calling "Kitty, kitty" followed by throwing cold water on the cat) is continued a number of times, the response to the call will be running away from instead of running toward the experimenter. (We should like to add, however, that in this series of responses, when the cat has formed the habit of running away from the experimenter instead of toward him upon the call of "Kitty, kitty," the experimenter is no longer able to throw cold water on it. Since the call "Kitty, kitty" is no longer followed by the stimulation of the cold water but by other stimuli which do not produce running away that response gradually disappears. The cat merely does nothing when called.) When the experimenter calls "Kitty, kitty" and then disregards the cat, it gradually ceases to answer the call. Gates says that "Later when the call alone is heard, the cat responds by doing nothing except being annoyed." He does not explain how he discovers that the cat "is annoyed."

Gates is not content to describe learning in terms of the process of conditioning, based upon the presentation of a sequence of stimuli and the occurrence of responses to these stimuli, but insists that the principle of satisfaction and annoyance must be introduced as an explanatory factor. The law of effect is not superfluous, he thinks, but is necessary because these cases can be explained only if we show that one response is *prepotent*. By prepotent, he means that one response is stronger than the other and will occur in preference to the other, when the stimuli for both acts are simultaneously present. He states that the important matter which determines learning in any situation is the answer to the question: "What *effect* will be produced by the new stimulus one is about to apply? What will be the *effect* of presenting along with the call 'Kitty, kitty' such a stimulus as a slap on the ear, a piece of fish, a rubbing the fur the wrong way? What will happen to the old stimulus depends entirely upon the new one."

How May Two Responses Be Related to Each Other?
Since the effect of the second stimulus (the response it
produces) determines what happens in response to the
old stimulus, it is necessary to inquire what relation-
ships can exist between the second response and the first.
(1) The second response may be based upon the first;
it cannot occur until the first has been completed, but
it cancels the result gained by the first. The cat approaches
the experimenter in response to the call; the slap, the
cold water, etc., drive it away. The chick gets the cater-
pillar in its mouth; the taste causes it to spit it out.
(2) The second response may be based upon the first; it
cannot occur until the first response has been completed,
but does not nullify, or in any way affect the result
gained by the first. The cat is given a piece of fish to
eat. The first response ends and a new one begins. (3) The
second response may be unrelated to the first. It does
not depend upon the completion of the first and does not
affect the result gained by the first response. The cat
comes in answer to the call but it is disregarded; it remains near by but further special stimulation is not presented. It is just as though it had not responded.

The Conditioned Reflex Theory. Now let us suppose
only the observed facts of conditioning—that when one
stimulus regularly follows or accompanies another, *there
is a tendency to make the response to the second stimulus
when only the first stimulus is presented.* In case *one*,
the cat should learn to run away when called; in case
two, the cat should learn to begin eating when called;
in case *three*, the cat should learn to do nothing when
called. How does this learning fit the observed facts?
Case *one* fits perfectly; the cat does run away when called.
(There is, of course, a second stage in which by another
process of learning the cat comes to disregard the call.)

Case *three*, fits the facts perfectly; the cat learns to disregard the call. (Remembering that coming in response to call is itself a conditioned response, its disappearance also fits the observed facts concerning the extinguishing of a conditioned response with repetition which is not occasionally reënforced by the unconditioned stimulus.) Case *two* fits the facts also if the cat, even before food is presented, begins all "eating" responses which can occur in the absence of specific food stimulation. Anyone who has ever observed a cat under such a situation will agree that such "eating" responses do occur soon after the call is heard.

The principles of conditioning are, therefore, adequate to explain the disappearance of the first response in some cases and its continuation in others. We have shown that any behavior series in which the later stimuli are by-products of the responses to the earlier stimuli will be shortened as much as possible by dropping out any units whose results nullify each other or add nothing in the way of new stimuli. It is unnecessary to assume that any of the responses are "prepotent" or that there is any peculiar quality of "satisfyingness" or "annoyingness" attached to any of them. Stimulus-response units do not occur in isolation but any functioning of one such unit has as its "effect" the initiation of another; the two stimulus-response units thus occurring in succession set the stage for the formation of a conditioned response which will unite the stimulus of the first unit with the response of the second unit—this is the law of effect in terms of double stimulation with satisfiers and annoyers left out.

If the principles of conditioning are adequate to explain learning, why are responses conditioned in the laboratory so transitory while learning in life situations is often so permanent? In life situations the unconditioned stimulus occurs as a normal consequence of the response to the (to be) conditioned stimulus, and not merely at the whim of the experimenter. Whenever the conditioned response fails, it is at once reënforced by the unconditioned stimulus. "School" learning, like responses conditioned in the laboratory, is likely to be transitory, and for the same reason—the unconditioned stimulus appears only at the whim of the teacher. James' statement, that in habit formation no "exceptions" must be permitted, is a recognition that the conditioned response must be reënforced by the unconditioned stimulus, whenever it is in danger of failing.

The Conditioned Response Theory Falls Short of Real Explanation. Do the principles of conditioning furnish a real explanation or are they at best a mere description of the course of events? Apparently they furnish only a description of the changes in behavior; an *explanation* of these changes must relate them to other known facts or principles—to underlying neurological changes, for example: Max F. Meyer has proposed a plausible theory of the way in which these neural changes occur. The Gestalt psychologists, however, say that any explanation based upon the building up of specific nerve paths of low resistance is wrong. Further study of the neurological conditions of learning is needed.

Does the Conditioned Response Theory Apply to the Development of Motor Skill? We have thus far confined the discussion to the continuation or elimination of comparatively large units of behavior which produce an appreciable effect in changing subsequent stimulation. Does increase in skill within a unit occur in the same manner? The cat learns to come when called, but how is "skill in running" increased? A man learns to play golf or to avoid playing golf, but how is skill in playing increased? A child learns to use the word "mother" to apply to a particular person, but how is skill in pronouncing or writing the word increased?

Learning a motor activity, such as driving a golf ball, seems to take place in the following fashion. The position of the feet, body, arms, etc. (the stance), together with the club and the ball mechanically limit the movement of the drive to some extent. The total stimulating situation—golf course, ball, subvocal movements, etc.—set off the first trial. This first trial provides additional stimulation—kinesthetic from the muscular contractions and body movement, visual from the flight of the ball, etc. This second group of stimuli in turn leads to other movements—walking after the ball, subvocal or vocal movement, etc. Each separate response of the series may be repeated indefinitely without learning; mere use does not change the movements made.

The important question to answer in order to understand learning is: How do the sensory consequences of the movements made operate to produce variation at the next trial? This variation is produced because of *double stimulation*, one stimulus response unit occurs in conjunction with another. At the end of the back swing of the golf club certain stimulation, mainly kinesthetic, is present in consequence of the back swing. This stimulation is followed by the downward and forward movement of the club; again the kinesthetic stimulation is altered and the "follow through" unit occurs. Minute analysis of the movement of driving the golf ball would show a continually changing set of kinesthetic stimuli as effects of immediately preceding movement, these new stimuli are in turn followed by more movement. The total number of stimulus and response units may be very great.

The requirements for conditioning—double stimulation—are present. Variation in movement will therefore occur. The variations will be in the direction of smoother movement by the elimination of any conflicting muscular contractions.

The flight of the ball will be affected by every variation in the muscular contractions, but will the effect be to increase distance and improve direction? If the mechanical factors of stance and clubs have been properly adjusted such will be the case. Taking the proper stance and choosing the proper club require adjustment to the visual factors on the golf course. It is through the mechanical factors of stance and clubs that the visual stimuli from the layout of the course and the kinesthetic factors controlling the course of the movement are brought into mutual relation to secure a good drive.

Increased smoothness of muscular coördination, then, is based upon conditioning of many small movement units to kinesthetic stimuli, the adjustment of the total movement as a larger unit to the demands of the external environment, and the occurrence or non-occurrence of the total unit are based upon conditioning to external stimuli, visual, subvocal, auditory, etc. External factors determining the selection of the appropriate movement unit are often comparatively simple so that such learning is rapid, kinesthetic factors controlling smoothness of coördination are likely to be highly complex so that increase in skill is often very slow. Each change in a small detail of the form of the movement may change many of the kinesthetic consequences all throughout the movement, thus leading to the introduction of many new changes in the movement, good or bad. Increased smoothness of coördination is truly a matter of progressive variation of response, the final form used by the expert may consist almost entirely of coördinations not represented at all in the early stages of learning.

Does the Conditioned Response Theory Apply to Thinking and Problem-solving? We have pointed out earlier, that from the objective viewpoint thinking and problem-solving are based upon the existence of patterns of conditioned responses, whose movement aspect is implicit. To understand the building up of such a system which is consistent and logical—for example, demonstration of a geometrical theorem or arguments supporting a political principle—it is only necessary to assume that implicit responses are conditioned in the same manner as the explicit responses discussed in the preceding pages. If the same principle holds true, then we should expect the contradictory and superfluous elements in a system of thought gradually to disappear and the others to remain. The time required for building up of a consistent system should depend upon its complexity, just as the time required for establishing a high degree of skill in an overt physical activity such as tennis, golf, or swimming depends upon its complexity.

Peterson's Completeness-of-response Theory. Peterson recognizes that learning a complicated task and problem-solving call for an interaction of many stimuli with many responses. Some of the stimuli inhibit action, others produce and continue action. In any complicated situation where choice must be made between two or more lines of action—maze learning, swimming, solving a problem in arithmetic—the first responses must be more or less incomplete because all the possibilities of action cannot take place at once. When any activity begins it will, if erroneous, soon be checked. The check may not be serious, however, for other response tendencies are going on at the same time and tending to produce other actions—perhaps the correct ones. These other tendencies now prevail when the first one is checked, and other action—perhaps correct—continues. When the goal has finally been reached all remaining delayed action tendencies disappear; the act as a whole is complete.

Peterson's theory stresses the integrative character of learning. It is non-teleological and explains the elimination of error as well as the fixation of correct responses. If it were applied in detail to the learning of a complicated skill, taking account of each stimulus-response unit in turn, it would seemingly approach the conditioned response theory.

The Æsthetic Basis of Learning. These previously quoted theories are based upon the assumption that there is an original group of responses, some of which are to be classed as errors and eliminated, others of which are to be classed as correct and fixed in some manner. The Gestalt psychologists reject this fundamental notion. They object to this minute analysis of movement into S-R units. They have not, however, given any satisfactory explanation of learning as a substitute. They are content with saying that there is an æsthetic basis for learning or that learning depends upon "insight." Some responses *feel* right and are perpetuated just because they are right. The learning process occurs rapidly if the person has insight into the problem, slowly if a trial-and-error procedure must be followed.

This view of the Gestalt psychologists reminds us somewhat of Thorndike's Law of Effect, but it is not to be considered as its equivalent. An illustration will help to make this clear. If we are walking along a path and happen to stumble over a stone and fall, the stumbling and falling are to be considered as unæsthetic and awkward. Our activity would not be classed as graceful by any person who happened to be watching us. It is just this lack of grace which the Gestalt psychologists consider to be lack of skill. If we practice falling as a gymnastic stunt until we have learned a good manner of falling, then this action will give the impression to an onlooker of being graceful and well-coördinated, and we, while engaging in it, will have the feeling that it is æsthetic and well done. It is just in this matter of feeling right that the skilled activity is different from the unskilled one. Learning, then, takes place whenever we hit upon a method of falling which feels right. We will hit upon this method more quickly if we have insight into the problem, if we understood body mechanics and principles of muscular contraction and relaxation.

The Gestalt psychologists do not offer any explanation of the underlying neurological processes except to say that there is "maturation" and that the nervous system as a whole is concerned.

This explanation of learning is a description of the process in terms which may prove useful to a teacher or parent in much the same way that Thorndike's Law of Effect may prove useful. There is included in this description the purely subjective element of the æsthetic feeling of the child who is engaged in learning. This subjective statement helps to make the *description* more popular and easily understood without adding anything to its value as an explanation. The insistence upon the importance of insight seems to mean merely that the problem must not be too difficult but must be adapted to the stage of progress of the learner.

Learning as Inner Development. Most of the theories and laws which have been developed assume that learning is a process of changing behavior by applying external stimulation. The objection has been offered that these theories assume the child to remain more or less passive.

This criticism is not fully justified. The child is the raw
material which is to be made into a finished product
by means of environmental influences. These environmental influences can be applied, however, only when
the child is active. The child's activity is the starting
point for learning. It is not assumed that the child has
any "insight" into the process, but merely that it is active.

There is an increasing number of educators who think
of learning as creative self-expression, a development
from within which is relatively independent of environmental influences. These people take, as their fundamental principle, Rousseau's statement that nature is
right. They adopt very much the same attitude as does
Froebel in his kindergarten. They believe that the function of education is merely to permit natural development, rather than to attempt to change it in any important respect. For them learning is not a matter of
imposing habit formation from without, but it is rather a
matter of permitting development from within. Their
view is supported by the early attitude of biologists toward heredity. It was assumed, for many years, that
hereditary characteristics worked themselves out in a
fashion quite independent of environmental influences.
The individual was supposed to develop as a result of the
unfolding of germinal characteristics, rather than as a
result of the imposing of any plan of development by the
environment.

The biological attitude toward the development of
hereditary characteristics has changed within recent years.
It is believed now that the environmental factors do enter
actively into the changes that take place in the developing individual. It is believed that the uniformity which
we find in individual development is due to the fact that
a considerable amount of standardization has occurred

in the range of environmental accidents to which the developing individual is exposed (Chapter IV). Individual peculiarities are supposed to be, in part, the outgrowth of the variable factors in the environmental situation, which cause a constant disturbance of the direction and rate of development which might be expected to occur as a result of the germinal characteristics alone. When we assume that an individual, left to his own devices, permitted to work out his education by a process of creative self-expression, will develop into a highly desirable type of individual, we can do so only on the assumption that chance influences in the environment will give better direction to development than controlled influences in the environment. Development will be controlled by environmental factors; we should not leave this environmental control to chance, but should arrange it to the best of our ability in the interests of the developing individual.

V. Summary

The laws of association, formulated by Aristotle, have been redefined and clarified by modern experimental psychologists. The terminology has been changed by the objective psychologists of the twentieth century; the words "learning" and "conditioning" have replaced "association," and "stimulus" and "response" have replaced "sensation," "image," "idea," and the like. Interest in the development of skill has been added on to the interest in the purely "conscious" mental activity, and the psycho-analysts have discovered the subconscious mind; but no fundamentally new approach to the problem of development in behavior—i.e., learning, association—has been made until the present generation.

Atomistic views of association favor the theory that

learning is a trial-and-error process involving the fixation of correct responses and the elimination of errors. The accepted neurological theory assumes the existence of specific nerve pathways whose resistance is lowered with repeated use. This atomistic view of learning has been challenged by the Gestalt psychologists, who emphasize the fact that the entire organism participates in every action, however localized it seems. Physical skills involving large muscle groups (athletics) seem to be acquired by a progressive variation of response rather than by an elimination of errors and fixation of correct response.

The occurrence of habitual actions requires the immediate presence of sensory stimulation. Because this fact is sometimes easily overlooked there has grown up the popular misconception that habits may initiate themselves, that they have internal driving power. Habitual actions are based upon bodily structure, especially nervous structures. The exact nature of the neurological basis of habits is not well understood.

The law of use has long been considered of fundamental importance in learning. It is now believed by many that repetition does not cause learning but merely gives opportunity for the true causes to operate. Apparently learning occurs during some repetitions and not during others. The law of effect has been developed to explain this observation. In its subjective form, based upon satisfaction and annoyance, it has met with much criticism. If it can be reduced to the principle of double stimulation— i.e., conditioning—it loses its objectionable features and becomes merely a description of the manner in which the stimulating conditions requisite to learning are set up as a natural consequence of responding to a single initial stimulus.

Some educators believe that the environment control of learning has been overemphasized and insist that learning is a process of inner development. It seems impossible, however, in the light of modern biology and psychology, to think of any development which is independent of a measure of environmental direction. The problem of education is to direct wisely inner development by means of proper environmental control.

CHAPTER VIII

TESTS AND MEASUREMENTS

Modern Experimental Psychology Had Its Beginning in the Attempt to Make Mental Measurements. About a century ago the first measurements of reaction times were made. It was noted by astronomers that there were individual variations among different observers in recording the time at which a fixed star passed the meridian. This variation could be accounted for only by the assumption that time was required for the passage of the nerve impulse from the retina of the eye to the parts of the body concerned in making the record. During the first half of the nineteenth century considerable interest developed in the measuring of the intensities of sensations. Much research was conducted to determine the laws governing the changes in intensity of sensations and the correspondence of these changes with changes in intensity of the stimulus. The name "Psycho-physics" was applied to this phase of psychology. The first psychological laboratories were founded mainly for the study of psycho-physics and reaction times.

This type of measurement is not usually included in mental tests as used in school work. It is, however, finding some application in tests for discovering special abilities in trades and vocations.

The Great Development of Mental Tests Has Occurred under the Leadership of the Functional Psychologists. In 1890, Cattell at Columbia University attempted to devise a type of examination for college freshmen which would be more valuable for predicting their scholastic success than the usual type of entrance examination based upon knowledge of subject matter. He used essentially the assumptions of the functional psychology, which were to be explicitly formulated only a decade later. This school of psychological thought believes that mind can be understood as being composed of a large number of functions or ways of acting. The names which have been assigned to these functions are attention, memory, reasoning, association, and the like.

In developing mental tests, it was at first believed that it would be necessary to test each of the mental functions separately. The testing movement in America began according to this plan. *Association* tests were devised based upon controlled and uncontrolled word associations. A controlled association test consisted of a list of words, such as *good, outside, quick, tall, big.* The subject taking the test was required to write down their opposites as quickly as posssible. Another test consisting of words such as *window, leaf, pillow, button* would be presented, the requirement being that the wholes of which these things were a part should be written down as quickly as possible. The words used and the type of association demanded depended only upon the ingenuity of the test maker. In the uncontrolled association tests, a word such as *play* would be given as a starting point; the person being tested would then write down one after another all the words that occurred to him during a space of three minutes. These tests could be given as pencil and paper tests to groups of school children or orally to individuals. *Attention* tests consisted of such activities as crossing out all the *A's* from a page of printed matter. *Memory* tests consisted of lists of words with or without some form of connection, lists of numbers, short stories, etc., which were read aloud to the subject, who was required to at once write down or repeat aloud as much of them as possible.

By 1912 tests of this general nature had been devised covering many different mental functions. It was hoped eventually to devise good tests for all the mental functions. By combining these tests it was hoped that we could arrive at an estimate of the general mental worth of an individual.

Binet Developed the Concept of "Mental Age." Shortly after 1900, Binet and Simon in Paris set to work in connection with the public school system on the problem of picking out those children who were likely to fail to profit from their public school work. They hoped, after picking out these children, to devise a plan of education which would bring them up to the level of ability of normal children and enable them to resume their place in the regular public school. This second part of their problem has as yet proved impossible; with the first part of their problem, the devising of tests for picking out such children, they were much more successful.

Binet began his work with the psychological assumptions in vogue in this country; that is, he assumed that there were many mental functions, each of which it was desirable to test. However, he made one additional assumption which radically changed the character of the tests. He assumed that *mental functions of all kinds develop at approximately the same rate.* That is, if a mental function, such as memory, has developed up to a given point of efficiency, all other mental functions, such as attention, association, reasoning, have also developed up to that same point.

This assumption of Binet's made it unnecessary to devise tests for more than a few mental functions. It also made it unnecessary to be greatly concerned about just which mental function was being measured by any given test. Binet's first attempt at a measuring scale of intelligence was simply a list of tasks of a simple nature which children in the elementary school might be expected to successfully accomplish. These tasks were not arranged in any special fashion.

By 1909 Binet had worked out his theory a bit further. Since all mental functions were supposed to develop at the same rate, it was possible to conceive of different *mental levels*. Binet expressed these mental levels in terms of *age*, that is he conceived of a five-year mental level, a six-year level, etc. He proceeded to arrange his tests in accordance with this idea of mental ages. The ability to perform certain tasks which the average five-year-old could perform was taken as indicative of the attainment of a five-year level of development. Certain other tasks represented a ten-year level of development, etc.

When Binet's work had reached this stage it began to attract attention in America. Goddard tried to adapt Binet's measuring scale of intelligence to his work in the training-school for feeble-minded at Vineland, New Jersey. He published an American revision of the Binet tests which was essentially a mere translation of these tests into English. In 1911, Terman published his first revision of the Binet tests, adapting them to American conditions. This type of test gained rapidly in popularity and seemed about to displace the tests of the separate mental functions which had been developed in the United States.

The Development of Group Tests of Intelligence. The Binet tests, however, could be given to only one individual at a time, while the tests of mental functions as developed in America had included written group tests which could be given to large numbers of children. Our system of public education demanded that all children should be tested. The logical answer to the problem was the combination of the already existing separate tests of mental functions into a single unit which could be used as a group intelligence test. If Binet's assumption that the various mental functions develop at the same rate was valid, then there was no reason why these pencil and paper tests should not be combined into batteries—*i.e.*, unitary groupings—and the concept of mental level applied to them. The group intelligence tests as used to-day are essentially a miscellaneous combination of these earlier tests of the separate mental functions. Instead of a separate score being given for the test of each function as was formerly done, a single score is obtained for the entire test battery.

The occurrence of the Great War gave an impetus to the entire testing movement. It was thought desirable to classify the drafted men in the army according to their mental ability so that they could be assigned to the tasks for which they were best fitted. For this purpose it was essential to have tests which could be administered to large numbers of the men at the same time. After the war this method of group testing was applied very extensively in the public school system.

The "Intelligence Quotient" Was Developed as an Index of Brightness. When Terman made his revision of the Binet tests it occurred to him that an additional statistical term was needed properly to express the findings of the tests. Binet had developed the concept of "mental age." Two children might, however, have the same mental age, such as ten years, and yet differ very widely in their possibilities of development. If the one child had a chronological age of eight and the other a chronological age of twelve, the younger of the two children had future possibilities immensely greater than the older. As a means for expressing this relationship between mental age and chronological age, Terman developed the concept of "Intelligence Quotient" (I.Q.), which is the figure obtained by dividing the mental age by the chonological age. The intelligence quotient may be considered as an index of the brightness of a given child. It indicates the rate at which he is developing. It has turned out that this rate is relatively consistent from year to year. That is, a six-year-old child who is developing rapidly will at twelve or fifteen still be developing rapidly and will attain a much higher final level of development than another child whose rate of development is slow.

What Is "Intelligence?" The testing movement has seen the concept of mind as composed of a large number of separate—even though coöperating—mental functions replaced by a concept of mind as a unit which manifests its worth by a certain *level* (stated in terms of mental age) of intelligence. Each mind has a certain degree of brightness (stated in terms of I.Q.) which is commonly assumed to be constant and fixed for the lifetime of the individual.

The development of this concept of intelligence as a fixed unitary thing has not been without opposition. The chief advocate of the theory that there is a unitary something which influences all the individual's mental life is Pearson. He has sought to show by statistical treatment of test results that the scores can be explained only by the assumption of a common factor. For many of the statistically-minded he has proved his point. Some, however, assert that the test results can be explained as well by the assumption of a number of group factors (separate functions) and that they do not require the existence of a common factor. Pearson himself assumes the existence of these group factors and the existence of many specific factors *in addition* to the general factor of intelligence.

Assuming that there is something of far-reaching importance in an individual's mental life which can be called "intelligence," many attempts have been made to define it. The most popular definitions identify it with ability to learn, ability to profit by experience. Those who believe that there is no one general factor in mind, use the word intelligence to mean a composite or an average of all the separate mental abilities which an individual possesses. The most satisfactory practical definition (even though it is tautological) seems to be "that which is measured by intelligence tests" or "score on an intelligence test."

The Effect of Behaviorism upon the Theory of Mental Measurement. Since 1913 there has been a widespread shift in psychological theory from the functional to the behavioristic or objective psychology. The question at once arises: if we discard our belief in the existence of mental functions, such as association and memory, what becomes of the system of mental tests which has been developed based upon this theory? For the objective psychologist, mental tests do not represent an attempt to determine the strength of any individual function or capacity or of any general mental factor called intelligence; they are, rather, attempts to obtain samples of behavior in the hope that these samples may be useful as an indication of a child's present behavior equipment or for purposes of predicting future behavior.

An illustration taken from another field may help to make this theory clear. When a carload of wheat is delivered at an elevator it becomes important to determine what is the grade of the wheat. The price which is paid for the wheat depends to a very large extent upon the determination of its quality. In order to determine its quality, samples of the wheat are taken. These samples are taken with great care so that may be considered as truly representing the wheat contained in the carload. A very small quantity of wheat is taken from different parts of the car, that is, from the ends, the middle, from deep down in the car, and from near the top. These samples are put together and on the basis of the mixture the value of the entire car is estimated. The amount of wheat actually taken as a sample and used as a basis for determining the value of the entire carload is very small. Nevertheless, on the basis of this very small sample the car of grain is bought and sold.

Objective psychologists consider that in administering mental tests we are doing something of a very similar nature. We are taking small samples of behavior in the hope that by using them we shall be able to estimate the child's present behavior status and make predictions concerning the kind of behavior which he may be expected to show in the future. It is at once apparent that if these behavior samples, which we call *mental tests*, are to be of real value for these purposes, they must be systematically taken and treated. That is, we must be certain that our samples are really representative of the kind of behavior in which we are interested. We must use the very best technique in obtaining these samples. Treatment of them in a statistical way must be very careful and accurate. Failure in care and accuracy at any point in obtaining and treating the samples will cause them to lose their value and become misleading. The requirements that the *validity*, *reliability*, and *objectivity* of tests must be established, and that tests must be administered and their results evaluated and used by people with a sufficient degree of training is a recognition of this necessity for care in the taking of samples and intelligence in their use. For the objective psychologist the question: "What is measured by this test?" is meaningless. He would restate the question in this form: "What use can I make of this sample of behavior?"

All Psychological Tests Are "Achievement" Tests for the Behaviorist. It is customary to classify mental tests into two groups,—tests of *native ability* on the one hand and *achievement tests* on the other. So long as we hold to the belief that there are mental functions which may have a certain innate strength, this classification is important and necessary. It is desirable to test the inherent strength of such functions as memory, association, reasoning, and attention. It is also desirable to have measures for determining what these mental functions have accomplished during the lifetime of the individual. Particularly is this important in connection with school work. Here we wish to know what a student *could accomplish* if he only would. We also wish to know what he *has* accomplished. An important aim of educational procedure is found in the attempt to let a child work up to the limits set by his native ability. Whenever a score, as shown on an achievement test, is lower than it apparently ought to be as a result of his native ability, it is assumed that the training of the child has been defective, or that he has been lazy or indifferent.

When we adopt the attitude that testing is merely a process of taking samples of behavior, then the classification of tests into native ability tests and achievement tests becomes absurd. All tests are of exactly the same nature, whether tests of subject matter, as geometry or history, tests of general intelligence or of mechanical aptitude, and they represent merely systematic attempts to take behavior samples. We may use these samples in different ways. Depending upon the use we expect to make of the test results we may sample a child's behavior in school situations (subject-matter tests), in social situations (social aptitude tests), in mechanical situations (mechanical aptitude tests), etc. When we consider the results of a test alone, without relation to other factors in development, we have a measure of achievement, of level of attainment, of development. The concept of mental age taken alone is such a measure as well as the result obtained by an achievement test in history. When we take the results of any test *in relation to other known factors of development*, we are able to make predictions concerning the future course of development. The tests which have been called tests of *native ability* are almost invariably used in this fashion. For example, if we take the mental age of a child in relation to its chronological age, we are able to make an estimate of its future course of development. In a like manner, if we take a score on a modern language test in relation to a pupil's opportunity to learn that language, we are able to make a prediction concerning his future language development. If we relate the same score to the score on an intelligence test and chronological age, we are able to determine whether he has made good use of his opportunities or has been loafing. When we develop a test and use it for prediction exclusively, we are likely to call it a native ability test or a prognostic test, but it is in no respect different from the other test which we have called a test of achievement.

We can conclude that no test taken alone gives anything more than a measure of achievement. With tests it is just as in geometry, a single point may have any number of straight lines passing through it. If we wish to determine a single straight line in a given direction it is necessary to have at least one additional point of reference. Likewise, if we wish to determine the direction and rate of a child's progress, it is necessary to fix at least *two* points in his course of development. One of these points may be obtained by the use of a single test, but *only one*. We must have some additional information before we can make any prediction concerning the future. Even then we must assume that development takes place in a straight line and at a constant rate. If we do not wish to make these two assumptions, we must collect as much additional information as possible and use it all in making predictions concerning the future course of growth.

Development Is Fairly Consistent. We are able to make predictions concerning the future only because there is a certain amount of constancy in human behavior. We assume, and the assumption seems fairly well justified, that the direction and rate which development has taken in the past will be continued in the future. This assumption is not always correct. In studies of the constancy of the intelligence quotient, it has been found that over a period of several years the intelligence quotient of 90% of children will not change to any important extent. In the case of 10% of the children, however, there will be important changes, and in the case of a few, these changes will be very great. In other aspects of mental development there seems to be a similar consistency, although it is well known that many times important changes do occur in temperament, personality, and character.

The Gestalt Psychologists Are Very Critical of Mental Tests. They say that these tests may have some practical value but that they are theoretically of no importance unless we know what is being measured by them. When they ask the question "What does a test measure?"

they are consciously or unconsciously assuming the existence of a mental something which can be measured. We have seen that early in the development of mental testing the attempt was made to let each test or each part of a test represent an attempt to measure a specific function. We have seen that this attempt was discarded because it was assumed by Binet that all mental functions develop at the same rate. The Gestalt psychologists seem to be insisting that we should return to the earlier attitude toward tests. When tests are conceived of as samples of behavior, there is no point to the question, "What does a test measure?" No test measures anything; it is merely a sample which, if handled intelligently, can be made useful.

The Psycho-analysts Have Not Had Much Interest in Mental Tests. They are not interested so much in the general level of mental development as in mental abnormalities and disturbances. They believe that mental disorders can be better understood in terms of suppression and unwise direction of mental driving forces; any person, whatever his level of general development, may or may not show proper direction of his motivating forces. Their method of procedure, too, is fundamentally opposed to the testing program. Tests represent attempts to gain information concerning mental life in a very limited space of time; psycho-analytic method requires the patient and painstaking unraveling of all the complicated threads of development. Their analysis requires months and even years of effort for each individual, while the testing program calls for the determination of an individual's mental status in a few minutes, an hour or two at most.

The Educational Uses of Standardized Tests. Tests were first developed by teachers for use in solving problems in which teachers were interested; they have turned out to be useful instruments. By using intelligence test score in connection with other information which has been obtained about a pupil, it has been found possible to predict fairly well the course of his future scholastic development. It has been found more difficult to determine with (or without) the aid of tests exactly which school subjects a child will find easy and which he will find difficult. Estimates of future development in matters of morals, character, temperament, and personality are even more difficult to obtain through the use of tests or in any other way, in spite of the fact that many attempts have been made. Failure in this type of testing seems to be based upon the fact that there are strong social taboos which prevent the examiner from using the kind of test which would be valuable. Even if this restraint could be removed, difficulties in technique would still exist, concerned with getting the person tested to respond normally in the test situation.

The standardization of subject-matter tests has met with varying success. Where there is general agreement upon specific objectives and sequences of subject matter for gaining these objectives, standardized tests have proved very useful. Such tests are widely used in many elementary school subjects, as in arithmetic, spelling, reading, and writing. In high school and in college where there is less agreement upon specific objectives and sequences of subject matter, the use of standardized tests is necessarily more restricted. The labor involved in standardizing a test seems not worth while unless large numbers of students are to be tested by it.

Other Uses of Mental Tests. Since tests turned out to be so useful for prediction of school success, it was assumed that these same tests should prove equally useful in predicting success in life after school. They were not developed for this purpose, and it turns out that they are not very valuable when used in this way. Many attempts have been made to develop highly specialized tests for predicting success in special occupations. Some of these attempts have been reasonably successful. If such tests are developed with the needs of a specific occupation in mind, we may expect them to be as successful in their field as the general mental and educational tests have been in their own field, but where attempts are made to carry the general mental and educational tests over into the vocational field, they are uniformly unsuccessful. We can sum the matter up in this fashion: general mental tests were made by school teachers for their own special purposes; whenever we attempt to use them for the purposes for which they were designed they are good, but the farther we get away from their original purpose the less valuable they become.

SUMMARY

While the measurement of reaction times and intensities of sensation began a century ago, the use of standardized tests as aids in solving educational problems is an affair of the twentieth century. Mental tests were first developed by the functional psychologists as measures of the separate mental functions. Binet was able to introduce the concept of mental age by making the assumption that all the various mental functions develop at the same rate. The concept of intelligence quotient was originated to describe rate of development, this rate has been found to be fairly constant for any individual during his period of physical growth. The general mental worth of an individual has been summed up in the word "intelligence," but it has not been satisfactorily defined.

Behaviorism has abandoned the assumption that there are mental functions. In consequence, tests must be regarded from this point of view as samples of behavior. The value of a behavior sample is determined by the care with which it has been taken and the use which is made of it. Any behavior sample represents the child's present status in that class of behavior. In this sense all tests are achievement tests. Tests can be used for prediction when they are related to other known facts of development, they then become prognostic or native ability tests.

Gestalt psychologists point out the need for definition of the things measured by tests. Psycho-analysts have not been much interested in level or rate of development.

Standardized mental and educational tests were first developed by school teachers for the use of school teachers. They have proven their value in helping to meet educational problems. When used for other purposes—in business, for example—they have less value and require adaptation to the new demands made upon them.

CHAPTER IX

INDIVIDUALIZED INSTRUCTION

I. INDIVIDUAL DIFFERENCES IN PSYCHOLOGY

The Study of Individual Differences Requires an Objective Approach. As long as a psychologist holds fast to a purely subjective method of investigation he will learn nothing concerning individual differences. The psychology of individual differences is always "the Psychology of the Other One." Comparison between individuals must be made; the only person the investigator can study subjectively is himself. Scientists have been traditionally interested in discovering laws which have *general* application. The subjective psychologist can discover such laws only if he assumes that he is *typical of the whole human race.* Differences between individuals are disturbing factors in his investigations; he wishes to eliminate them.

Just as soon, however, as experimentation is carried on in an objective fashion, it becomes possible to subject a number of individuals to the same experimental situation. Whenever this is done it is evident at once that individuals differ markedly in sensory capacity, in learning ability, and in behavior traits of every kind. It is just this background of individual variation which causes the really *common* traits to stand out and makes the formulation of valid laws possible. In addition to the generalizations concerning common human traits which emerge from the accumulation of observations upon different individuals, many important facts and principles concerning the nature and range of individual variations and peculiarities are discovered. The understanding of these peculiarities of individuals, fully as much as the discovery of general laws of human nature, is rapidly making over the whole educational system.

The Various Psychologies Have Different Attitudes toward the Facts of Individual Differences. For the structural psychologist, whose approach is wholly subjective and introspective (in theory at least), the variation between individuals is a disturbing factor which he wishes to eliminate. The fact that such differences could not be wholly eliminated from psychological experiments was one of the important causes for the origin of the functional psychology. The objective experimentation of the functionalists, particularly the systematic attempts to study child development, soon gave rise to an extensive literature concerned with individual differences. In behavioristic psychology, the subjective method has been almost completely discarded and the objective approach is the customary procedure. Individual differences are taken as a matter of fact; no attempt is made to dodge them.

Psycho-analysis has frequently been called "Individual Psychology." It is concerned primarily with tracing out in great detail the development of individuals. The method of operation *seems* to be wholly subjective; but it is recognized that each individual stands alone, that his development can be understood and explained only by reference to events in his own past life. Generalization and discovery of *laws* of mental life which were the objectives of the structural psychology are not matters of interest to the psycho-analysts. Two important generalizations, it is true, have been made: that mental driving forces are back of all individual actions and that abnormalities usually arise in early childhood. These are generalizations which have been made by the physician who compares the case histories of all his various patients. This relation of physician to patient is, in fact, the foundation of psycho-analytic method. The responses of the patient to the circumstances of his past life are examined in great detail by the physician. Psycho-analysis reduces in fact to the "Psychology of the Other One." What appears to be a subjective method is in reality objective. Psycho-analysis differs in method from behaviorism and what has been called objective psychology chiefly in the manner of collecting data; reliance is placed upon *recall of behavior in previous situations* rather than upon *observation of behavior under controlled experimental conditions.* Psycho-analytic method, being essentially objective, is adapted to the study of individual differences; nevertheless, in their insistence upon the importance of instinctive driving forces, psycho-analysts have tried to fit all individuals to a common pattern.

The Gestalt psychology in its experimentation and theory has been quite ready to recognize the importance of individual differences, although it has been almost wholly occupied with the enormous task of making over the previously accepted laws and generalizations to fit its own peculiar assumptions.

Purposive psychology insists that behavior must always be explained in terms of the purposes and goals of the individual. But in its insistence upon the number and importance of innate desires and instinctive driving forces which are common to the race it tends to fit all individuals to a general pattern. The well-springs of behavior are believed to be racial; it is only the particular means of their expression which can be individual.

Instinct Psychology Tends to Ignore Individual Differences. So long as the belief in the existence and importance of a large number of instincts and emotions has a prominent place in a psychological system, individual differences are likely to prove troublesome. By definition, instinctive and emotional characteristics are universal and present in all individual members of the race. From the first use of objective observation of human behavior, it was apparent that these tendencies were not universal. To account for this lack of universality various principles were developed: (1) delayed appearance, (2) maturation, (3) waning, (4) modifiability, (5) specialization, (6) inhibition, (7) breaking up into partial tendencies (cf. Chapter IV). These principles, which permitted individual differences in instinctive behavior, had to be called into operation so often that psychologists began to wonder whether there was not a fundamental error in attaching so much importance to instinct.

Individual Psychology Has Modified the Meaning of "Law." There has persisted in psychology an attitude toward "laws" and "principles" which has disappeared from the natural sciences. In the natural sciences laws or principles are recognized as being the statement merely of *probabilities*, rather than of *absolute uniformities*. They are merely theories which fit a finite number of facts. Through mathematical treatment attempts are made to extend the theories and make them absolute, but it is recognized that such attempts are subject to errors and limitations of observations. When we make a subjective approach to psychology and ignore individual differences, we are more likely to look upon the "laws" of mind as *absolute* and not, as in the other sciences, merely probabilities. With an objective approach which entails a recognition of individual differences, "laws" and "principles" come to have the same meaning as in science generally, namely a *high degree of probability*.

Individual Differences Are Quantitative Rather than Qualitative. A child or a man may have more or less ability of a particular kind than another, but he will not be wholly lacking in any ability. It is true that we sometimes speak as if a person totally lacked some ability. We say that a child has no ability in music, that another child has no athletic ability, that another one lacks mathematical ability, etc. What we mean by such statements is not that the ability is wholly lacking, but that the degree of ability possessed by the child is so small that it can be disregarded when considering the kind of occupation he should enter. It seems to be possible for any child— unless handicapped by extreme physical defect such as blindness, deafness, loss of arms, etc.—to engage in any of the types of work found in the ordinary school or the average community. His *degree* of success may, however, be great or small and the *amount of time* required for learning a given task may be great or small. It is probable that he will be able to attain a higher degree of success in some kinds of work than in others and that he will be able to develop a given degree of skill more quickly in some activities than in others.

How Great Are the Differences between Individuals? We know that some persons have such a low degree of ability in general intelligence that they are helpless idiots who cannot even feed themselves, while others are geniuses who make important contributions to the welfare of large numbers of other people. In musical ability there are, at the one extreme, people who have very poor ability to discriminate pitches and people who are almost monotones, with little ability to produce different pitches; at the other extreme there is the musical genius. When attempts are made to express such differences in mathematical terms, it is difficult to find a suitable unit of measure. It is probable that some people have abilities many times greater than those of others.

Individual differences in school subjects have been more accurately measured. We know that within a given class, a fourth grade for example, one child may be able to read two or three times as fast as another; in ability to understand what is read the differences are likely to be even greater. In addition or subtraction the best pupil in the class may work four or five times as fast or as accurately as the poorest. In a college class in psychology the best person in the class can learn two or three times as much in a given period as the average member of the class. If we could so organize school work that each pupil could progress at his own rate, some pupils should be expected to do as much in half a year or even less as others do in a full year. Within a large class, children will be found to differ from those nearest them in ability by very small amounts in any given trait. The group as a whole will range all the way from very low to very high ability. The majority of individuals will be grouped closely about the class average while a very few will possess low, and a very few high ability.

Individuals Cannot Be Grouped into Types or Discontinuous Classes. It was customary for many years to speak of *imagery types.* According to this theory it was believed that some individuals could learn much more readily through the medium of some one type of sensory experience than another and would recall past experiences primarily in terms of one dominant type of imagery. Some children were supposed to be of the visual type, that is, it was believed they could learn quite well when material was presented to them visually, and would recall past events in terms of visual images, but could not learn readily in any other manner, as for example, through the ear, and would not recall auditory images. Others were supposed to be of an auditory type or a kinesthetic type.

Investigations of the manner in which learning takes place show that any one of us may learn through any kind of stimulation. Whether we learn primarily through visual stimulation depends in part upon the general habits of learning which we have developed, but it depends as well upon the kind of habit which is to be formed. In thinking about trees and learning about trees, most of us perhaps are of what has been called the visual imagery type. This means simply that the experiences which we have had in connection with trees are almost entirely visual. However, those of us who have had the experience of cutting down a tree may think about it in terms of kinesthetic imagery, of labor involved in cutting the tree, or we may think of it in terms of auditory imagery based upon the sound of the tree in falling and the sound of the ax and saw in cutting. Whether our imagery and our learning with respect to any particular feature of our environment is primarily visual, auditory, or kinesthetic depends, then, simply upon the kind of experience which we have had with that feature of our environment. We are all of us fully capable of learning and learning well through any class of stimulation, by means of any one of our sense organs, so long as the sense organ is in good functional condition.

The general conclusion is that differences which exist between individuals are not of such kind as to justify the classification of children into types, if by types we mean children who possess some one ability and lack certain others. Differences between individuals are, as we previously pointed out, quantitative rather than qualitative.

Individuals Differ in the Degree of Difficulty of Tasks Which They Can Learn. It is commonly recognized that material presented to pupils must be adapted to their stage of progress in the subject taught. The learning of any given task is always based upon the existence of habits which have been formed at some earlier time or upon instinctive tendencies which were present as a part of the original equipment of the individual. As we find children in any grade in school, their previous preparation differs, and in consequence the degree of difficulty of the tasks which they are ready to learn differs.

Whenever a task is too difficult for a learner this difficulty is based upon the fact that his previous learning is defective. His previous learning may be defective merely because of lack of opportunity, or because he is such a slow learner that the same opportunity afforded other pupils is not sufficient to prepare him for the difficult task. In mathematics, for example, we know that multiplication is too difficult for a child until that child has first learned addition, that division is too difficult for a child until he has first learned to add, to subtract, and to multiply. If a child is such a slow learner that he learns to add only after years of practice (if, that is, he is feeble-minded) we are likely to say that arithmetic has such a high degree of difficulty that he cannot learn it, meaning that the usual opportunities are not sufficient in his case and that the amount of time and effort required is not justified by the results obtained. At the rate of progress of which he is capable in mathematics he will not live long enough to acquire much skill. Some other student may be ordinarily a good learner. He may have successfully completed elementary school and high school and be doing good work in college. If he has not done much work in science it will be easy to find problems in chemistry or physics that are too difficult for him, but he is capable of learning with sufficient rapidity so that the problems in chemistry or physics which are difficult for him to-day will not be difficult after a comparatively short period of training.

The statement that individuals differ in the degree of difficulty of tasks which they can learn means, for one thing, that they differ in their present preparation for learning the task. Some individuals are not merely deficient in preparation, but have a rate of learning so slow that it will be impracticable for them ever to learn the task.

Individuals Differ in Method of Learning. Individuals in school have formed many study habits but they have not all formed the same ones. One pupil make like to read in a quiet room; another may not object to a certain amount of noise. One pupil may like to underline pages in the book he is reading; another may not make use of this device. One student may like to take notes upon his reading; another may not care to do so. One student may like to read rapidly through material to be studied and then go back over it more slowly and carefully a second time, while another may like to make his first reading of the material slow and careful. One student may wish to discuss the material being studied at considerable length with other students or the teacher; another student may feel that such discussion is unnecessary. These and many other differences in method of study are clearly dependent upon habits which pupils have developed during the course of their school life. We are likely to assume that out of these conflicting habits we should be able to determine an ideal method of study suited to all pupils. A considerable amount of experimentation has been conducted in the attempt to work out these most economical methods of study. Up to the present, however, the results are incomplete and inconclusive. It seems desirable in the present state of our knowledge to give such advice as we can concerning methods of study, but to leave much leeway for pupils to choose those methods which they prefer.

II. Methods for Adapting School Work to Individuals

1. Since children differ in degree of ability for different kinds of work it is desirable to have some *flexibility in the selection of subject matter*. Each child should be permitted to spend most of his time studying those things which he can learn easily and well. 2. Since some individuals can and do learn more rapidly than others, it is desirable to arrange school work in such a fashion that different children may be permitted to spend *different amounts of time* on a given unit of the curriculum. Pupils must be permitted to progress in each special subject at their own rate. 3. The ways in which children learn an activity may vary on account of variations in previous experience and in methods of study. The teacher must, therefore, *vary her methods of instruction* to suit the needs of her various pupils and must allow a certain amount of freedom for individual methods of learning. 4. Since there is a difference in degree of difficulty of tasks for which pupils are prepared, because of different amounts of preparation, there must be *provision for a graded curriculum*.

Organization of the School to Provide for Individual Differences. The attempt to work out educational procedures which make use of the facts of individual difference has attracted attention only recently. It was formerly believed that all individuals were very much alike and that differences in learning were based upon differences in industry rather than differences in abilities. During recent years many devices have been adopted with or without good reason in the attempt to provide for individual differences. Each special plan for providing for individual differences has usually been concerned with only one of the four phases of adaptation which we have mentioned.

The Graded Curriculum. Almost since the beginning of formal instruction it has been recognized that all learners are not ready for tasks of the same degree of difficulty and some attempt has been made to suit the instruction to the stage of advancement of the learner. Definite provision for a rough adjustment of degree of difficulty of tasks to the stage of advancement of the learner is provided in modern school systems by the organization of pupils into school grades or classes, and by the provision that a pupil can progress from one grade or class to another only when the work of the first grade has been satisfactorily completed. While this principle has been generally recognized and generally provided for, its application is still conspicuously lacking in the work of physical education. This failure to provide for graded work in physical education is doubtless due to the fact that it is a relatively new part of the curriculum. Its aims and objectives are not well understood by school administrators and the importance of adapting physical education to the stage of advancement of the pupil has not been appreciated.

Within a given year's work there is ordinarily a certain sequence of subject matter which is believed to be based upon the requirements of the pupils for learning. Presumably work given during the first month of a school year is a necessary prerequisite for the work of the second month; work during the first week is a prerequisite for the work of the second week, etc. This arrangement of units of subject matter is, however, often purely arbitrary or based entirely upon some logical scheme. The organization may be one that appeals to a person who is thoroughly familiar with the whole field, but it is frequently not an arrangement which makes learning easiest for the pupil. That particular arrangement of subject matter which is based upon the requirements of the learner rather than upon the logical divisions of the subject is properly called "psychological" as opposed to "logical."

Sometimes the psychological and logical arrangements of subject matter coincide but not always. For example, a logical arrangement of mathematics divides the subject into arithmetic, algebra, plane geometry, solid geometry, trigonometry, analytical geometry, calculus, etc. We commonly teach each subdivision during a separate year or half year of school work. There is no reason, however, in the necessity of learning, why a student should be familiar with all the algebra taught during the freshman and sophomore years in high school before he can undertake the study of geometry. It is wholly unnecessary for him to be familiar with geometry as it is taught in high school before he begins a study of trigonometry, and it is wholly unnecessary that he should have completed all three of these and in addition analytical geometry before he begins a study of calculus. From the standpoint of the learner, it is entirely possible and even desirable that some of the more important principles of geometry, trigonometry, analytical geometry, and calculus shall be taught during the first year of high-school mathematics. Such a grading of subject matter, adapting it to the needs of the learner, is properly called a psychological arrangement.

Specialization. For centuries it has been recognized that students should prepare themselves primarily for one or another occupation in life and that this preparation requires a certain specialization in choice of subject matter. Presumably this specialization is based upon the special abilities of the student. Since the school has been concerned mainly with literary and professional activities, the earliest types of specialization recognized were in theology, medicine, and law. Specialization in theology, medicine, or law was not, however, based upon any good understanding of the abilities of the student, but depended rather upon social and economic pressures, interests of family, etc. With the increasing complexity of civilization and the increasing accumulation of knowledge, the necessity for specialization has increased. During recent years we have recognized that specialization should depend not merely upon the whims of the student or his family but should be based upon an understanding of his special abilities. The program of vocational and educational guidance in the public schools has developed as a means for meeting this problem.

Free Electives. In recognition of the fact that students differ in their special abilities, there has been introduced into the curriculum of many schools much freedom in choosing subjects to be studied. This freedom of choice ordinarily begins on the high-school level and is quite extensive in the college curriculum. The introduction of electives into the curriculum at first took place in such a way that any student might choose to study any subject. A few schools still proceed on this basis. Now, however, it is generally recognized that freedom of choice of subjects to be studied should not be absolute, but that studies elected should fall largely within some one chosen field, such as natural science, social science, philosophy, literature, etc. The belief that the facts of individual differences in special abilities require complete freedom of choice has been replaced with the belief that the facts of difference in special ability are better recognized by setting up fields of specialization.

Orientation and Try-out Courses. Along with the recognition of the desirability of permitting freedom of choice and opportunity for specialization, there has arisen the difficulty of discovering what the special abilities and interests of a student actually are. As a means for aiding a student in his choice of a field of specialization, special courses have been introduced which give a sample of the various types of work to be found within that field of specialization. A general course in science, for example, gives a student an introduction to physics, chemistry, zoölogy, botany, etc. On the basis of this introduction he can discover whether he likes science in general and which phase of science appeals most to him. In the vocational subjects try-out courses are frequently found in which the student spends a week or two working at each of several types of work, such as woodworking, ironwork, typesetting. These try-out courses are based upon the assumption that a week or two will be a sufficient period to enable the student and the instructor to determine fairly well the student's ability for that kind of work so that he can be guided wisely in his future choice of a field of specialization.

Supervised Study. One of the earliest forms of the modern interest in individualized instruction made use of the substitution of a supervised study period for a part of the traditional recitation period. It was believed that students if left to their own devices would study ineffectively; it was thought that they gained little of real value in the formal question-and-answer type of class recitation. Students were required to be present in study rooms under the immediate supervision of a teacher who gave them such advice and help as seemed to be needed. It was possible in this way to treat each pupil as an individual. No attempt was made either to permit one pupil to progress at a faster rate than another, or to change the character of the subject matter to fit the needs of individual pupils in the class. The provision was solely for difference in method of learning and the attempt was primarily to gain greater efficiency in learning.

Ability Grouping. Where a large number of students are engaged in studying the same subject, they may be divided into two or three groups according to their ability. This division into groups may be based upon an analysis of previous school marks, upon the judgment of teachers, or upon the results of mental tests. When the division into groups has taken place, an attempt may be made to use different methods of instruction with each of the three different groups. Such attempts have not been very successful because there seems to be no uniform difference in method of studying which is correlated with degree of ability. The attempt may be made to permit each of the different groups to progress at a different rate. The dull group may be taught by the same methods as the bright group, and they may follow the same curriculum but be given more time. One public school attempted to work out ability grouping on the following basis: Upon entering school the pupils were divided into three groups according to ability; the dull group was permitted to follow the usual school curriculum, completing the work ordinarily done in the first six grades in eight years; the middle group was permitted to follow the usual curriculum completing the work of eight grades in eight years; the bright group was permitted to complete the work of eight grades in six years. At the end of this period of elementary instruction, all pupils were graduated into the high school, each pupil being permitted to engage in that part of high-school work for which he was best fitted. Sometimes an attempt is made to modify the curriculum for the different ability groupings. Dull pupils may be provided with a simplified curriculum, and bright pupils with an enriched curriculum. Each pupil completes one school grade each year. In high school this provision for brighter pupils may be made by permitting them to carry more subjects, completing the usual four-year course in three years, or remaining for four years but completing a larger number of subjects.

Contract Plan. The subject matter of the year is divided into a number of logical or psychological units. Each unit is prepared in the form of an assignment which is issued to the pupil in mimeographed form. Considerable freedom in preparing the work of each unit is permitted. Pupils may use their own methods of study, receiving advice and suggestions from the teacher. The same time limit for completing the contract is given to all pupils so that each pupil completes all the work of a given subject during the year. The brighter pupils, however, are required to do more work than the dull pupils. The differentiation between bright and dull pupils is made by providing two or more levels of work for each unit. For the dull pupils a contract is provided which contains the minimum essentials of the unit. The brighter pupils are given additional work concerned with additional details or with applications of the important principles contained in the unit. The teacher and pupil usually agree beforehand that the pupil is to undertake the minimum contract or a contract at a higher level. It is assumed that the pupil will master whatever contract he undertakes. Half learning is not to be permitted. This contract plan, therefore, represents an attempt to provide for individual differences by permitting fast learners to learn more within a given time than slow learners, at the same time keeping all the pupils together in a single class and permitting them to progress from grade to grade together.

The Dalton Plan. Each pupil is provided with mimeographed assignments or contracts as in the Contract Plan. Pupil freedom is encouraged. The rooms are considered as subject workshops. Pupils are permitted to come and go freely. There is no class schedule, but the pupils are expected to group themselves periodically for conferences with the teacher. No definite time limit is set for the completion of any contract, but a pupil must complete one contract in a given subject before he is allowed to receive any fresh contract. He may spend his entire time for a day or a week working at a single contract in a single subject, such as history, or he may divide his time during the week between contracts in history, mathematics, English, etc. He is required to budget his own time. To help him in budgeting his time and estimating his progress, graphic devices are provided showing expected progress and his own actual progress. This plan requires self-testing devices to be used periodically to check the amount of progress made. The Dalton Plan, therefore, provides that each pupil may progress at his own rate. It permits considerable freedom in choice of method of studying, and it provides for an enriched curriculum for those students who can progress rapidly.

The Unit Plan. Pupils are provided with mimeographed assignments which outline in some detail the procedure to be followed in learning. This procedure may be definitely divided into five divisions,—exploration, presentation, assimilation, organization, and recitation. A definite date for the completion of the unit is specified. This plan permits students to work as individuals and does not require class recitation. It does, however, prescribe rather definitely the kind of subject matter, the rate of work, and the method of study, so that not much real provision for individual differences is present. It becomes, rather, a correspondence method of study, the pupils doing all their work in written form, the teacher accepting and grading it. The instructional activities are determined largely by the mimeographed assignment sheets. The teacher is merely a kind of examiner.

Individualized Instruction. The aim of this plan is self-instruction. The pupils are provided with specially prepared textbooks which are in the main self-instructive and self-corrective. The teacher, as in the Unit Plan, is merely a kind of examiner. The quantity and quality of work done is determined by the use of objective tests. There are no formal recitations. The curriculum and the units of study are the same for all pupils. Each pupil is, however, permitted to progress at his own rate and complete the work of the curriculum in a longer or shorter time, depending upon his own ability.

Opportunity Rooms. Some pupils are always found who do not adapt themselves readily to the ordinary school procedures. These maladjusted pupils may be of any age or grade. Sometimes they are dull and sometimes normal or even bright. A small number of such pupils is placed in the care of a specially trained teacher. An attempt is made to analyze the difficulty of each pupil as an individual. Based upon this analysis of each pupil's difficulty, he is given the instruction which he individually needs and is restored to the regular school class as quickly as possible. The primary object of the Opportunity Room is to provide special opportunity for individual instruction by a teacher who is especially capable. The Opportunity Room is not to be thought of as a class for defectives but as a special class for pupils who have experienced some temporary difficulty which can ordinarily be overcome, permitting their return to the usual type of instruction.

The Project Method. It has been thought that many of the difficulties which arise from the traditional plan of class instruction are based upon the fact that the subject matter is not concerned with the immediate interests of the pupil, and that the method of instruction is too formal and impersonal to arouse their fullest effort. The project method is an attempt to provide subject matter that has more immediate interest and to permit a method of study which is more informal. Ideally it is expected that pupils will on their own initiative choose worthwhile activities to engage in. Examples of such activities are an investigation of the milk supply of the community, a study of the local electric-lighting plant, a study of the community government, the building of a boat, etc. It is believed that by engaging in these activities which arise out of their own experience pupils will be able to learn the traditional subject matter in an informal and incidental fashion. Arithmetic, for example, will be learned as an outgrowth of the mathematical computations needed in the project. Language will be learned as an incident to the discussion and the writing which are needed in carrying on the project. Historical information will be gathered as it has a bearing upon the project.

In practice, knowledge of arithmetic, language, history, etc., gained through the project method of instruction is likely to be one-sided and defective. Important matters are likely to be neglected because they are not needed in the projects which are being carried on. It is very difficult to devise projects which will include all the necessary drill in arithmetic, language forms, etc. Learning in these subjects is likely to be only half learning. Furthermore, it is necessary that there shall be a certain unity of effort among the pupils grouped together in a given grade. They must all engage in one project together. This project may be of interest to some of the pupils but not of interest to others. While in theory the choice of the project to be undertaken is left to the pupils, in practice this choice is largely determined by the teacher, based upon the availability of materials and the desirability of certain kinds of learning. In consequence, the amount of pupil initiative and freedom involved in this plan is easily overestimated. The project method has the advantage that the projects chosen are likely to be of more immediate interest to the students than textbook material. It represents an attempt to provide for individual differences by permitting informality of learning and adaptation of subject matter to the interests of the particular group.

Special Classes for Defectives. There is always a large number of children in any community who because of physical or mental defect cannot profitably engage in the usual school work. Such children are the deaf, the blind, speech defectives, feeble-minded, neurotic, etc. Whenever the community is large enough, attempts are usually made to provide special classes for each special type of defect. In these classes special methods of instruction are necessarily used. The blind must be taught to read by the use of the fingers and according to a radically different plan than is used with normal children. The deaf must be taught to talk by the use of special devices. On account of the difficulty which defectives may have in learning the usual school subjects, the curriculum is ordinarily radically modified to suit their special needs. Such classes provide for extremes of individual difference by radical modifications in method of instruction and type of curriculum.

Comparison of the Traditional Plan of Instruction with Individualized Plans. The objection to the traditional plan is that it is adapted to the average pupil and that it does not develop desirable habits of industry and initiative. Bright pupils are held back, thereby losing interest and becoming lazy, while dull pupils are forced to work beyond their capacity, thereby becoming discouraged. The attempt is made to attain a dead level of mediocrity. Pupils spend too much of their time in listening. They develop habits of unthinking obedience rather than habits of initiative and industry. The individualized plans of instruction have as their objective the correcting of these evils.

The division of pupils into groups according to ability has been criticized because it does not go far enough. Instead of one general level of mediocrity there is a substitution of three different levels of mediocrity. Individualized plans of instruction, such as the Dalton Plan, the Contract Plan, the Unit Plan, etc., eliminate this dead level of mediocrity and increase the amount of pupil activity and initiative. The assigning of names to these various plans has, however, tended to obscure the important issues. The important results to be gained through individualized instruction are: (1) permitting specialization in accordance with special ability, (2) adaptation of subject matter to the stage of advancement of the pupil, (3) provision for learning at that rate to which the pupil is suited, and (4) provision for individuality in method of study. The various plans have usually emphasized one or more of these four requirements and have neglected the others. The Contract Plan, for example, permits individuality in studying and provides for an enriched curriculum. The enrichment of the curriculum is provided to take care of increase in rate of learning, but is not necessarily concerned with providing additional subject matter which is specially suited to the needs of the pupil. The Dalton Plan permits each pupil to progress at his own rate and choose his own method of learning, but is not concerned with the other two phases of individual differences. Individualized instruction permits pupils to progress at their own rate, but ignores the other three phases of individual differences. The Unit Plan does not provide satisfactorily for any phase of individual difference. All of these plans are likely to degenerate into a kind of correspondence course between teacher and pupil, even though they are present in the same building or in the same room. The function of the teacher may become that of a taskmaster and examiner. The amount of aid given the pupil is frequently small. These difficulties are not inherent in the plans but usually appear as the plans become formalized. This danger is likely to be increased when the various plans are assigned formal names. It seems highly desirable to keep in mind the facts of individual difference which are to be provided for rather than to attempt to work out a definitely organized plan of procedure to be adopted as a cure-all for the evils of the traditional class recitation.

III. Summary

The facts of individual difference in mental activity emphasized the defects of introspective method in psychology and had much to do with the origin of functional and objective psychology. Psycho-analysis has been interested in individuals from its origin. Gestalt psychology is adapted to the study of individuals but has as yet contributed little. Purposive psychology, because of its emphasis upon racial driving forces (instinct and emotion) tends to ignore the facts of individual variation.

Individuals do not totally lack any ability unless handicapped by gross physical defect; differences in degree of ability may, however, be very great. Individuals cannot be divided into types, but differ from those closest to them in ability by very small amounts, and range in ability from the very deficient to the genius.

School work may be adapted to individuals in four fundamental ways: (1) by permitting variations in selection of subject matter; (2) by permitting pupils to spend varying amounts of time on a given unit of work; (3) by varying methods of instruction and permitting freedom for individual methods of learning; (4) by providing a psychologically graded curriculum. The various new plans of instruction which are designed to supplement or replace the traditional class recitation provide for one or more of these four phases of adaptation to individuals with greater or less success.

CHAPTER X

VOCATIONAL AND EDUCATIONAL GUIDANCE

Educational and Vocational Guidance Are Interrelated.
Educational guidance has in view a pupil's preparation
for a particular occupation or class of occupations. It requires, first, the determination of the kind of education that
the child is capable of receiving and, second, the direction
of that education—in part at least—toward meeting the
requirements of a particular vocation. The selection of
a vocation toward which training is directed requires
an understanding of the special abilities of the child and
an understanding of his educational possibilities as well
as a knowledge of the requirements of many vocations.

*Human Nature and the Nature of Vocations Demand
Individual Guidance.* The need for vocational and educational guidance is based upon two classes of facts,—
that individuals do differ from one another in many important ways, and that different occupations demand
different human qualities. Even if we should agree with
Watson in his statement that he can train any child for
any kind of occupation if he is given the child early enough
in its development and is provided with the right kind of
environment to use in training the child, it would, nevertheless, be necessary to assert that the task of training
children for particular occupations could be made easier
by adopting some plan of educational and vocational
guidance. It is a matter of common observation supported
by scientific evidence that children, as we find them at
school age, do differ greatly in their aptitudes for specific

tasks. Whether the difference is due to native differences in bodily and nervous structure, or due exclusively to their individual background of experiences, as Watson maintains, it is easier to direct their future development in some directions than in others. The attempt to give educational or vocational guidance is further based upon the theory that any person will be happier and will be a more useful member of society if he follows the line of least resistance in his choice of an occupation.

Before we can offer intelligent advice to any child concerning his choice of a vocation or a particular kind of education, it is necessary to do two things. We must first carefully analyze the various occupations which are open to the child, discovering their peculiar demands upon human nature; we must next carefully examine the child to discover his own peculiar and special abilities. Having made this analysis of vocations and of the personality of the child, the advisor is called upon to exercise his understanding and intelligence in matching up the two sets of data in such a way that just that occupation will be selected which demands primarily just those abilities that the child has been found to possess.

Occupations Must Be Analyzed in Terms of Tasks to Be Performed. Certain procedures have been found useful in analyzing an occupation and discovering the kind of personality traits and skills which are needed for its successful prosecution. The beginning is usually made by securing interviews with experts in that field of work. On the basis of such interviews a preliminary list of the duties of the occupation is developed. With this list as a guide, further interviews with other experts are obtained for the purpose of verifying and extending the list of activities found in that occupation. This preliminary list of requirement must be made up in terms of work done by people engaged in the occupation. The attempt is made to gain a purely objective statement of tasks and duties, with no reference at first to the kind of human qualities which are needed successfully to accomplish and perform these tasks.

When such a list has been worked out in a fairly complete form on the basis of interviews with workers expert in that occupation, the second step can be taken. Careful and detailed observations are made of work actually performed during the course of a working day. This observation must be extended throughout weeks and seasons. It frequently happens that work on Monday is different from work on Wednesday or Saturday, so that observation must be extended throughout the week in order to get a complete picture of the occupation. Likewise, at the beginning of the month there may be a different form of work than that at the middle or end of the month. There may be seasonal or other variations in the type of work which is performed. Careful observation of work actually carried on must be extended over a period of at least a year before the list of tasks and duties as found in the occupation can be considered complete.

When this list of activities has been completed by observation of work actually performed, it must be subjected to further verification and extension by a second interview with experts in which the list previously worked out is examined, systematized, and revised. Only after the list of activities which are actually performed by people engaged in the occupation has been completed is it desirable to undertake a statement of the human qualities needed in the occupation.

The Statement of Work Done in an Occupation Must Be Translated into Terms of Abilities Needed to Perform the Work. There are two recognized approaches to this problem. The first procedure is again to seek the advice of successful members of that trade or occupation. These experts should be interviewed, with the statement of work to be done in the occupation before them. The details of the occupation should be checked over, item by item, and the experts' opinions obtained concerning the personal ability required for successfully doing each task.

This method has some value. It turns out, however, in practice that the list of personal qualities and abilities needed for one occupation as determined by this procedure is very similar to the list of qualities and abilities needed for almost any other occupation.

The Opinions of Experts Can Be Verified and Supplemented by the Use of Psychological Tests. Workers who are actively engaged in the vocation may be examined to determine what traits and characteristics they possess. If, as a result of extensive and careful observation and psychological examination, successful workers in an occupation can be shown to possess traits that are lacking in people who have tried the occupation and failed, we have the beginning of an important list of traits which are needed for that occupation. If successful workers in two different occupations, such as plumbing and carpentry or medicine and engineering, can be carefully examined and found to have certain characteristics in common but certain other characteristics which are *peculiar to the one occupation or the other*, we have, then, an important basis of differentiation between the two occupations. This procedure is promising but requires a large amount of careful and detailed work.

Some such attempts to analyze the characteristics of workers have been made, but they are largely inconclusive. One of the great obstacles is the fact that the words which are available for describing personal traits are generally very vague and indefinite in their applications. A procedure of this kind seems to be of value only for determining the requirements of certain broad, general classes of work. Mechanical work, for example, can be distinguished from work of a purely literary nature. Social and business activities on the one hand can be distinguished from more purely individual work as found in scientific occupations. The distinction between two professions, such as medicine and engineering, or law and the ministry, or between two trades, such as plumbing and carpentry, can scarcely be made on the basis of lists of characteristics arrived at by such a consensus of opinion of experts or by the use of psychological tests.

Abilities Needed in an Occupation Can Be Stated in Terms of Score in Trade Tests. It will be worth while to examine the procedure by which such tests are developed and administered. A first requirement is that large numbers of individuals who are doing almost exactly the same kind of work must be found. The standardization of a test—the determination of its validity, reliability, and objectivity—depends upon a statistical treatment which demands the collection of a large number of test scores. This condition can be met in some of the simpler trades and occupations. It is a condition that is very difficult to fulfill in connection with the more important trades and occupations in which there is a high degree of specialization or in which individuality of the worker plays an important part in his success. Most of the more important business and industrial occupations and most of the professions contain these elements of specialization and individuality which make it exceedingly difficult if not impossible to carry on this kind of testing.

When this first requirement for the development of a

test has been met, it is necessary to devise a number of relatively simple tasks which will constitute the "test." The kind of tasks chosen will depend only upon the ingenuity of the psychologist and the limitations of time and equipment. It is usually believed that such tasks should meet certain requirements. 1. Their administration should require a minimum of time, not more than one or two hours in all. 2. They should be relatively inexpensive. This is a practical consideration. Employers are not willing to spend much money in selecting employees. Prospective employees are not willing or able to pay a fee for being tested. It may be that employers can eventually be shown the financial saving to be gained by a more careful selection of employees and become willing to spend more money in a testing program. 3. They should be highly selective. Successful workers in the vocation should succeed in the tests, unsuccessful workers should fail in the tests. 4. No attempt should be made to develop the tests as measures of psychological "traits." The aim should be to discover tasks diagnostic of success or failure in the occupation, with no reference to personality, intelligence, or the like.

When such a test series for a particular vocation has been devised, it must be standardized by the use of appropriate statistical technique. After determining its predictive value by administering it to workers on the job, it must be applied to prospective workers and predictions of their probable success made. Their later success must be compared with the predictions made on the basis of the test. The test can be considered as complete only when it has been found to yield good results when used in practice for selecting employees. It must, however, be revised whenever changes in the vocation make new demands upon the worker.

Educational Guidance Requires Differentiation between School Subjects in Terms of Human Traits. Certainly no one up to the present has succeeded in discovering what personal traits and characteristics are needed for success in one school subject, such as science, which are not needed for success in another school subject, such as mathematics or literary work. Until we have worked out the list of traits which distinguish the ability to succeed in one school subject from ability to succeed in another school subject, we can scarcely make a beginning in giving educational guidance. The problem seems to be similar to that of distinguishing between vocations on the basis of personal traits. The same technique should be used and the same difficulties will be encountered.

How Can Tests Be Used in Educational and Vocational Guidance? There has been worked out a long and imposing list of tests, both of general and special abilities. We have a great variety of so-called general intelligence tests, of mechanical aptitude tests, a few tests of social intelligence, some tests of personality and morality traits, many tests of special abilities, and many trade tests. A rational program for the use of such tests can be worked out, although it involves a large amount of labor. It would seem, however, that we should not be disturbed by the fact that labor and expense are needed. We do not hesitate to spend time and money in physical and medical examinations of students, and we should no more hesitate to spend a similar amount of time and money in psychological examinations.

If we wish to discover the particular traits and abilities possessed by an individual child with the intention of relating these special traits and abilities to some vocation, the procedure seems to be that of gradually narrowing down and limiting the field of choice. We should begin by subjecting the child to a general intelligence test. On the basis of this test we can determine fairly well the level of his educational possibilities. We can determine whether he can successfully complete grade-school, high-school, or college work. When we find that he can expect to complete high-school work, but cannot expect to complete a college course, we have already gained certain valuable information concerning his vocational possibilities. We know that certain vocations require graduation from college as a prerequisite, while others do not require so much formal education. Having determined in a very general way by intelligence tests the class of occupation in which the child can expect to succeed, the next step is still further to narrow the field of choice by administering tests concerned with mechanical and social aptitudes. These two classes of tests are not so well developed as the general intelligence tests. Their results will be somewhat more inaccurate. We may, however, as a result of the administration of such tests, determine that the child under consideration should or should not enter a mechanical or social occupation.

When, as a result of an intelligence test, we have discovered that a boy can successfully complete a college course, the whole range of professions and vocations are open to him. If in addition we discover that he has a social rather than a mechanical aptitude, we know that from the whole range of professions and vocations he should choose one which involves contacts with other people. If we discover that his aptitude is mechanical rather than social we know that he should choose from the wide range of occupations which do not involve social contacts but depend rather upon the manipulation of materials.

When we attempt to make such a choice between vocations we at once get into difficulties. A profession such as medicine demands of some of its practitioners a high degree of ability in understanding and dealing with people, while a research worker in the field of medicine or a laboratory technician may be quite successful without any such ability. He may require, rather, the kind of ability which we have called mechanical. The success of one lawyer may be determined by his ability as a public speaker and his social qualities, another lawyer may be successful because of his range of legal information and so-called general intelligence. One engineer may be successful because of his ability to deal with men and thus obtain contracts for construction and manage his subordinates, another engineer may be successful because of his technical knowledge.

For the occupations requiring a lesser degree of formal schooling the task of guidance is equally complicated. The abilities which make for success or failure are likely to be highly specialized and obscure. It is only when there are large numbers of individuals doing essentially the same work that we can apply statistical procedures and discover the particular traits which determine success or failure.

Guidance in the choice of school subjects by means of tests is equally difficult. From the administration of intelligence tests, we can learn only that a certain level of attainment can be reached. Mechanical aptitude tests may indicate the desirability of manual or laboratory courses. Social aptitude does not usually enter into success or failure in a special school subject. Attempts further to narrow the field of choice can be based upon the use of prognostic tests in special subjects, but such tests are not well developed. Trying out a course still remains the usual procedure.

Who Is Qualified to Give Vocational and Educational Advice? Teachers have always advised pupils concerning continuance in school. Recently, with the introduction of diversified courses of study and electives, they have been forced to give advice concerning choice of courses and fields of specialization. Such advice has been more or less guesswork and has usually reduced to a tryout of courses. With the increasing use of a variety of general and specialized tests, accumulative record cards, etc., many data have been collected concerning the abilities and special traits of pupils. Such data can be made useful in giving advice only when it is matched up with similar data concerning the demands of school courses and vocations.

Teachers are for the most part peculiarly unfitted to understand the demands of occupations outside of school. Their whole life has been devoted, in most cases, to obtaining a formal school education and to teaching. They have been trained to understand pupils, but not to understand the vocations into which the pupils will go.

In the vocations are many intelligent practitioners who are capable of understanding the demands of their vocation in terms of human traits. For the most part, however, they have been too much occupied with the details of their work to think much about the traits required to be successful in it. They are not accustomed to making nice distinctions between mental characteristics.

Neither the teacher nor the vocational practitioner, therefore, is qualified to give sound vocational advice, although the two together possess the information upon which such advice could be based. In practice, which will be the easier, to give the teacher an understanding of a great variety of vocations or to give representatives of the various vocations training in the analysis of human nature? It seems unreasonable to expect any one person to combine a detailed knowledge of several vocations and of human nature too. Apparently no one person, whatever his training, can combine all the knowledge needed by the vocational adviser. The rational solution seems to be the finding of some method for pooling the knowledge of teachers and vocational practitioners, and at the same time encourage teachers to get outside vocational experience and encourage vocational practitioners to interest themselves in the advising and training of children. When teachers have worked at some job besides teaching, and vocational practitioners have interested themselves in education, a successful program of vocational and educational guidance will become possible.

What Is the Function of the Guidance Expert? It is highly desirable to have someone who is especially trained in coördinating the efforts of teachers and vocational practitioners. The administration of tests, the collection of personality data, the analysis of vocations, all these require a special technique. The guidance expert should have special training to enable him to aid vocational practitioners and teachers in doing these things, and should have special training in matching the various sets of data for the purpose of giving advice. He must be a person of wide experience, both educational and vocational.

The Requirements of a Good Guidance Program. Guidance will be placed on a sound basis when we have adequate records of pupil abilities, adequate analyses of the important vocations, teachers who have done something besides go to school and teach, successful vocational practitioners who will take time to understand educational problems, and guidance experts who can coördinate the efforts of teachers and practitioners and interpret the data which they furnish.

Summary

Since human beings differ in their abilities and since vocations make varied demands upon human nature, educational and vocational guidance are needed. Guidance must be based upon an analysis of vocations and of school curricula in terms of human traits and upon an analysis of the traits possessed by individual pupils. A technique of occupational analysis has been developed to meet the first part of the problem and general and special ability tests have been devised to aid in meeting the second part. Neither part of the problem has as yet been met with more than moderate success.

Even when the results of the two kinds of analysis are available, the vocational or educational advisor must exercise almost superhuman ingenuity and intelligence in matching up the two sets of data in order to give good advice. Such advice cannot be given satisfactorily by an expert who has had only a formal school education. Vocational and educational advising must be a coöperative project of teachers, practitioners in the several vocations, and guidance experts.

CHAPTER XI

PRE-SCHOOL EDUCATION

I. The Origin and Nature of Pre-school Education

What Is Pre-school Education? A pre-school class, or a nursery school, is an institution providing for the care and training of children too young to enter the traditional type of elementary school. The ages of the children participating in such a class are usually from two to five years. Such a pre-school class has two recognized functions. It provides close personal care of the individual child involving provision for its comfort, rest, suitable nourishment, physical and medical supervision, and training of a physical, mental, moral, and social nature. The attempt is made to develop good habits in the widest sense, by means of the guidance of a skilled and intelligent teacher, and through the supervised association of young children in common games and occupations.

The Pre-school Movement Originated in Europe. Froebel developed his kindergarten with the object of supplying the physical and mental needs of the young child. The kindergarten has, however, not usually concerned itself with children as young as are found in the modern pre-school class or nursery school. In Belgium there have been schools for young children since 1889, partially supported by the state. In Italy, Dr. Maria Montessori founded her school for young children in 1907. In France, schools for the very young have been an integral part of school life since 1833. There are more than 3500 nursery schools, of which about 2700 are state supported. They are, however, not usually good schools—sanitary conditions are poor, equipment is unsatisfactory, there are too many pupils to a teacher.

In England the nursery school grew up to meet the needs of mothers of low economic status, who were forced to be away from home during the working day. Children were cared for throughout the working day, during the absence of the mother. There was provision for food and rest with a minimum amount of supervision of play and little or no positive education. The object was merely to provide a substitute for the mother who was forced by her economic situation to be away from home. After a time this problem of caring for young children attracted the attention of educators. Grace Owen and Margaret McMillan are the pioneers of modern nursery education in England. The English government now has a special school for training teachers for very young children.

Nursery Education in the United States. In 1922 Columbia University brought Grace Owen to the United States to lecture and to establish a model nursery school. During the same year nursery schools were founded in Boston and Philadelphia. The Merrill-Palmer School had its beginning in Detroit in 1922, and has rapidly gained favorable attention, through its efforts in training teachers for pre-school children and through its stimulation of research in pre-school education.

Pre-school groups have been established rather widely in the United States. They are usually founded by the coöperation of mothers in a neighborhood. They are more likely to be found in college and university communities than elsewhere. In Madison, Wisconsin, there have been for the past five years from three to five such nursery schools. Each school has from five to fifteen children. Most of them care for the children for a two-hour period during the morning or the afternoon.

In Seattle, at the University of Washington, a pre-school group was organized during the summer of 1929 in connection with the school of education. This class was much larger and more systematically organized than most such groups. The school had a total enrollment of about eighty. Transportation to and from school was furnished; a registered nurse was employed to make a brief physical inspection of each child each morning; there was individual and group play under the direction of competent supervisors; definite attempts were made to develop desirable social attitudes.

What Are the Educational Objectives of Pre-school Education? In the Montessori system of schools emphasis was placed from the beginning upon training the children to do useful tasks. The primary object of the Montessori schools seems to be the training of children to take care of the daily routine concerned with dressing themselves, helping the mother in the preparation and serving of food, etc., at as early an age as possible. Such activities as buttoning and unbuttoning clothing, tying strings, carrying dishes of food without spilling, and others of a purely practical nature occupy the training period. The training took this form because the Italian families were ordinarily large and the mothers were hard pressed for time to care for all of the children, to carry on the routine of housework, and at the same time to aid the father in earning a living for the family. The Montessori training was primarily a training in motor coördinations of a practical nature.

In America pre-school education was introduced in the interests of a different economic and social group. People of moderate economic circumstances in America ordinarily have small families of one to three children. On account of the small number of children in the family, they do not receive at home the kind of social training which they might get if there was a large number of brothers and sisters. The Merrill-Palmer School and other similar schools in this country have appealed largely to this social and economic group. The children are placed in the pre-school group for a few hours during the morning or the afternoon, or for the entire day. It is believed that by putting these children together with a considerable number of other children of similar age, they will receive a valuable social training which they cannot get at home. This social training is an outgrowth of the play activity in which the children engage; reliance is placed more upon the incidental training received as members of a group than upon any specific program of education in social behavior. The attempt is made in these schools to provide healthful physical conditions in the form of regular feeding, prescribed amounts of sleep, and proper exercise. Medical inspection has also been added to the activities of this type of school. The primary objectives seem to be the development of right social attitudes and proper physical development.

The Daily Program of an American Nursery School. The typical program during a two- or three-hour period is as follows: Upon arrival at the school there is a brief medical examination, followed by a short period of play with very simple toys. These toys are of such a nature that they call for initiative and constructive ability on the part of the children. This period of individual play is usually followed by story-telling, singing, and simple rhythmic activities. If the weather is at all favorable, a certain amount of outdoor play takes place. The outdoor activity is followed by another short period of indoor play. The social training which the children get is merely an outgrowth of their association together as a group. No attempt is made to give training in the activities which are ordinarily found in the schoolroom, except as the kind of activity just mentioned happens to furnish a preparation for this later school activity. During the course of the morning the children are given milk or orange juice. When the children are kept for longer periods, beds are provided and regular periods of sleep are a part of the routine.

Social and Economic Causes for the Development of Nursery Schools. Changes in social and industrial conditions have given a great impetus to the development of schools for children during their earliest years. Life in cities and the development of factories have relieved women of many of the occupations which they formerly performed at home. They have thus gained a certain amount of leisure time which makes it possible for them to be away from home for a considerable part of the working day. Poverty has made it necessary that some women should work away from home to supplement the earnings of the male members of the family. The great difficulty which stands in the way of women working away from home is the proper care and training of the children while the mother is away. In Europe, the nursery school has developed to meet this need.

In the United States economic pressure has not usually been so severe as in Europe. Mothers are not so much under the necessity of working to supplement the father's income. They do, however, have outside interests in the form of clubs and organizations of every kind. They believe their social interests to be of sufficient importance to justify frequent absence from home. These same mothers ordinarily do their own housework. Domestic servants are not so commonly employed as in Europe. The American mother feels the desirability of being freed from the care of her children while she is attending to her household duties or her social obligations. Nursery schools have developed in part as a means of relieving such mothers for a part of the day. Most commonly the nursery school cares for the children for two or three hours during the morning while the mother is doing her housework; sometimes there is a similar afternoon period while the mother fulfills her social obligations.

We have previously pointed out that decrease in the size of families has deprived children of valuable social training formerly gained at home. The nursery school provides the social contacts which are no longer found in the family groups.

The Relationship of the Philosophical Theories of Rousseau to Pre-school Education. The theories of Rousseau and his followers emphasized the importance of development during early childhood. It was believed that a newborn child was the most natural and therefore the most perfect type of human being. It had not been subjected to the contaminating influences of the civilized world and therefore, represented an ideal type of creature. It was believed that the primary objective of education was to promote the growth, in the sense of enlargement, of the infant with as little interference with his natural course of development as possible. With this aim in view, Froebel developed his kindergarten. The object of the kindergarten was to supply the physical and mental needs of the child in such a way that his development would be promoted, not changed. This kind of thinking has its counterpart to-day in the so-called child-centered schools or progressive schools in which primary emphasis is upon child nature and the primary attempt is to promote hygiene, both mental and physical, with the belief that the internal forces within the child will lead to its proper and correct development. When this line of thinking is adopted it becomes increasingly important to understand the nature of the child during its earliest years. It also becomes evident that possibilities for interfering with a child's development and leading it astray from its natural path are greatest early in its life. The tendency of Rousseau and Froebel and their followers to emphasize the importance of early childhood has given a strong reason for pre-school education.

Psycho-analysis Has Emphasized the Importance of Education during Infancy. Freud and his followers have pointed out that the development of personality, character, and temperament is dependent largely upon the events of the first five years of life. They have shown that mental abnormalities usually have their origin in the incidents of early childhood. The influence of this group of psychologists upon education has become increasingly evident during the past decade and has had much to do with the growth of interest in nursery schools.

The Scientific Study of Early Childhood Is an Affair of the Twentieth Century. The first attempts to study childhood were forced to go on without the aid of the orthodox psychology. The psychology at the beginning of the century was structuralism which, in theory at least, depended upon introspective method. Small children could not be trained to introspect, therefore it was impossible to study their mental life by the accepted psychological procedures. It was possible to arrive at conclusions concerning their mental activity only by assuming that they resembled those of adults, or by asking the adult to remember what his mental states were when he was a child. Neither of these two approaches to child psychology could be considered at all satisfactory. The attempt to study child life directly was an important factor in developing an entirely different attitude toward psychology as a whole. This new attitude toward psychology has produced functionalism and behaviorism.

Studies of Animal Behavior Furnished a New Child Study Technique. Early in this century a new attitude appeared among zoölogists. They became interested in studying animals, not merely from the standpoint of their anatomical structure, for the sake of classifying them according to family and species, but they developed an interest in their mode of living as well. The fundamental question in biology shifted from interest in form and anatomy to interest in an animal's mode of living and method of adapting itself to its environment. As an outgrowth of this interest in the manner of living of animals, there developed a distinct line of interest which has been called "animal psychology."

Soon an attempt was made to apply the methods of animal psychology to the study of children. Among the earliest of such attempts were the observations of Watson upon the behavior of infants. These early attempts were made primarily as a demonstration of the fact that human behavior could be studied without the aid of introspection. The net result (for child study) of this interest in animal psychology was, therefore, an increased interest in child study and the discovery of a method of investigation which proved to be very valuable. This interest in child study and the use of this method led to the discovery of facts and principles which emphasized the importance of early childhood and furnished a scientific basis for preschool education.

II. The Physical and Mental Characteristics of Early Childhood

Pre-school Education Requires an Understanding of the Nature of Childhood. Rousseau's theories emphasized the educational importance of early childhood. Froebel developed the kindergarten to give practical application to the ideas of Rousseau. Neither Rousseau nor Froebel, however, had an adequate understanding of the facts of child nature. Both began with theories concerning the nature of man—*adult* man—and by a logical process arrived at an opinion concerning the nature of children *as they ought to be.* It has remained for the scientific child study of the twentieth century to make a first-hand study of children and learn to know them *as they are.*

The founder of the modern child study movement was G. Stanley Hall. He was handicapped by the recapitulation theory and the culture-epoch theory—legacies from Rousseau, Froebel, and the early biologists in the one case and from the Herbartians in the other. The science of psychology, too, was still in its infancy, and scientific methods for studying children were undeveloped.

During the twentieth century the psycho-analysts, the functional psychologists, and the behaviorists have given us much needed information concerning the mental development of infants. The importance of physical growth has been recognized and many anatomical and physiological studies of infants have been made. A great mass of facts and a few important principles of child development are now available to furnish a scientific basis for pre-school education.

Physical Characteristics of the New-born Infant. During prenatal development the trunk and viscera of the body are developed first. As a matter of fact, at the time of birth an infant is scarcely more than stomach, heart, lungs, and nervous system. Its legs and arms are still very short and poorly developed. It is incapable of any effective motor activities aside from the purely physiological processes of metabolism.

The heart is small in proportion to the size of the arteries and must beat at a rapid rate in order to maintain proper circulation. It doubles in size during the first two years and continues to grow at a rapid rate on to maturity. The amount of blood during the first few years of life is relatively great. There is a deficiency in the number of red corpuscles so that oxygen is not so readily supplied to the tissues as in the adult. On this account the child fatigues rather rapidly. Work and exercise periods must be short, with frequent rest. The infant must sleep a large part of the time. The white corpuscles are not functionally so well developed as later; their ability to destroy disease germs is low, so that the infant is much more susceptible than the adult to germ diseases.

Because of its small size the child has a relatively large amount of radiating surface. Its body loses heat much more rapidly than that of the adult. To make up for this rapid loss in heat, the child must produce relatively more than the adult; that is, it requires more food and must assimilate this food more rapidly. On account of the rudimentary development of many of its physiological processes and on account of the small reserve store of energy, the infant is much less capable of regulating and quickly increasing its heat supply than is the adult. It therefore has much less power for resisting cold. Proper clothing and protection from exposure of all kinds are therefore quite important.

The digestive system of the child is relatively large at

birth. The child needs much more food in proportion to body weight than the adult because it must supply material for growth as well as for maintenance, and also because of its rapid radiation of heat.

The head is much larger in proportion to the rest of the body than it will be at maturity. The brain of the newborn infant is correspondingly large. The total number of nerve cells is probably fixed in rudimentary form about three months before birth. A large part of the increase in size of the brain has been completed by the time the child is three years of age. It is true that not all of the neurons are functionally active at this time. They continue to develop and to come into functional activity on up to maturity or even to middle life.

Physical Growth during Infancy Is Directed toward Increasing Possibilities of Motor Activity. The increase in size of the child during its first few years is due to a considerable extent to the growth of the arms and legs. At birth the arms and legs are very short and poorly developed. The child is not able to walk because its legs are mechanically not ready for walking. The child is incapable of any efficient motor activity, because its arms and legs have not yet reached a size and mechanical efficiency which make good motor activity possible. They grow at a very rapid rate from birth and contribute a larger percentage to the child's growth in height and weight than any other part of the body up to about fifteen years of age, at which time they have outstripped the trunk and are actually too long. The first few years of a child's life are, therefore, characterized by a development in motor activity.

The child learns to walk at a year or a year and one-half of age, because at this time its legs have developed sufficiently to make walking possible. Its learning to walk is probably dependent upon proper coördinations between reflexes of straightening the knees in response to pressure on the soles of the feet and certain other reflexes concerned with balancing. The primary learning seems to be that of balancing and standing alone. Once this set of coördinations has been developed learning to take steps and actually to walk is a comparatively simple and more or less accidental matter.

The use of the hands for grasping and holding objects is dependent upon increase in the mechanical efficiency of the arms and fingers and must wait until these organs have attained their proper size and development. The speed of muscular movement increases considerably during childhood. That is, during early infancy movements are relatively slow; with increasing age the speed of movement increases. A child's ability to run, for example, is based upon several sets of facts. Although it may have learned to walk, it has not yet perfected its habits of balancing to such an extent that they will function during rapid movement. Its legs are still too short and too imperfect mechanically to make running possible. Its speed of muscular contraction is still too slow to permit any very rapid to and fro movement of the legs. In a similar way we can explain the inability of a child to perform other motor activities as due primarily to the stage of development of arms and legs.

Rhythm in Movement Is a Kind of "Motor Generalization." Simple rhythmic ability (ability to *reproduce*— not merely produce at random—simple rhythmic movements) begins to appear at about two or two and one-half years. Its appearance is definitely dependent upon the attainment of a certain degree of motor development. In the first place the motor organs, that is, the arms and legs, must have developed sufficiently to make rhythmic activity possible. In the next place fundamental motor habits, such as are involved in walking, must have been developed as a preliminary to other rhythmic habits. Rhythmic behavior, when it appears, seems to be nothing more than a *motor generalization*, based upon the accentuation and subordination of movement elements such as are found in walking and other motor activities which are present early in a child's life. Walking, for example, involves a simple combination of movements in groups of two, one of these movements being accented due to the fact that the child has begun to develop a right or a left sidedness by the time it has learned to walk. Being one-sided, the child in walking places more weight on one of its legs than on the other, thus furnishing the accent in the simple two-part activity of walking. Other motor activities in a similar manner build up two- and four-part rhythms. The average child of four years has already fairly well developed the ability to appreciate and reproduce two, three, and four-part rhythms. It is not uncommon to find five-part rhythms in children, although the ability to produce such rhythms seems to be rather uncommon in adults.

Mental Development Must Wait upon Motor Development. The development of motor ability during the first few years, especially learning to walk, is of far-reaching importance for the child's mental development. So long as the child cannot walk it is dependent in its development upon the kind of stimulation which comes to it. Just as soon as the child is able to move about from place to place, its horizon is greatly widened. It then comes into contact with a variety of objects and situations which it could never meet so long as it remained stationary. From the standpoint of the child, it is this broadening of its horizon which is the important consequence of walking. (From the standpoint of the mother walking owes its importance largely to the fact that the care of the child is somewhat less burdensome than previously.) What is true of walking is true of motor development as a whole. As a child becomes better able to use its hands in catching hold of and manipulating objects, the range of stimulation to which it is subjected is greatly increased. The emphasis of pre-school education upon motor activity, therefore, is not misplaced.

The Function of Language in Mental Development. Learning to talk, aside from its value as a convenience to parents, has the same value for the child as the development of motor activity. An immensely important source of stimulation is opened up with the acquisition of language. The child has been able to respond to sounds all during its life, but the fine differentiations as found in language furnish an endless source of variety in the environment. The only other event of a similar nature is learning to read, which will occur during the elementary school period.

How Children Learn to Talk. The development of language seems to be dependent upon the acquisition of two kinds of habits, (1) imitation of sound, and (2) connection of words with objects or events.

First the child must learn to imitate sound, that is, he must develop a habit such that when a sound is heard he will imitate it with his own vocal apparatus. Frequently the imitation of sound has been called reflex and inherited. It is possible, however, to show how such imitation can be developed as a result of learning and many psychologists believe it is so developed. Let us assume, for example, that a noise or a light or a change in temperature or *any other stimulation whatever* happens to produce an activity of the vocal apparatus, resulting in making a sound such as "ah." When the sound is produced, the child's ears are stimulated by it. Now it usually happens in the case of infants as well as in the case of adults, that when our physical organism is so arranged that a stimulus will produce an activity, that activity is likely not to occur just once but several times. That is, there is a tendency for actions to be repeated rather than to occur in isolation. The waving of an infant's arms, for example, are of this nature. Now, if any stimulation whatever sets off a sound such as "ah," it is likely to cause it not once but several times in succession. Each time the sound is produced the child's ears are stimulated by it.

Passing now from the original stimulation which caused the sound to the production of the sound itself and the stimulation of the ear by it, it is clear that all conditions are present which are necessary for setting up a conditioned reflex; that is, there is vocal movement followed by a sound, which is in turn followed by the same vocal movement, that movement is again followed by the sound, which is again followed by the movement, etc. It is necessary only that this sequence shall occur a few times until the sound, however it is produced, will have become a sufficient stimulus for the production of the vocal movement. The first production of the sound "ah" on the part of the child is therefore more or less accidental, a by-product of movement of vocal organs. After this accidental production, followed by the process of conditioning just described, it may happen that another person will produce the sound "ah." The latter is now a sufficient stimulus to lead the child to make the vocal movements which will produce that same "ah." When this stage has been reached, the child has learned to imitate sounds. It has taken the first important step in learning to talk.

Once the child has learned to imitate sounds it is easy to show how it learns to use words on their proper occasions by a second process of conditioning. It is necessary only that a word (as sound and vocal imitation) be produced a number of times in connection with the object or event to which it refers. After making due allowance for peculiarities in its vocal organs the child's accent, pronunciation, choice of words, and every other detail of its spoken language are determined by the models which are furnished it for imitation by parents and associates.

When a child is born deaf, it fails to learn to talk, even though it is well able to make all the necessary sounds. Being unable to develop the habits of imitating sounds, it can learn to talk only when special substitute devices are adopted by its teacher to replace the normal auditory stimulation.

The only native thing about language seems to be merely the possession by the child of a normal nervous system, normal ears, and a vocal apparatus which is not defective. If the child possesses these three things, the normal course of stimulation and response will in time result in building up the whole complex set of language responses which the child finds in the world around it. It should be unnecessary to point out that the particular kind of language which the child develops, whether English, Chinese, or Arabian, will depend not upon the child's ancestry but upon the language which happens to be spoken by the adults who surround it.

By the time the child has reached school age it has already developed a vocabulary of about two thousand words. These two thousand words are the ones which are most common and most fundamental to the child's native tongue. During the school life it normally adds to its vocabulary many thousands of new words, most of which are, however, used far less frequently than those fundamental ones which were acquired during the early years of life. In a very important sense, the usage of spoken language is fixed during the pre-school period.

Important Traits of Personality and Character Are Established during Early Childhood. The psycho-analysts and other psychologists have pointed out that the early years of life are particularly important in the development of personality and temperament. This statement does not mean that new personality and temperamental characteristics cannot appear during the later stages of development. It means, rather, that the general attitude toward life which is developed during the first four or five years tends to persist throughout the entire remainder of the child's career. Human beings are relatively consistent in their development. If a child develops negative habits, such as fear, timidity, and bashfulness, during its first few years, this general attitude toward life is likely to prevail indefinitely. It can be changed when demanded by circumstances, but it is not easily changed. If a child, on the other hand, has a positive attitude toward life, that is, if he is aggressive and bold, he is likely to continue this attitude throughout the remainder of his lifetime. Whether a child develops the one attitude or the other, seems to be largely dependent upon the accidents of early training. It does not seem to be a matter which is much influenced by heredity.

Some Behaviorists Believe that Intelligence Is Determined by Training during Early Childhood. We know from the use of intelligence tests that by the time a child is five or six years of age we can predict quite well the final degree of intelligence which he will achieve. A child who at five years of age is developing rapidly is likely to continue to develop at a rapid rate on up to maturity, while a child who is developing slowly at five years is likely to continue developing slowly on to maturity. It has been commonly assumed that this difference in brightness of children is a matter of heredity. This view has been challenged by such people as Watson, who insists that intelligence, as well as character and temperamental peculiarities, is dependent upon the kind of treatment which the child receives during its earliest years. Whether or not this extreme view is true we are at least justified in stating that the kind of training given and the kind of development which takes place during the first five years of a child's life will have very far-reaching and important effects upon the whole future course of intellectual development.

The Modern Tendency to Make Special Provision for the Training of Children before They Have Attained School Age Is Fully Justified. It is justified from the standpoint of psycho-analysis, which has been especially concerned with the development of character and temperament. It is justified from the standpoint of the objective psychology, which has been concerned with behavior as a whole. It is justified upon the basis of the facts of physical, physiological, and motor development of young children. Nursery schools which originated from philosophical, social, and economic considerations find justification as well as guidance in the scientific study of the nature of childhood.

III. Summary

Pre-school education provides special care and training for children of two to five years in age. The movement originated in Europe in the nineteenth century and has been introduced into America during the last decade. The primary objectives seem to be provision for physical well-being, motor training, and the development of good social attitudes.

The social and economic sources of pre-school education are to be found in the increasing tendency of mothers to work away from home and in the decrease in the size of families. The philosophy of Rousseau emphasized the educational importance of early childhood. Psychoanalysis has shown the importance of early childhood in the development of social attitudes. Functionalism and behaviorism have furnished methods of studying the mental development of young children and have contributed an important body of facts and principles.

Physically and mentally the young child is very different from the adult. Early growth is directed toward increasing the possibilities of motor activity, which furnishes the basis for later mental development. The habits of walking, manipulating objects, and talking are basic to mental development because they open up new avenues of stimulation and furnish new contacts with the environment. A few extremists believe that the final degree of intelligence attained by an individual is largely determined by the kind of development which occurs in early childhood. Pre-school education seems destined to find a larger and larger place in the educational system.

CHAPTER XII

ADULT EDUCATION

I. THE NEED FOR ADULT EDUCATION

Full Membership in the Adult Community Requires Knowledge of Important Laws and Customs. In early primitive communities formal education consisted of a simple initiation ceremony in which the adolescent was inducted into the secrets and mysteries of the tribe. Once the adolescent had been initiated, he took his place as an adult on an equal footing with the other adults of the tribe or community, and no further formal education was given to him. As the amount of ceremonial and magic increased, the period of instruction preparatory to initiation had to be lengthened, but throughout the history of the human race we find education primarily has been concerned with imparting information to the physically immature members of the community. By the time the children have reached physical maturity (which has ordinarily been taken to be equivalent to sexual maturity) their formal education has been concluded.

The Origin of the Belief that Only Children Can Learn. After centuries in which the school has been concerned only with education of *children*, there has gradually grown up the tradition that *none but children* are capable of being educated. We have come to assume that when physical maturity is reached ability to learn either decreases or disappears. It has been assumed that long before we reach middle life we become so fixed in our ways, and lose so much of the plasticity of childhood that we are no longer capable of developing any new ideas or acquiring any fundamentally new skills. This assumption has grown up and has been widely accepted, despite the fact that adults are constantly learning and are constantly developing new ideas. The fact that the "wise men" of the tribe or the community are always old men has not overcome the belief that the young learn far more easily than the old.

Adult Education Already Well Developed. This belief that education is finished when a child leaves school is being challenged more and more. We have developed a great many agencies which are concerned with educating the adults of the community. There are public evening schools, educational departments of the Y.M.C.A. and Y.W.C.A., various philanthropic agencies concerned with the welfare of adults, correspondence schools, vocational schools, and university extension divisions. These organizations are directing the study of thousands of adults throughout the United States, and are very clearly doing important work. In addition to these formal agencies which are concerned with adult education, much incidental learning is going on. Workers are constantly being trained to use new machines and new methods of working. Individuals are constantly learning through the use of public libraries, public lectures, the newspapers, and in other ways which are outgrowths of their daily life.

There is a tendency at the present time for some people who are interested in the teaching of adults in the community to minimize the importance of the agencies which are already at work. These people are inclined to think that learning of a vocational or practical nature is not educational in the true sense. They are interested primarily in a so-called liberal education. They say that agencies, such as public evening schools, correspondence schools, and university extension departments have been concerned mainly with giving an immediately useful and practical training. They overlook the fact that these same agencies are giving to many people training of a much more liberal and cultural nature. At the University of Wisconsin, for example, the Extension Division is training many adult students in vocational subjects (accounting, mechanics, agriculture, etc.). It is, however, also training many people in the more liberal subjects of English literature, economics, sociology, and psychology. Each year there is offered a short course in agriculture which is concerned primarily with the vocational problems of farming. It does, however, include a certain amount of more liberal and general education.

This activity of the University of Wisconsin is typical of activities which are being carried on by most of the state universities in the United States. The people who are engaged in directing such adult education are very enthusiastic and are thoroughly convinced of the value of their work. The students themselves find this work valuable, as shown by the fact that they are enrolling in constantly increasing numbers. The enrollment in the extension division of many universities greatly exceeds that of students in residence. Our universities are recognizing their duty in the matter of educating the adult population of the state, and are meeting this obligation in a more and more effective manner.

Formal Education as a Preparation for Further Learning. Morrison's conception of education, which was described in the discussion of individualized instruction, definitely takes account of the fact that the period of formal education is only the beginning of the educational life of an individual. He points out that the task of the primary school is to set up certain fundamental adaptations, which he calls the reading adaptation, the writing adaptation, the mathematical adaptation, and the social adaptation. The chief object in arranging the elementary school so that the child acquires these fundamental adaptations is to enable him to use them in acquiring further information, skills, and attitudes. They are not to be considered as ends in themselves, but rather as a means to further learning. When we recall the historical development of schools in America, we recognize that the elementary schools or the grammar schools, as they first existed, were intended merely to develop the first three of these four adaptations, that is, the reading, the writing, and the mathematical adaptations. It was clearly recognized by the founders of the elementary schools that the abilities to read and write were merely tools which were to be used by the adult in the community for the purpose of taking his place in the religious and political life of the times. We see that even in the beginning of our school system there was the underlying assumption that education should not end with the completion of formal schooling.

When the academy or the high school was added on to the public school system, it, too, was not considered by its founders to represent a finishing of education. It was intended to add to the child's equipment additional facility in the use of language and mathematics; it was believed that during the process of studying language and mathematics, mental faculties would be trained so that they could be used in meeting practical problems in life and in gaining information of a religious, political, and professional nature. It is quite clear that high-school education was considered in part as a preparation for further learning.

The colleges and universities likewise had the two functions which have just been mentioned. They had the task of giving a professional training as represented primarily by facility in the use of language; but the leaders in the colleges and universities clearly recognized that this facility in language was more than an end in itself. It was understood to be also a valuable means for *continued acquisition of knowledge throughout the individual's lifetime.*

Economic Conditions Have Restricted Learning by Adults. As education has become universal, understanding of one of the fundamental aims of formal schooling, as preparation for later learning, has been lost to many people, or rather has never been understood by more than the few educational leaders of each generation. The attitude of the average parent who wishes to give his children better opportunities than he himself has received is that their education is fully determined by the number of years which they spend in school. He sees that in his own life he has been so much occupied with the business of earning a living that he has not had an opportunity to maintain his contacts with many fields of thought and interest. He recognizes that the same situation is likely to be repeated in the life of his children. When they shall have finished their formal schooling and shall have founded families of their own, they will be so occupied with earning a living that they will have little opportunity for more than the routine tasks of life. He wishes to see that their education has progressed further than his own before the sterner duties of life are forced upon them. He therefore tries to keep them in school a little longer. As this attempt on the part of parents becomes more common, there is increasing enrollment in high schools and colleges, but no change in their belief that education is an affair of the early years of life, and that it must be an affair of the early years of life only.

We have pointed out that although in practice formal education is an affair of the early years of life, there is no reason in the nature of education itself why it must be confined to them. The only reasons for letting a person's education be finished when he has finished formal schooling are economic and social; there are no psychological reasons why he should be through with learning.

Modern Life Demands Continued Learning by Adults. During the early development of the human race, when political, industrial, and social changes were slow, education of the adult was not a matter of such great consequence as now, when changes are occurring at an increasingly rapid rate. Formal educational institutions have therefore not concerned themselves much with adult learning. The world in which we live is so rapidly changing when we compare it with the world of even a half-century ago, that it has become highly desirable from religious, political, social, and economic considerations that education shall not be completed early in an individual's lifetime. The boy or the girl who leaves school at fifteen, or even at twenty or twenty-five, has before him an expectancy of twenty or thirty years of membership in the adult community. If nothing is learned during this period of twenty or thirty years of adult life, he is certain to find himself hopelessly old-fashioned and religiously, politically, and socially conservative before the end of his period of physical and intellectual vigor. A review of the industrial, political, and social changes during the first thirty years of this century will show most strikingly the necessity for learning by all adults who wish to remain abreast of the times.

Increased Complexity of Life Has Required Use of the Entire Period of Childhood for Instruction. The age of beginning instruction was first pushed back from the age of puberty to the age of six or seven years in order to provide more time for learning the increasing store of knowledge. Up to the twentieth century the eight-year period, from six to fourteen years of age, had been thought sufficient to meet the educational needs of the average citizen. Those who were to enter the skilled trades were provided with a further vocational education, continuing until maturity, by an apprenticeship system. Secondary schools, colleges, and universities were thought to be worth while only for a chosen few who were to occupy the higher positions in life. During the present century a larger and larger proportion of the population is continuing its education in the secondary schools and colleges. There is now developing a strong movement (nursery schools) setting the beginning of organized instruction at about two years.

Even with this lengthening of the period of formal education to include twenty years of an individual's life (ages two to twenty-two) it is clearly impossible to acquaint him with all the accumulated knowledge of the race.

Undesirable Consequences Follow the Concentration of Education into Early Life. Even when the future vocation of a person can be determined years in advance so that suitable selection of subject matter can be made, thereby avoiding the necessity for teaching the pupil *all* accumulated knowledge, the formal school system encounters many difficulties. Many of these difficulties are due to the fact that such a great amount of training is needed as a preparation for the more important vocations, and for life as an intelligent citizen, that much of the important training must be given years in advance of the time when it is to be used. It is a generally recognized principle in the psychology of learning, that an activity ought to be learned as nearly as possible at the time when it can be put into use. This principle leads to a greater willingness on the part of the child to engage in the learning and to a greater effectiveness in the learning itself. As an example, we may take the content of courses in home economics for girls. Such courses are finding their way into the seventh and eight grades and the high school. A girl in such a course is taught many things concerning household activities, including perhaps the care and feeding of infants. If she has small brothers and sisters, so that she can put this training into immediate use, it will undoubtedly prove highly valuable and profitable. If, however, we are interested in training her to care for her own children, this training is put into the course of study much too soon. It will be perhaps ten years before she needs such information on her own account. During such a period of ten years, ideas concerning the proper care and training of infants can, and certainly will, be greatly changed, since knowledge of hygiene, dietetics, and psychology are advancing at a very rapid rate. By the time a girl who has received training in the care of infants in the eighth grade is ready to use such information in her own home, she will be hopelessly out of date and misinformed even though she has not forgotten what has been learned. It is true that unless we give her this training while she is in the eighth grade, she may never receive it at all, since most girls drop out of school at about sixteen. This fact merely emphasizes the need for adult education. If we seize our opportunity and give the training while the girl is in school, it will be given too early in her life to be of much value. If we do not seize our opportunity we may be wholly unable to give this training at all, because the girl may pass beyond our reach. The organization of adult education helps to avoid this situation.

Can the General Level of Intelligence Be Raised by Adult Education? The application of mental tests to soldiers during the recent war showed that their average mental age was about fourteen. This finding has been interpreted by some people as meaning that intelligence ceases to develop on the average at about that age because the internal growth forces have been exhausted. Another interpretation which is equally plausible and which holds much more promise is that this discovery that the mental age of the average man in America is fourteen years is merely a consequence of the fact that children ordinarily drop out of school soon after that age. When a person drops out of school he ordinarily becomes so occupied with the routine business of gaining a living that he ceases acquiring information except of a strictly vocational character. Hence we should not expect intelligence as shown by mental tests to improve much after fourteen when schooling has ceased. If there was wide-spread effort concerned with the education of adults, we should expect the average mental age of men and women to be increased. This should be true particularly if the adult education were concerned not merely with the development of vocational and other highly specialized skills, but also with the further development of skills and attitudes of more general social importance.

II. THE LEARNING CAPACITY OF ADULTS

The Question of Fundamental Importance Is Whether the Adult Is Capable of Learning Effectively. We have pointed out that as a matter of common experience adults do learn. Adults do change their kind of work and find it perfectly possible to learn the duties of new occupations. Adults do gradually acquire new ideas with respect to religion, politics, and social action. The organized agencies for adult education—evening schools, university extension divisions, etc.—do find it possible to carry on valuable and effective work.

The Reasons for Differences in Learning with Increasing Age Are Rather Difficult to Single Out. Old learners, for example, may be especially ambitious and may put forth special effort, while the younger learners may not try so hard; the old learners, as we ordinarily find them in evening classes and the like, may be the dull learners who did not learn when they were young and are now trying to make up their deficiency. The young learners may be more willing to engage in the detailed routine work which is necessary for learning, while the adults may be so occupied with a variety of interests that they are unwilling to give the time and effort which are needed for learning. The old learners may have the advantage because they have developed habits of work and industry, which have not yet been developed by the young ones. We see, then, that there are a variety of conflicting factors which tend to cover up the real ability to learn in the sense of modifiability of the nervous system.

Experimental Evidence concerning Learning by Adults. In psychological laboratories, many learning experiments have been carried on. In them adults have taken part and there is no question that learning has occurred. The most extensive experiments which have been concerned directly with comparing the learning ability of adults of different ages with the learning ability of younger people, are those which are summarized by Thorndike in his *Adult Learning*. His general conclusion is that ability to learn increases until about 22 years of age. This ability remains at its high point for a few years and then gradually declines with increasing age. The adult of 40 has lost about

20% of the learning ability which he had at 22, but he is still as well able to learn as the child of 16. Thorndike used in his experiments university students, prisoners in penal institutions, evening high-school students, and students in secretarial schools. These learners performed a great variety of tasks, such as learning to draw lines of a specified length, writing with the wrong hand, learning a code, learning Esperanto, learning numbers to fit nonsense syllables, learning elementary school, high-school and university studies, and learning typewriting. His general conclusion is that "the old are considerably inferior to those around twenty-two in general basic modifiability, but compensate for this inferiority somehow (probably by better appreciation of what is learned, possibly by greater interest) when learning typewriting or stenography or school studies." The special difficulties which the adult is likely to encounter in forming new habits are such things as the awkwardness of adults in certain social situations, the difficulty of securing the adult's complete coöperation, and the inhibitive force of previously acquired habits and customs. The special difficulties which young people are likely to encounter in learning are the lack of incentives, lack of proper habits of study, and the lack of a sufficient factual foundation upon which to build.

The Age Factor in Learning among Animals. In the attempt to determine the influence of the age factor in learning uninfluenced by habits of learning, motives, incentives, and the like, some experimentation has been made upon animals. Hubbert, in his experimentation with rats, says that "young rats learn the maze more rapidly than the old ones, the rapidity with which the habit may be formed decreasing with increase in age." His results, however, are statistically inadequate to support his conclusion and the work of other experimenters has not borne out his results. Stone studied the learning of rats in an inclined plane box and two types of maze. He found that differences in rate of learning could not be correlated with differences in the age of the rats: age differences in the maze records of the learning of rats may be due to difference in motivation; one group may not be exercising its maximum learning ability. In general, we can say that experiments with animals have failed to demonstrate variations in learning ability which can be definitely attributed to difference in age.

As a General Conclusion, We Can Say that Adults Can and Do Learn Quite Effectively throughout the Middle Period of Their Lives. We have no evidence which would lead us to assume that there are intrinsic neural changes which can operate as a causal factor to make the learning of adults easier or more difficult than the learning of children. The common belief that children are more plastic than adults has no factual basis in neurology or experimental psychology. It is probably based mainly upon the traditional attitude toward the time at which schooling should take place. This traditional attitude is based mainly upon custom and upon the fact that we are more willing to allow time for learning during childhood when the economic value of the individual's production would be small, even if he should engage in productive work instead of learning.

III. SUMMARY

In order to take his place in the adult community each citizen must be familiar with the more important laws and customs. Among primitive peoples the only formal education was a brief initiation ceremony shortly after puberty. With the increasing complexity of civilization the period of formal instruction has been extended downward to include all of childhood. The extension of the period of instruction upward to include a part of adult life has been prevented, except for the chosen few, by economic pressure. Because of the restriction of formal education to childhood and in consequence of the absorption of the adult in the routine tasks of gaining a livelihood, there has grown up the tradition that only children can learn.

Until recently habits formed in childhood were likely to remain effective for the remainder of any individual's life; but during the last century rapid changes in industrial and social conditions have made desirable a continued process of learning all through the active period of life. This need has been partially met by evening schools, correspondence schools and the like. Many agencies for adult education have arisen to meet specific needs, but organization and coördination are lacking.

So long as education was primarily disciplinary and literary, its concentration into the early years was not objectionable, but with the introduction of vocational subjects there has followed a violation of the principle that an activity ought to be learned as nearly as possible at the time when it can be put into use. The concentration of all liberal education into childhood results in the adult losing touch with new developments in the humanities as soon as he leaves school so that he soon finds himself old-fashioned and conservative.

During recent years, as a result of investigations into the learning capacity of adults, it has been concluded that adults can learn quite effectively all through the middle period of life. There seems to be no insurmountable psychological reason why adults cannot be educated to meet the rapidly changing social and industrial demands. It seems that in the near future the adult who is not systematically continuing his education will be subject to the same social disapproval that is now accorded the child that is not in school.

CHAPTER XIII

EXTRA–CURRICULAR ACTIVITIES

Basis of Selection of Curricular Activities. The traditional task of the schools has been to train students in literary and professional activities. Nevertheless, during the past century in America we have introduced into the school system many vocational activities of a manual character. We have proceeded on the theory that school work should be definitely a training for life in the adult community after school has been finished, and that any socially acceptable activity which is found in the adult community may very well be represented in the work of the school. While we have proceeded upon this theory there have remained a large number of activities which we have believed to have no rightful place in school work but which are to be considered rather as distracting influences.

In consequence of changing social attitudes, some of these distracting influences have found their way into the curriculum, while others have remained partially or wholly outside. It is only a comparatively short time since literary and debating societies were frowned upon by educators as being types of activities to distract the students from the more serious work of a school. Anything in the nature of play, especially physical play, has until recently been considered an invention of the devil, an activity which could not be tolerated in connection with the school system. It was believed that children, if they were permitted to play, would develop into adults who would also play. It was considered as true beyond the possibility of argument that one ought not to play but should take life seriously and do some useful work in the world without wasting any of his energies. The attitude of educators toward many of these things has radically changed. We have definitely made a place for debating, dramatics, physical activities, and even play in our regular school work. Many activities however, still remain outside and are looked upon by teachers as distractions.

The Development of Extra-curricular Activities. Some of these distractions have been recognized as necessary evils. An attempt has been made to organize them in such a fashion that they will do the least harm possible. We have even gone so far as to recognize that some extra-curricular activities have a positive educational value and we have attempted to organize them in such a way that this educational value can be realized. Such extra-curricular activities are athletics of all kinds, student publications, various social activities, debating teams, dramatics, etc.

Not All Students Are Permitted to Engage in Extra-curricular Activities. Our present attitude toward these activities is that while they are valuable in some cases and necessary evils in others, they are in no case of so much importance as the regular curricular work. We have, therefore, set up eligibility requirements for participation in these extra-curricular activities. We do this on the theory that a student, before participating in them, must prove that he can afford to waste a certain amount of time or, at least, he must prove that he can spare some of his time for these less necessary activities. If a student has good standing in all his regular curricular work, we permit him to do something else, but if his standing in the regular curricular work is low we insist that other things must be eliminated and the regular work of the school must come first. On this theory we set up a grade standard for eligibility in athletics, debating, student publications, etc. On this theory we require fraternity and sorority groups to maintain a certain scholastic average as a condition to good standing and continued existence in the school community.

Growing Recognition of the Educational Value of Extra-curricular Activities. This conception of extra-curricular activities as mere distractions is being challenged by a few people. It is believed by some educators that the school should sponsor only those activities which have a real educational value. If an activity is recognized as being educationally valuable, then it is very doubtful whether we should make high standing in some other phase of educational work a prerequisite to participation. That is, if debating is an educationally desirable activity, it seems absurd to debar a student from this activity because of low standing in mathematics or physics or any other phase of school work. This would seem to be just as absurd as telling a student that he could not be permitted to enroll in a course in German because he had during the preceding year received a low grade in physics. Likewise, if athletics have a distinct educational value, it would seem to be absurd to debar a student from athletics because he has received a low grade in some academic subject or even because his average as a whole is low. If fraternities have a value in the social development of students, it would seem that we should aim directly at securing this social value and should not regulate fraternities and sororities in a merely restrictive and negative fashion on the basis of academic standing. This recognition of the educational value of extra-curricular activities is being forced by the discovery that later occupational success is determined as much by participation in them as by good standing in academic work.

The Basis for Scholastic Requirements for Extra-curricular Activities. The setting up of academic requirements as a pre-requisite to participation in any extra-curricular activity may be based upon one of four theories. (1) We may assume that the extra-curricular activity represents a distraction from the real work of the school and in that sense is a waste of time. We are, therefore, justified in requiring a student to prove that he has time to spare before permitting him to engage in this distracting activity. (2) It may be assumed that extra-curricular activities are not worth while in themselves but may be held out as a bait to induce students to work more industriously in the regular curricular activities. (3) We may assume that students participating in extra-curricular activities, especially inter-collegiate contests, are in a sense representatives of the school. In this case they should be *bona fide* students and not imported especially for the sake of winning contests. The setting up of academic standards is in this case intended to insure that the participants in an inter-collegiate contest are students in fact. (4) A fourth possible reason for setting up academic standards of eligibility, which has never been applied, could be based upon the considerations that efficient performance in the extra-curricular activity could be expected mainly of those who have high academic standing and could not be expected of those who have low academic standing. If this were found to be true of any extra-curricular activity, then the eligibility rule should be based upon the requirements of the activity itself and should be different for different activities.

The School Should Sponsor Only Educational Activities. A school should stand sponsor for an extra-curricular activity only when it has a definite educational value. If such an activity has an educational value it is doubtful whether we can logically exclude any student from participation except upon the same basis that we use in excluding students from the regularly established courses in the curriculum. These reasons for exclusion are: first of all, the inability of the student to pursue the activity profitably; second, the elimination of the activities which are of least value to the individual student since he does not have time to participate in all; and third, exclusion by reason of limitation of numbers imposed by lack of equipment and other facilities. The real basis for excluding any *bona fide* student from athletics, for example, should be first of all the lack of the needed physical and mental qualities on the part of the student, together with the probability that he would be unable to develop these qualities after a reasonable course of training; in the second place, he might be excluded from athletics if it could be shown that he has greater ability and talents in other kinds of work so that participation in athletics is for him, in a sense, a waste of time; in the third place, he might be excluded from athletics if there were not sufficient facilities and opportunities to permit him to engage in them. An inter-collegiate athletic team can have only a few members, so that many students are necessarily excluded. This exclusion should, however, be based upon lack of ability in athletics or at least upon greater ability in some other kind of work, and should not be based upon any purely arbitrary rule.

The same thing may be said of participation in debating teams, dramatics, student publications, or any of the many other extra-curricular activities. If the activity lacks educational value it should be excluded from the school; no student should be permitted to waste time upon it. If it has educational value students should be encouraged to participate according to the principles just enumerated.

Eligibility Standards as a Means of Increasing Scholarship. It is assumed that since the student is greatly interested in the extra-curricular activity he will make a special effort to increase his scholarship standing so that he may participate. The extra-curricular activity is held out as a kind of bait or reward to induce the student to swallow the less desirable scholastic work. This is a view which cannot be defended. In practice it has led to many evils. One of the outstanding evils which has been produced in many colleges has been the development of special funds to pay for special tutoring of backward athletes. Such special tutoring enables the athlete to pass examinations and so to meet his scholastic requirements, but does not contribute much of real educational value.

Whether students do work more industriously for the sake of becoming eligible for extra-curricular work is a debatable question. At most, only a few students are affected, so that there can be little effect upon the school as a whole. Outside activities can be used most effectively for promoting scholarship when they are used not as a bait or reward, but are made an integral part of the school work, as is done in the project method of teaching. This method has been used mainly in the elementary school and has not been applied effectively in high school or college except in isolated cases.

Making Athletes "Representative" of the School. If we wish to make certain that the members of athletic teams are real representatives of a school, it is doubtful whether we can achieve this end by setting up any academic standard at all. Whatever grade standard we may set up is purely arbitrary. It might just as well have been placed either higher or lower. We cannot say that the student who is in the upper 10% academically is any more representative of the school than the student who is in the lower 10%. All groups of students represent certain phases of school life. Every student whom we are willing to accept as a member of the school is just as truly a representative of the school as any other student. The standard for participation in athletics from this point of view should be of such a nature that every *bona fide* student should be eligible. We should still avoid the bringing in of students for the special purpose of participating in inter-collegiate contests. This can best be done by a direct attack upon the problem instead of the indirect attack through grade standards.

We are all familiar with the fact that in many of our colleges and universities athletes are brought in for the special purpose of participating in athletic contests, their academic work remaining for them a necessary evil. Such students are not being eliminated by grade requirements and seemingly *cannot* be eliminated in such a manner even though the grade standards are raised far above the point which is commonly used at present. The people who are directly responsible for the conduct of athletics could easily discover who these students are. They may not be responsible for recruiting these athletes and in many of our leading colleges and universities we may feel quite certain that they are not responsible. They are, however, in a position easily to discover such students if they are given incentive for doing so. The simplest and most effective means for eliminating the kind of athlete who has been recruited for the special purpose of taking part in athletics would seem to be to place the responsibility directly upon the members of the athletic department.

It is true that the members of the athletic department

are under pressure to turn out winning teams. On this account they may be inclined to overlook the presence of athletes who are academically undesirable. If this pressure for winning games can be removed by having security of tenure for coaches and by having an administration which will support them in an attempt to gain the educational values from athletics rather than to concentrate their effort only on winning games, then the coaches will be found much more than willing to eliminate all athletes who are not at the same time *bona fide* students. This problem has been very successfully met in high schools; it is true that in high schools outside pressure of alumni and "friends of the school" is not so great and it is easier to give precedence to educational values.

The standards of physical education are rapidly changing at the present time. Physical educators are developing a much greater interest in the real educational values of their work. They are themselves rapidly reaching a point where they will be ready to assume new responsibilities. The best arrangement for eliminating professionals and other undesirables from athletic teams would seem to be the appointment of a director of athletics who is primarily interested in the educational value of his work. Such an athletic director, if given full responsibility, could quickly achieve the results which we have been trying quite unsuccessfully to achieve through a multiplicity of eligibility rules and requirements. There are many physical educators at the present time quite willing to accept the responsibility of administering athletics so as to secure the maximum educational return.

Scholastic Requirements as a Cure for Over-emphasis of Athletics and Social Life. Recently as an outgrowth of the undue emphasis upon inter-collegiate athletics in high schools and colleges, there has been a general tendency to raise the minimum scholastic requirement for athletes. This tendency is based upon the theory that by reducing the number of students who are eligible for the athletic teams interest in athletics will somehow be decreased. At the University of Wisconsin, for example, there has recently been much agitation of this character. This agitation has been carried on by the people who are in general opposed to athletic contests. If they are not opposed to athletic contests in general they are at least disturbed by the large attendance at football games, the great amount of student interest in such contests, and the large financial interests in the game. They are apparently attempting to reduce student interest, reduce attendance at games, and check the increasing financial aspect of football by a slight increase in academic standards. This procedure is, of course, utterly illogical and can have no important effect in this direction. If it is desired to decrease the attendance at games and the financial returns from football games, a much more direct attack upon the problem is needed.

While the publication of the scholastic standings of fraternities and sororities and the setting of minimum requirements for initiation of pledges has caused some students to work more industriously for the sake of their social group, the emphasis upon social activities has not been decreased. The requirement is met because of necessity, but no love for study is created. The effect is rather the opposite; study becomes a task to be completed as a prerequisite to the more interesting social life.

If the evil phases of social life in high schools and colleges are to be overcome, the problems must be attacked directly, instead of indirectly through scholastic requirements for participation. Educators have too long regarded the gaining of satisfactory school grades as the panacea for all student ills. They must now recognize that many important educational influences are at work in the school community outside of the classroom. They must organize the school on a wider basis to take advantage of these other factors in the life of their pupils.

Eligibility for Extra-curricular Activities from the Standpoint of Individual Psychology. During recent years, we have made many attempts to apply our knowledge of individual differences to educational problems. What should be our attitude toward scholastic requirements for participation in extra-curricular activities, based upon our knowledge of individual differences, and in particular, upon the knowledge which we have of the correlations between motor and mental skills? It is a common practice to fix certain minimum scholastic requirements for participation in extra-curricular activities of all kinds. It is commonly believed that the same minimum requirements should apply to all forms of extra-curricular activity.

When we approach these requirements from the standpoint of the correlation between motor and mental skills, considerable doubt is thrown upon this assumption. The correlation between two mental skills such as knowledge in mathematics and history, or knowledge in history and ability in debating, dramatics, student publication, or the like, is high. On the other hand, the correlation between the academic subjects, such as history and mathematics, and the motor activities, as found in shop work, manual work, and athletics, is low. On account of this high correlation between the academic subjects and the extra-curricular activities such as debating, dramatics, and student publication, few students who have sufficient ability to participate in these extra-curricular activities fail to meet scholastic eligibility requirements.

On the other hand, on account of the low correlation which exists between motor skills and mental skills, many students who have good motor ability can be expected to fail to meet the minimum scholastic requirements.

The eligibility problem is most acute in the case of the student who has good motor ability and is able to participate successfully in athletics, but who lacks sufficient ability of the so-called mental type to enable him to maintain a sufficiently high scholastic average to meet the eligibility requirement. If such a student fails to maintain an acceptable scholastic standard on account of laziness, there can be no question but that a minimum requirement should be applied. If the student, however, fails to maintain the minimum scholastic standing not because of laziness or indifference, but simply because of low ability for that kind of work, there is reason for doubt as to whether the minimum scholastic eligibility requirement should be applied in his case.

When we are willing to accept as a student a person who has a low degree of ability in the academic subjects, we assume certain obligations toward him. It is our duty to give him the kind of training for which he is best fitted. We recognize this duty and attempt to fulfill it in connection with that part of our school system which belongs to the regular curriculum. We do not exclude a boy from the study of mathematics on the ground that he has made a low grade in history. We do not refuse to permit a boy to study French and German when he likes them and gets along well in them, merely because he *does not* get good grades in history. We believe that the study of any subject in the regular curriculum should depend only upon ability profitably to engage in that kind of work, and not upon ability to do something else.

Toward participation in extra-curricular activities we

have adopted a very different attitude. When a boy demonstrates that he can profitably engage in basketball, football, baseball, or some other sport, we do not at once grant him permission to do so. We first examine his scholastic standing, and, in many cases, refuse him permission to receive any benefits from athletics because he has failed to get the expected amount of benefit from one or more of the subjects in the regular curriculum. When we feel that he is spending an undue amount of time on athletics and neglecting other things of importance, we properly deny him permission to participate in them until he readjusts his efforts; but, in the case of the student who is working industriously but is nevertheless failing to reach high standards in his regular curricular work, we are doing an injustice when we prevent him from participating in athletics or any other extra-curricular activity, for which he has shown ability. We are forcing this student to spend his time engaging in work for which he has little ability and are refusing him permission to spend his time working at the things which he can do well. This state of affairs is certain to have an extremely harmful effect upon personality and character development. Because of the low correlation between athletic ability and ability in academic subjects, there are certain to be many students who are thus harmed by scholastic requirements for participating in athletics. A new approach to the problem of eligibility is needed to take care of the interests of this group of students.

The ideal method for handling problems of eligibility for activities seems to be to place the responsibility in the hands of a person who has a good understanding of students and their needs and to give him authority to treat students as individuals. For participation in athletics a student should be required to be making an earnest effort to get what he can out of his school work as a whole, that is, he should be a *bona fide* student. When a student is making this effort he should not be denied permission to participate in any extra-curricular activity which can contribute to his education.

Permission to play on an athletic team, or engage in any other extra-curricular activity, should be accorded to any student whom we are willing to retain in the educational institution, and who, in the judgment of a responsible party, is making an earnest effort to profit from his school work as a whole. Under a rational system, which takes into account known facts of correlation between motor and mental abilities, many a student who has low scholastic marks will be permitted to play on athletic teams while other students with higher scholastic standing will be denied such permission. The point of this discussion is that the modern tendency to treat students as individuals should be extended to include extra-curricular activities.

Extra-curricular Activities Present a Problem in Individualized Education. In conclusion we can say that evils of extra-curricular activities can best be corrected if we approach them in the effort to determine their real educational value and accept the responsibility for treating students as individuals in determining whether they shall be permitted to participate in these extra-curricular activities. There is no educational reason why all students should be treated alike. Indeed, from the standpoint of education, equality of treatment is undesirable unless we wish to turn out a highly standardized product. In a political organization it may be desirable to proceed upon the theory that all men are created equal, that all men should be equal before the law. In an educational organization, on the other hand, it is highly desirable to proceed on the theory that all students are different, that all students should be treated as individuals, that any general rules and regulations are educationally undesirable. A few such general rules and regulations may be needed to enable the educational machinery to run smoothly, but their effect if they increase too much in number and importance is to defeat the primary aims of education. What we need at the present time is the acceptance by educators of a larger measure of responsibility for the direction of *individuals* in the school system.

SUMMARY

Many of the activities of pupils which were frowned upon as distractions a few years ago have found their way into the curriculum, and many others have been organized under the sponsorship of the school as extra-curricular activities. This change is an outgrowth of the abandonment of the disciplinary conception of education and the substitution of the ideal of education as a training in the activities of the contemporary adult community.

Teachers absorbed in curricular teaching are likely to regard extra-curricular activity as distracting from the "more important" scholastic work. In consequence, scholastic standards of eligibility for extra-curricular activities have been set up. Teachers have become alarmed at the increasing interest of students in extra-curricular activities, especially athletics and social organizations, and have sought to lessen this interest by raising scholastic eligibility requirements. They have rationalized this attitude by saying that they seek to make the participants real representatives of the school. Eligibility requirements, however, are ineffective instruments for combating undue interest in extra-curricular work.

Prohibition of participation in an extra-curricular activity because of low scholastic standing violates the modern tendency to treat students as individuals and violates the principle that students should be encouraged to develop along the lines of their special abilities. The program of individualized instruction should be extended to include extra-curricular activities and teachers should assume the responsibility for advising students according to their individual needs. Blanket prohibitions should be discarded as educational instruments.

CHAPTER XIV

PHYSICAL AND HEALTH EDUCATION

I. Origin and Aims of Physical and Health Education

The Importance of the Human Body in Ancient Education. Public schools in recent times have been concerned mainly with teaching literature, science, and mathematics. Physical and health education have been either ignored or forced to occupy a secondary position. Among the ancient Greeks and Romans, however, the development of a healthy body and the acquisition of skill and grace in movement were considered legitimate parts of the cultural development of every educated citizen. Every citizen owed a certain amount of military service to the State and was expected to maintain himself in proper physical condition to fulfill his obligation. Physical grace and skill were ends in themselves as worthy and honorable as literary and intellectual excellence. Much of the program of the schools was concerned with this phase of education.

Medieval Education Believed Physical and Mental Development Were Incompatible. Early in the Christian era there began to develop the belief that there was an opposition between the physical and the spiritual. It was believed that the physical world as a whole and the human body in particular represented a kind of prison for the spirit. If not a prison, it was at best only a temporary shelter for the soul and its neglect need not cause much concern. The first end and aim of life in this world was to escape from it. Man was supposed to be in this world

313

but not of it. His soul was considered to be something of a higher nature. It could best be freed for its higher spiritual functions if the demands of the world were minimized, and the body weakened. This belief—that the soul could not attain its fullest development unless the body was kept weak—extended to the mental life as well. It was considered that the scholar must necessarily have poor physical development and poor health if he was to do the highest type of mental work. All during the Christian era, however, the physical well-being of the majority of the population was provided for by the necessities of military training.

Sources of the Revival of Interest in Physical Education. The first definite movement for physical education in modern times grew up in Germany in an attempt to build up a strong race which might eventually restore Germany's military position, which had been destroyed during the Napoleonic wars. The German military idea led to the great development of formal gymnastic work. This type of work dominated central and northern Europe and America for many years. At the present time it is rapidly giving way to a program of plays and games and natural activities which can be considered an outgrowth of Rousseau's work. Rousseau, in the eighteenth century, advanced the doctrine that nature is always right. As a part of his doctrine, good physical development was considered to be natural and therefore right. It is the development of this idea of Rousseau which is responsible for the modern emphasis upon plays and natural activities in physical education.

Psychological Interest in the Relationship between Mental and Physical Development. Toward the close of the nineteenth century psychology began to make rapid development. The basic philosophical assumption of psychology at that time was psycho-physical parallelism. It was assumed that for every mental event there is a corresponding physical occurrence. At first the consequences of this theory for physical education were not understood, but by the beginning of the twentieth century these implications had been formulated in the statement that the aim of education is to develop "A sound mind in a sound body." It was considered that a sound body was essential for the existence of a sound mind, since the two were believed to be in every respect parallel.

This idea was developed more explicitly with the beginning of the functional psychology, which, as we have earlier pointed out, considered mind to have as its chief function the adaptation of man to his environment. An important phase of this adaptation was necessarily physical. In consequence, there quickly grew up an interest in physical adaptation as well as mental adaptation.

During the first ten years of the twentieth century there was great interest in the problem of working out the correlation between mental and physical characteristics. It was believed that this correlation ought to be positive and high. This should seemingly be true since the underlying assumption of the functional psychology was that of a parallelism between the mental and the physical. Many measurements were made of mental functions and physical characteristics, and correlations between the two were worked out. These correlations turned out to be disappointingly low. It was found, for example, that while there is a positive correlation between brain weight and intelligence, this correlation is very small. Likewise, the correlation between mental traits and such physical traits as speed of tapping, strength of grip, strength of muscles in the arms, legs, and back, height, body-weight, etc., were found to be positive but very small. As a result of these disappointing findings, the scientific interest in measurements of physical development began to lag.

The Great War Showed the Need for Physical and Health Education. An impetus for physical education in the schools had been established, however, and this interest in physical and health education was again revived because of military necessities. It was found as a result of the physical examinations of young men called in the draft that a very large percentage of them were unfit for military service because of physical or health defects. This information concerning the extent of physical defects and organic disorders and the desirability of good physical development for military reasons led to a renewed interest in physical education, both in Europe and in America.

Behavioristic Psychology Favors Physical Education. At about the time of the Great War a new movement—objectivity—appeared in psychology. For the objective psychologist, physical habits are on exactly the same level as the so-called mental habits. All skills and all activities are of one general kind, which the objective psychologists consider to be physical. Whether the emphasis in education should be placed upon the finer adjustments, such as are found in language or verbal activity, or whether an important place should be made for grosser activities, such as are found in athletics and physical education, is purely a question of usefulness. If the adult in the community finds physical activities useful, then they have a place in education exactly as important as any other activity (mental) which is equally useful. This type of psychology makes possible a return to the Greek ideal of physical education in which physical grace and skill are considered a valuable part of the cultural life.

Revival of the Greek Ideal in Physical Education. The development of physical education in modern times has emphasized the one function of exercise for the sake of good health and good physique. It has occurred to only a few that physical education may have other equally important aims. The introduction of physical education into the school curriculum has ordinarily occurred purely upon the basis of the need of the children for exercise. In city school systems physical education has therefore developed to a considerable extent. In the rural districts physical education has scarcely been introduced because of the general feeling of parents that their children get a sufficient amount of exercise during their work at home and during play outside of school. Only recently has it been recognized that physical activity has a cultural and recreational value which is something in addition to the mere maintenance of good health through exercise. It is coming to be believed that physical grace and skill and the ability to participate in physical activity are an essential part of a cultural education. It is now believed that physical education should develop habits of exercise and recreation which will last after school work has ended.

The Type of Physical Activity Demanded by the Cultural and Recreational Aims. With this emphasis upon the cultural and recreational aspect of physical education there necessarily goes a change in the type of work which is considered worth while. Team games, such as football and baseball, for example, furnish the needed exercise and physical development, but they are types of activity which cannot ordinarily be continued after school work is finished. The student who has participated in such a team game has gained a valuable physical development. In addition, he may have formed certain desirable habits of character which will carry over into later life, but he has not learned any physical activity which he can use for recreation during his middle age. On the other hand, the student who plays tennis or golf or handball for his physical education work in school has learned an activity which may continue to be valuable for many years to come. At the present time a rapid re-assessment of the work in physical education is taking place. A change in emphasis which will lead to a recognition of the importance of such games as bowling, golf, and tennis at the expense of team games such as basketball, football, and baseball, is the inevitable outcome. There is likewise an increasing interest in those forms of physical activity which are primarily æsthetic and recreational—natural dancing especially.

The intramural program of schools has been designed to provide recreational activity for all the students. If this intramural program is confined largely to the development of team games, it will fail in one of its most important functions, that of training the students in cultural and recreational activities which can be used not only during school life but later, when such violent and active games as football can no longer be continued.

There is certainly a place in the educational system for active team games. Through participation in athletic contests as members of teams, students can develop many desirable character traits. It is doubtless true that some of the qualities developed through playing football, baseball, and basketball can, under favorable conditions, carry over into later social and industrial life. These games contain a valuable kind of training which should not be lost. In addition to this training, however, athletic and recreational habits should be formed which can be made directly valuable for leisure-time activity throughout the remainder of an individual's active life. A rational program does not require the elimination of team games,

but demands a decrease in the emphasis upon them together with increased emphasis upon individual physical
activities which can be carried on by an adult in an average American community.

*Claims for the Development of Personality and Character
through Physical Education.* Of considerable importance
in physical education is the problem of the extent to
which character traits and ideals are developed through
athletic and physical activities. Many extravagant claims
of this nature have been made concerning them. No experimental work has been done, however, to substantiate
these claims. The chief problem involved is that of the
transfer of training. If we wish to know the extent to
which the playing of football will result in the formation
of habits of loyalty, coöperation, persistence, and so forth,
which will show themselves in later social, political, and
industrial life, we must understand the conditions under
which these habits are formed in the first place, and then
the conditions under which they can be transferred to
new situations. We must first ask the question whether
the members of a football team develop habits of loyalty,
coöperation, and the like in connection with the work of
the team itself. We know that this is sometimes done.
We know, however, that such habits may be conspicuously
lacking in the work of a football team. In determining
whether physical activities develop these characteristics
we must make certain that athletes who possess them
have not merely been selected because they already possess desirable traits; it must be shown that the athletic
activity itself is responsible for the habits.

Coaches, for example, are inclined to drop from athletic squads any players who show evidence of being "yellow," and keep only those who show a certain amount of
courage. These same coaches give themselves and the

sport they are teaching credit for the development of the quality of courage. A true test of the ability of a coach or a sport to develop courage would be furnished if the coach should take the boy who is "yellow" and make a good player out of him, developing the quality of courage during the course of the training. We need more such assumption of responsibility by the coach and definite efforts to discover the ways and means by which valuable character traits can be developed in and through athletic activities.

When we have established the fact that character and personality can be developed by physical activity and have learned something about the kind of training which will best develop them, we will be ready for the second type of experimentation which is concerned with measuring the conditions under which these character and personality traits are carried over into the later life of the individuals. We shall then be ready for experimentation concerned with increasing the amount of transfer from physical and athletic activities to later social, industrial, and political life.

From knowledge of the psychology of learning and especially of the transfer of training, certain possibilities are apparent. It may well be possible so to conduct physical and athletic activities that habits of fair-play, co-operation, etc., are not developed, even in the physical and athletic activities themselves. On the other hand, some methods of coaching and training may result in the development of these characteristics in connection with the physical activity. Assuming that we have found a method for developing these traits in the physical activity, it is possible that a method of training can be found which will result in a greater or lesser amount of transfer to later life.

II. The Technique of Physical and Health Education

Technique for Developing Personality and Character Traits through Physical Activities. By way of illustration let us choose a specific trait—"team-work." Let us take a boy at the beginning of his high school work who has had little opportunity for indulging in team games. This boy undertakes to learn to play basketball. In his early efforts at playing he develops a series of individual skills concerned with catching, handling, and throwing the basketball. He proceeds for a time on the assumption that he will be a good player in the measure that he can properly catch and throw the basketball. Soon, however, his coach may point out to him that, instead of attempting to throw the ball into the basket himself, he should have passed it to another member of his team. The coach may tell him that passing the ball to the other member of the team, instead of throwing it into the basket himself, would have been good team-work. As training continues, on one occasion after another, the coach may point out specific things that the boy should do which would constitute good team-work. Gradually the boy learns to connect the general descriptive word "team-work" with a large number of specific activities. If he continues playing basketball and other team games throughout his high-school course and possibly thoughout his college course, he will eventually connect this word "team-work" with a very large number of specific activities, so that he knows the meaning of the word. He knows its meaning, not only in the sense that he can give a dictionary definition, but he knows it in a much more personal sense in connection with a large number of his own personal actions. In a similar manner, traits of loyalty, fair play, sympathy, etc., can be developed in connection with specific playing situations. Unless special effort is made to give training in these characteristics they may fail to appear. With the wrong kind of training bad traits may be developed.

Conditions under Which Transfer Is Favored. We know something of the conditions under which such transfer takes place, but we need experimentation that is concerned directly with this problem in physical education. We know that the students who are the more intelligent are likely to secure a greater amount of transfer. We know that the coach who is more intelligent, and who has a wide range of information in addition to his knowledge of athletics, is likely to secure more such transfer than the coach who is merely a narrow specialist. We know that training which makes room for pointing out possibilities in the development of valuable character traits and pointing out their possible applications in later life will secure more such development and transfer than training which is concerned merely with the narrow problem of developing athletic skill. We know these things because we assume that transfer from physical activities to later life will be favored by much the same conditions that favor transfer in other situations. We need, however, experimentation dealing with these specific problems so that we will not have to rely entirely upon general principles whose application has not been checked and tested.

The Acquisition of Physical Skill. The rules and principles of learning which are found in books on methods of teaching and educational psychology have been worked out very largely from investigations of such activities as learning to read, memorizing poetry and prose, and learning arithmetic. These studies have been supplemented by investigations of the learning of animals, particularly the learning of white rats, cats, and other animals to run through mazes or to find their way out of problem boxes. Investigations which are directly concerned with learning by school children of the physical and manual activities are singularly lacking. It is dangerous to apply literally and in detail the rules of learning and teaching gained from such studies to the teaching of motor skills.

Let us put the problem of developing physical skills in the form of a question. What can the administration and the teacher do to aid the pupil in learning?

The Importance of Good Equipment. In recognizing the importance of contact between teacher and pupil, there is danger of overlooking the great importance of proper equipment, materials and the like. Pupils can learn without much aid from a teacher if only they are given an opportunity. This opportunity consists of good equipment for working—good equipment on the playground and in the gymnasium. Providing for these things is, of course, the responsibility of the administration. When they are properly provided for, pupils can learn even with a poor teacher, and even the best teacher is helpless without them. In teaching the academic school subjects—history, literature, language, mathematics, and the like—the teacher can draw on her own knowledge and understanding. Her own contacts with the pupil are the all-important factors in the pupil's education. The administration can merely provide a well-lighted and attractive place to work. But in the physical activities no knowledge or skill on the part of the teacher can successfully replace defective equipment or lack of equipment.

The Importance of a Graded Physical Program. The teaching of physical education suffers from another special handicap which is largely the fault of the administration. Effective teaching and learning require that the skills taught shall be arranged in some kind of sequence or order. Certain things must be taught first, these skills form the basis for those which come later. Work must be graded and suited to the stage of advancement of the pupil. This principle is just as true in physical education as it is in arithmetic or history. The administration usually makes it impossible for physical education teachers to do their work effectively, especially in the high schools, when it makes out a program of studies which ignores the needs of physical education. The physical education program in a high school should present a four-year sequence, just as much as in English, history, or mathematics. The physical education program in the elementary school should present a graded program, just as in reading, arithmetic, or language. If the physical education teacher is to work effectively, his work must be given a place in the program of studies which makes possible a graded program of work adapted to the age and stage of progress of the pupil.

Motivation through the Use of Standard Tests. In teaching a special skill to a pupil who is ready for it, what can a teacher do? First the teacher can motivate the work. (Chapter VII.) By this is meant merely that somehow the pupil must be made to *try* to learn. We will not here point out all devices which can be used. Perhaps the most important is the setting of goals. The pupil must know what is expected of him. A certain standard of quality and of speed must be set up for each pupil. This standard must, of course, be suited to his stage of advancement. An impossible goal will discourage effort, while a goal which is too easy will demand no effort. Such goals are skill and accuracy tests in basketball, speed tests in running, accuracy tests in throwing a ball, etc.

Frequent use of such tests to show the pupil what progress he is making and how far he has yet to go to reach his goal is one of the most effective devices in motivation. Physical activities are ordinarily close enough to the life interests of the pupils that little else will be needed for their motivation.

The Use of Verbal Directions, Demonstrations, and Manual Guidance. In teaching a new skill what can the teacher do to aid the pupil in learning more quickly? In the beginning do not rely too much on words. It is almost useless to tell a child how to do a stunt in a gymnasium. He will not understand the directions. He may be able to give you the meaning of every word used; he may be able to repeat the directions; but he has not connected the words with the movements of his hands and body. Directions are just empty words until the pupil has already learned something about the new task, until he has already developed a fair degree of skill. He must first build up a *movement vocabulary*, before he can understand and profit by directions given in words. It is only after the fundamental skills have been developed by actual work that pupils can be expected to follow directions. But after these skills are learned, directions in words may be very much worth while.

In the beginning it is much more effective to show a pupil what to do than to tell him. But do not expect too much even then. Pupils can imitate only those things with which they are already somewhat familiar. There seems to be no escaping the fact that pupils must learn by their own efforts. Showing a pupil what to do helps to set the goal for him; he knows *what* to do, but a demonstration cannot show him *how* to do it, unless he already has the fundamental skills. Then the demonstration merely shows him which skills he must use from among those which he has already learned. But unless care is taken, attempts to show the pupil what to do are likely to have no value after the first few trials. Once the pupil has got well started, it is useless to give another demonstration unless it is split up into parts so that it helps the pupil to analyze the skill he is learning.

Learning may be aided somewhat by taking hold of the pupil's hands and actually putting him through the movement. This way of teaching cannot often be used, but when it is possible it seems to be worth about as much as a demonstration, and should be used in the same way.

It seems, then, that attempts to show a pupil how to do a physical task are worth something at the beginning, but are likely not to be worth much after the pupil has made some progress. On the other hand, directions in words are not worth much in the beginning, but will be worth more after the pupil has begun to learn.

Teaching by Analysis of Skills and Pupil Performance. Another important function of the teacher is found in the arrangement of the skills to be learned. She must be able to analyze a skill into its elements, and arrange practice so that none of those elements are overlooked, and so that they are learned in the most economical sequence.

The teacher must likewise analyze the performance of the pupils. She must be able to decide just where the pupils' errors are occurring, and by means of demonstration or directions in words show how to overcome the errors.

Summary of Teaching Procedure in Developing Physical Skill. Is there anything else which a teacher can do to aid pupils in learning? It seems there is nothing. The whole story seems to be just this: *first*, let the administration provide proper equipment and make possible the organization of a graded program of activities; *second*, let the teacher motivate the work by setting goals; *third*, get the learner started as well as possible by giving demonstrations and directions in words; *fourth*, watch the pupil's progress, repeating demonstrations and directions whenever errors occur. We might add that for the sake of motivation of future work it is worth while to pat the pupil on the back when he has attained his goal.

For the most part, the teacher is merely an onlooker during the learning process; the teacher gives a word of advice here and there, but the pupil must actively go through the process of trying himself out in the activity; he must overcome his own errors and develop his own skill.

Other Phases of Health Education. The problem of health education is broader than that of physical education. Health education includes, in addition to training in the desirable kind and amount of physical activity, a training in hygienic habits of life. Health education deals with such problems as diet, cleanliness, the proper amount of rest, etc. Health education of this kind has two aspects. It may be concerned merely with the giving of information. We may teach what combinations of food make up a good diet. We may teach the elements which go to make up cleanliness—the care of teeth, care of the skin, and care of the body in general. Health education, however, which stops with the giving of such information is far from complete. In many ways the most important aspect of health education is concerned with the development of good habits of living. A child must be taught not merely the value of clean teeth, but he must be trained in the specific habit of keeping his teeth clean. Children must be taught not merely what is good food, but they must be trained in good eating habits. Courses in health education in our public schools ought to combine these two elements, the giving of information and training in health habits. Giving of information is easy, while devising techniques for training in health habits is sometimes difficult. In consequence, health education tends to be informational rather than habit-forming. We need an increasing emphasis upon habit-formation without, however, discarding the information which furnishes the reason for the establishment of health habits.

III. SUMMARY

The ancient Greek ideal of physical grace and skill as a part of a life of culture was lost during the middle ages. During the Christian era the body came to be regarded as an undesirable encumbrance to the soul and mind.

The modern revival of interest in physical education has grown out of military necessity and the philosophy of Rousseau. Modern psychology, especially behaviorism, has contributed to a renewed interest in the physical. The ideal of physical skill as a part of the cultural and recreational life is beginning to reappear.

Cultural and recreational aims demand less emphasis upon exercise merely for strength and health and more emphasis upon exercise for grace and personal satisfaction, less emphasis upon vigorous team games whose recreational value soon disappears and more emphasis upon individual sports of a milder character.

Physical education has won its place in schools and in public confidence, in part because of its supposed value in developing valuable character traits. Experimental work is needed to substantiate these claims and to develop methods of training which will insure a maximum of character and personality development. The development of such traits is something in addition to the acquisition of physical skills, and must be made the object of special efforts on the part of teachers of physical education. The transfer of such traits from the gymnasium and playground to later social and industrial life probably occurs according to the general principles of transfer of training. It depends upon the intelligence of the pupil, the breadth of interest of the coach or teacher, and the method of training used.

The laws of learning and principles of economical learning worked out in the literary school subjects are commonly applied to the teaching of physical skills. It is uncertain whether they can properly be applied in detail. Experimentation is needed. Good equipment seems to be more necessary than in the academic school subjects. A graded curriculum as found elsewhere in the school seems to be essential. An increased use of standardized tests is desirable. To increase the effectiveness of the personal contact of teacher with pupil, the most pressing need seems to be the development of a movement vocabulary.

Good health should be a by-product of physical activity, rather than an immediate objective. Apart from physical grace and skill, good health demands training in hygienic habits of living. Information and knowledge are desirable as a background for health habits, but effective health education must be habit-forming rather than informational.

CHAPTER XV

THE DEVELOPMENT OF PERSONALITY AND CHARACTER

I. CHANGING ATTITUDES TOWARD MORAL EDUCATION

Restraint vs. Freedom in Education. Two opposing attitudes toward the training of children have existed throughout historical times. On the one hand it has been believed that education is primarily a process of disciplining and training the growing child by imposing all manner of external restraints and regulations upon him. On the other hand it has been thought that education is primarily an affair of inner development; restraints and regulations are to be considered as harmful rather than helpful from this educational standpoint.

The conflict between these two tendencies has been acute since the beginning of the Christian era. Christianity has traditionally assumed that man is naturally depraved and evil, and that his original depravity can be overcome only by a process of severe disciplining of his body. Most forms of Christianity have assumed that man does not belong in this world as a real part of it, that he is merely a temporary inhabitant who is preparing for a better and more perfect life in a world to come. His preparation for this later life requires that his original depravity be overcome as far as possible by the imposition of every manner of restraint and discipline. This view of the essential nature of man and of education prevailed during the Christian era, until the time of Rousseau.

Rousseau proposed the theory that man in a primitive

state is perfect, that his depravity is a result of his association with his fellows, the result of the fact that he lives in a "civilized" world. According to this view, the child when he is born is more nearly perfect than he will ever be at any time in his later life. The aim of education should be to preserve as nearly as possible this early perfection during the period of physical growth. If we can arrange conditions surrounding the child so that he can develop in accordance with his own inner tendencies, without being influenced by the civilized world, he should develop into the perfect man or woman.

Restraint vs. Freedom in Politics and Industry. It should be pointed out that these conflicting views of the nature of childhood and of man correspond in a general way to similar attitudes in politics, industry, and other phases of our social life. The attitude that man is naturally depraved and must be disciplined and restrained favors the monarchical system of government, with its view of the divine right of kings. According to this view, there must be some person divinely appointed and divinely fitted to control and discipline the rest of humanity. Likewise in industry, the centralization of power in the hands of a few people, with the rest of humanity on the level of workers who are following directions, is the ideal system.

When we start with the supposition that each individual, as he is born, is perfect, restraints succeed only in introducing imperfection. The political system which should logically be adopted is that which permits extreme individual freedom. In its most perfect form this system would be anarchism, a system in which there is no centralized government at all. It is interesting to note in this connection that communism corresponds more in its fundamentals to the monarchistic ideal, with many restraints and regulations, than it does to the system which would follow from the ideas of Rousseau. The republican or democratic form of government represents a compromise between the extreme view of Rousseau on the one hand and the extreme view involving restraint and discipline on the other.

Traditionally the School Has Given a Minimum of Freedom and a Maximum of Discipline and Restraint. Children have been required to march into the schoolroom in orderly formation, to sit in seats arranged in formal rows, to remain perfectly quiet except when asked by the teacher to make a recitation. The curriculum has been definitely and narrowly prescribed, and methods of teaching have been formal and have been identical for all the children in the school system.

The Introduction of Pupil Freedom into Education. With the development of Rousseau's ideas, a new ideal has begun to appear in education. Rousseau's successors (Pestalozzi, Froebel, and others) have tried to work out a scheme of education in which the child is permitted to develop according to his own individuality. In the direct line of descent from these educators are the so-called progressive schools of the present day. In these schools children no longer march in orderly fashion; they sit in chairs which can be moved about freely; they work with materials which permit individuality of expression; formality of method has been replaced by informality; and even the curriculum has been made to depend, in theory at least, upon the interests or even the whims of the children themselves. The function of the teacher has become that of an adviser rather than a disciplinarian.

Education as Adjustment. An intermediate view of education which has grown out of scientific interest in child study is that which considers education as adjustment.

It is considered that the child originally possesses many tendencies which must be taken into account, and made the most of in the business of education. These original tendencies must not, however, be permitted to develop unchecked and without direction. Education is rather a process of adjusting the tendencies of the growing child to the circumstances of the external world in which the child is living. It is believed that by the time the child reaches maturity, its original tendencies must have been so made over that they will fit into the social system of the community in which the child lives. They are not, however, to be fitted to the adult community merely by a process of discipline and restraint. The process is to be rather that of guidance and direction.

This process of adjustment has necessarily two aspects. There is the external world to which the inner tendencies must be adjusted. To this extent a certain amount of discipline and restraint is needed. There are, however, the original tendencies themselves which point toward certain lines of development. These lines of development must be promoted just as far as possible without producing an adult who will be seriously out of tune with the conventions of civilized society.

Behavioristic Psychology Favors External Direction. Recent developments in psychology have emphasized the importance of external direction in education. The concept of the conditioned reflex definitely places the burden of education upon the kind of stimulation which is presented; that is, upon the type of environment in which the child lives. In order to make a child into an adult of a particular kind, it is assumed to be only necessary to supply the right kind of stimulation so as to bring about the right kind of conditioning. This attitude toward education dominates in the Soviet Republic to-day. In that country there is no division of opinion concerning the immediate aim of education. It is considered that the aim is to develop a citizen who will fit into a communistic political system. In order to produce an adult of this particular kind, a definite system of stimulation is considered necessary. The schools are organized in a narrowly prescribed and rigid fashion. Instruction is not necessarily formal since it takes individual differences into account, but it is formal and restrictive in the sense that each child is to be made to fit into a definite pattern.

Child Nature as a Determiner in Education. A view which is closely allied to the belief that education is a process of conditioning or habit formation is that view which assumes that the child is raw material out of which an adult is to be made. From this standpoint the nature of the child is important in the sense that raw material of a certain kind limits the nature of the product which can be made from it. The process of education is important in the sense that it is the manufacturing process which is concerned with making over this raw material. The aim of education will depend upon the kind of finished product which is thought to be desirable. The nature of the finished product will be determined by the social system of the time. This does not, however, exclude the possibility that there may be a certain amount of anticipation of the social system of the future. That is, an attempt can be made to take the raw material (the child) and by the process of education (direction, guidance, discipline) make out of him an adult to fit the present social system and the social system of the future. The processes of education are not limited to adjustment to the present world, but can also allow for progress.

Discipline vs. Restraint in Moral Education. These different attitudes toward education show themselves in a striking manner in the problems of moral and character education. When education is considered as a process of disciplining, moral education depends upon the setting up of a large number of rules and regulations which the child must be made to follow by a system of rewards and punishments. The telling of a lie is considered as being an indication of man's natural depravity, as being a thing which is in itself sinful. Whenever a lie is told punishment must follow. The same attitude must be adopted toward other aspects of morality. It is taken for granted that the child will be guilty of many immoralities because he is naturally depraved, but by a constant process of discipline he must be taught to restrain his original tendencies, which are assumed to continue to exist in their full strength throughout life.

When education is considered as adjustment these original tendencies are thought to be somewhat less permanent. Since they are somewhat less permanent it is thought that the discipline and restraint which is necessary in early childhood may gradually disappear as education progresses. The original tendency which leads to telling a lie may be gradually adjusted to the demands of the civilized community in such a way that it will tend to disappear. An original tendency such as fighting may be gradually adjusted to the adult community so that it will receive desirable instead of undesirable outlets. The tendency to fight is assumed to remain even in the educated adult, but it now concerns itself with the right kind of fighting. The adult is supposed to have reached a point where he will fight against undesirable social conditions, where he will fight to procure worth-while necessities and conveniences of living.

When education is considered as a process of conditioning or habit formation, it is assumed that such an original tendency as fighting is produced by a certain particular situation. If we wish to make certain that the situation will no longer produce fighting, we have only to present along with the original stimulus another and different stimulus which leads to a different kind of response. If we present together for a sufficient number of times the two kinds of stimulation, the point may finally be reached where the original stimulus for fighting will produce a new and different response. In that sense, the fighting response is entirely lost so long as the new connection remains in good working order. Whether, then, the fighting response appears in an adult depends upon the kinds of situations he has met with during his period of development. This response or any other undesirable response with which the child is natively equipped can be made to disappear from adult life if only we so arrange stimulating conditions that it is replaced by some other and more desirable kind of activity.

When the child is considered as raw material out of which adults are made, we need to be concerned with these native responses only to the extent that they are the starting point for the work of education. These original forms of behavior can be made over in any fashion we choose, if only we have sufficient wisdom and patience to apply the right educational procedures. There need be little or nothing, in the behavior of the adult which represents the behavior with which he began as a child. Processes of education can presumably lead to something in human behavior radically different and almost wholly new. Original responses, such as fighting, are of interest in the educational program only because they are a part of the raw material which is to be used in manufacturing civilized adults.

The Theological Attitude toward Moral Education; Intuitive Knowledge of Right and Wrong. So long as education in matters of morality was in the hands of the church there was no doubt as to the proper procedure. The moral education which was carried on in the home was usually patterned directly after the procedures of the church. This procedure was simply that of the imposition of all manner of restraints. Rewards were held out to secure good moral behavior, and punishments were provided to insure the avoidance of bad moral action.

It was assumed that the process of moral education consisted first in giving information concerning right and wrong. This information need not be very elaborate, since it was assumed that as soon as we were "old enough" we should know intuitively what was right and what was wrong. This age of responsibility has been set at different points at different times in history; in any one period in history it has been placed at different ages for different purposes. The Christian church has ordinarily placed the age of responsibility at about the time of puberty. A certain amount of moral responsibility was supposed to begin, however, as soon as the child learned to talk. Until very recently, talking was supposed to be an affair of the soul. As soon as the soul had sufficiently developed that it could talk, it was assumed that it was also sufficiently developed to begin to be responsible for its moral behavior.

The age of responsibility from a legal standpoint varies for different purposes. From the standpoint of the criminal code the age of complete responsibility has been placed at ages varying from ten years to twenty-one years. Certain kinds of criminal responsibility are assumed to begin earlier than others. Responsibility for sex offenses is frequently supposed to begin at about the time of puberty, while responsibility for other kinds of criminal action is supposed to begin later. Full responsibility is ordinarily supposed to have been reached at about the age of twenty-one, when an individual assumes all his political responsibilities.

Giving Information as a Means of Moral Education. We have gradually placed more and more emphasis upon the giving of information concerning matters of moral behavior, and have come to place less and less confidence in intuitive knowledge of right and wrong. With respect to truth-telling, for example, it is assumed that a child must be informed of the evil nature of lying. The difficulties which arise from lying must be pointed out to him on many different occasions. Sex morality, which has been made the subject of educational effort quite recently, has been supposed to depend mainly upon the giving of sex information. It is assumed that if the child is informed of the nature and functions of his sex organs, and of the place of sex in the civilized community, he will then upon the basis of this information adopt the right method of sex behavior.

Moral Education as Habit Formation. As a result of increasing knowledge of the psychology of learning, we have come to understand that verbal knowledge is different from knowing in the form of habits of acting. We know that a person can build up many verbal habits descriptive of a certain kind of behavior and yet be wholly unable to engage in the behavior itself. We know that a person may have full knowledge concerning the evils of lying or full knowledge concerning the facts of sex, and yet not have the desirable habits of action. It seems impossible to dodge the fact that training must be given in action as well as in words. If we wish to teach a child to tell the truth we must provide him with occasions where he will be required to act by telling the truth. To state the matter in negative terms, if we wish to teach a child to avoid lying, we must put him in situations where

he has an *opportunity to lie,* so that by his own actions he
will discover the consequences of lying. It is not sufficient
to *force* him to tell the truth.

How Can Practice in Moral Behavior Be Provided? In
some aspects of moral behavior this problem of providing
opportunity for engaging in action, in addition to purely
verbal discussions, is difficult. It is not, nevertheless, impossible. The approach to the problem can probably be
made in much the same manner that we teach children
to avoid danger of physical injury. If we wish to develop in
a child habits of such a character that he will not be run
over by an automobile, it is not necessary to let an automobile run over him. It is, however, necessary to do
something *more than merely tell him in words* how to
avoid automobiles. This training in avoiding automobiles
has both a positive and a negative aspect. We provide
sidewalks which may be used instead of the street, and
we teach the child to walk on the sidewalks. We provide playgrounds which may be used for games, and
teach the child to use them instead of playing in the street.
In addition to this positive training, which is designed to
teach a child to avoid injury, he also gets practice in crossing streets accompanied by his elders, and in this way he
gains a much more intimate acquaintance with automobiles and their habits. He gets a certain amount of training in dodging automobiles, in estimating their speed, etc.,
while actually in the situation where an *error in judgment
might lead to injury.* The presence of the adult who is aiding him to make the crossing is an aid as a precautionary
measure to minimize the danger of his errors in judgment
leading to serious injury.

In the same way in matters of sex education, we need
positive training in the development of sex habits as a
part of the sex education program. In America this prob-

lem is simplified by the fortunate fact that we have almost universally a system of co-education. In their
daily contacts with one another in the presence of adults,
boys and girls develop valuable habits of behavior in
the presence of the opposite sex. When this system of
co-education is supplemented by education in the form
of sex information, it may be expected to go a long way
in the direction of providing correct sex education. If
teachers and parents are especially aware of the fact that
training in habits of behavior is important, and if they
direct some effort toward this end, we can expect fairly
good results to be attained. It should be pointed out,
however, that this training must not be purely negative.
There must be a certain amount of positive training in
acting under various circumstances which arise from contact between the two sexes. There must be opportunity
to practice this correct mode of behavior.

*The Possibility of Error Is Essential to Effective Learn-
ing.* From our knowledge of the psychology of learning
we feel certain that practice of an act when all opportunity
for making a mistake has been removed is not so valuable
as practice of the act when there is opportunity for error.
This means that in moral training supervision must exist
for the sake of *avoiding too great harm* as a result of mistakes, but this *supervision must not be too close.* A certain possibility for making mistakes even in such important matters as sex morality, truth-telling, respect for
property rights, etc., must be permitted if the child is
to develop the right kind of moral habits. We know
further that there is a considerable value in the making
of mistakes. We are coming to believe that learning does
not consist merely in repeating over and over a correct
mode of procedure until that procedure has somehow become fixed, we believe that education is more a matter

of *improving upon our ways of acting* and constantly discovering better and improved actions. Our actions at first in any kind of learning situation can be expected to be more or less wrong or incorrect. This incorrect action seems to be a necessary preliminary to the later correct response. If we carefully limit the kind of behavior which can occur so that errors are not permitted, the desired habit can never be well established. At some point in the course of training we must introduce the possibility of error, and even *permit error to take place*. In moral training, even in connection with actions where we consider errors to be sinful from the theological point of view, the *possibility of error* must be introduced and a certain amount of error must be expected. Our attitude toward moral mistakes on the part of developing children should be that they are a necessary part of the learning process and that they are to be as much regarded as mistakes in arithmetic or mistakes in language. A certain amount of freedom for making mistakes is necessary.

The mistakes which a child makes in arithmetic or in language are likely to have no serious consequences due to the making of the mistakes themselves. In some aspects of morality this same situation is true. A lie told by a child is not likely to cause any serious harmful consequence in itself. The value of articles stolen is not likely to be great. Errors in sex behavior may possibly have more serious consequences. In the effort to avoid errors we should be guided primarily by the principle that the mistake must not be permitted to result in serious personal injury; if, however, such consequence can be avoided the mistake is likely to prove a profitable part of the child's education.

We might illustrate this view by reference to an entirely different type of activity, that of learning to swim. In teaching swimming a certain amount of land drill is ordinarily given, the learner not being in the water at all. In this case there is no possibility of sinking under the water and certainly no possibility of drowning. When the learner has formed a few of the more fundamental habits, he is then permitted to enter shallow water. There is the possibility of sinking under the water but only a very remote possibility of drowning. While in shallow water the learner forms additional habits concerned with swimming. When he is able to maintain himself on the surface fairly well, he is then required to enter deep water, where there is still greater possibility of drowning—but the learner has already progressed to the point that by his own efforts he can fairly well avoid this danger. An additional safeguard is provided by the presence of the teacher. Finally if the learner is to become an expert swimmer he must have the experience of swimming in deep water without the immediate presence of a person to aid him. It is only when a person has been alone in deep water and developed a confidence in his ability to take care of himself without the aid of any one else that we can say that his habits of swimming have been fully formed.

A Program of Moral Training Which Includes Possibility of Error. In moral training we should probably follow some such program. The first training should be given in situations in which errors cannot possibly lead to harm. This should be followed by further practice in situations where slightly more responsibility is placed upon the learner, with a slightly increased possibility of harm resulting from the mistake, and eventually, before the process of training can be considered as complete, the learner must be placed in situations where he is entirely on his own responsibility, where a mistake might result in serious harm. It is only when the learner has tried himself out in situations where he is alone responsible for his own safety that he has formed his moral habits to such an extent that he can have confidence in his own ability and that he can be classed as being thoroughly dependable and reliable.

In practice, this manner of moral training is not so difficult as it might seem, even in connection with the kinds of moral training for which we have the strongest social conventions. In matters of sex morality, for example, the primary steps in training can and should take place very early in the child's life, where the possibility of harm resulting from sex errors is almost non-existent. This training in sex morality can have been carried a long way before the child reaches the age of sex maturity. When sex maturity, however, has been attained, further training is essential, due to the fact that new types of stimulation (organic) are introduced. The earlier training cannot possibly have made complete provision for sex behavior after sex maturity, just because new organic stimuli are introduced which could not be introduced earlier. Habitual reactions to these new stimuli must be developed *after they appear*. Beginning with puberty there is needed, then, a further course of training in habits of sex morality. The beginning steps of this training should be, as we have pointed out, conducted in such a fashion that errors made cannot possibly have harmful results, but by the time the child has reached maturity he must have had experience in which he is thrown entirely on his own responsibility; otherwise he cannot have confidence in his own behavior, and we cannot consider his behavior to be dependable on all occasions.

Effect of the "Double Standard" upon Moral Education of Girls. We have adopted different attitudes toward the moral education of boys and girls. We throw boys much earlier than girls upon their own responsibility. Ordinarily a girl is not permitted to depend entirely upon herself until she is married or leaves home to engage in some kind of industrial occupation. We have adopted the attitude that girls must be protected until long after the age when we are willing to dispense with such protection in the case of boys. From an educational standpoint, this long-continued protection is undesirable. It should be expected to result in a certain lack of responsibility in any except the conventional situations.

Effective Education Requires Progressive Relaxation of Supervision. Where children continue their education throughout a college course, they have ordinarily reached a fair degree of maturity by the time of graduation. By this time the course of moral training should have been completed in all its aspects. That is, the period of imposition of restraints should have been passed before the college course is ended. Certainly by the time students have reached their last year in a college, they should be thrown entirely upon their own responsibility for all aspects of their moral behavior.

It is true that we have not adopted this method of moral training in our educational system. We have not even attained this end in academic school work. It is still customary definitely to prescribe required reading, hours of attendance in class, and in other ways to refuse to place the student upon his own responsibility in his academic education. Since we have shown ourselves unwilling to permit the necessary amount of freedom even in academic work, it is not surprising that we still retain many rules and regulations to which students must conform in their social and moral behavior. At present there is a well-defined movement under way to remove many of the academic restrictions which have been placed upon college students. The movement, in the form of individualized instruction, is well developed in the elementary schools and high schools. This movement ought to be extended to moral and character training as well. There should be a progressive decrease in the imposition of rules and regulations, a progressive decrease in the closeness of moral supervision with each succeeding year of school life. The last year in college should be a year in which a student (boy or girl) has entire freedom in the disposition of his own time, entire freedom in all aspects of his behavior, the only requirement being that the year should be spent profitably, that by the end of the year the student should have gained a fair increase in knowledge and skill, a fair improvement in intellectual, social, and moral behavior, as the result of the year spent in the educational institution.

II. The Development of Personality

What Is Personality? Personality has always been a puzzling problem to psychologists. The word has never been satisfactorily defined, although many personality traits have been listed. The manner in which personality traits can be developed through education is a still more puzzling matter. Personality is usually taken to refer to a vaguely defined group of social traits. Perhaps as good a description of personality as we can give is that the word refers to the *total impression which one person makes upon others*. This total impression depends upon a variety of individual habits and peculiarities of behavior. It depends not only upon the habits and peculiarities of the individual, but upon the peculiarities of the person with whom he comes into contact. It is not so much the habit itself which is of importance in determining personality, but the *effect* this habit has upon other people. The only basis for a discussion of personality as an individual possession is the fact that *people as a whole have a community of interests and habits*, and tend to react in much the same way to the behavior of other people. A discussion of personality traits and the methods for developing them must be based, therefore, upon an understanding of the way in which certain traits will affect the average person or persons of a particular class or occupation.

Some personality traits are so wide in their effect that their discussion need not be restricted to individuals of a certain social or industrial class. Such traits are, for example, sympathy, tact, aggressiveness, leadership, cooperation, loyalty, and many others. Other personality traits are effective for a more limited group, as cleanliness, manner of dress, manner of speech, physical appearance.

Two Conditions Are Needed for Training in Personality. A personality trait such as sympathy depends upon two sets of conditions; there must first of all be a person who is in need of sympathy, and there must be a person who possesses a number of specific habits which we group together and call by the class name, sympathy. If we wish to develop this trait in an individual, the course of training must have *two aspects.* (1) The child must be taught to *recognize those situations* in which another person would like to be shown sympathy. (2) The child must be trained in those *modes of action* which we call being sympathetic.

Teaching a Child to Be Sympathetic. We may illustrate the development of this trait by referring to attitudes toward personal injury. One child may fall and hurt its hand. The child in whom we wish to develop the trait of sympathy must learn first that hurting the hand is an *occasion* which calls for a special kind of action. It must also be taught *what actions* are appropriate, such as giving aid, caring for the injured hand, speaking kindly and gently to reduce the excitement of the other person, picking up, fondling, petting, and other such responses that are designed to have a soothing, quieting, and helpful effect. When this *recognition* of the situation and the development of the *specific set of responses* in the situation have taken place, then the child has become *sympathetic* when another person is injured physically.

The child must likewise learn that there are many other situations in addition to physical injury which call for sympathy and he must learn the appropriate responses. The one child, for example, may break a toy or lose a ball. The child in whom we are attempting to develop this trait of sympathy must be taught the kind of actions that will meet with the approval of the child who has suffered the loss.

When a person has had a wide variety of experience in dealing with other individuals who have suffered injury or loss of some kind, and has developed ways of acting which meet with the approval of the person who has suffered the injury or loss, then we can say that this personality trait of sympathy is present.

Learning to Be Tactful Requires More than the Formation of Specific Habits. Tact refers to a certain way of acting as it affects people with whom we come into contact. Tact is usually called for when a person with whom we are associated wishes to do something which we should like him not to do, or when he wishes us to do something that we should like to avoid. Training in this personality trait depends first of all upon developing a *sensitiveness to the wishes of other people*. We must be taught to recognize quickly and to understand what their wishes are. This quickness in understanding the other person cannot be based entirely upon an understanding of words which the other person speaks but must be based upon a certain amount of skill in interpreting gestures and facial expression. When this skill in understanding the wishes of other people has been developed, a second phase of training consists in the development of a set of habits which will meet the wishes of other people and at the same time meet our own wishes. When the two are contradictory and cannot both be met, tact consists in deciding which of the two wishes should be gratified, that of oneself or of the other person, and then developing a line of procedure which will permit the gratification of the one desire or the other while at the same time *maintaining the friendly relationship*. Tact refers particularly to that kind of behavior which will result in changing the wishes of the other person to conform to our own wishes when there is a conflict.

This changing of the wishes of another person so that they will conform with our own is the central problem of many forms of social conduct. In business relations, for example, the influencing of another person to do as we wish is the central problem in selling; in political life it is the central problem of any candidate for office, the central problem of any member of a legislative body, the central problem of any political executive; in recreational social activities, this influencing of other people to meet our wishes is the central problem in social leadership. There is no one formula by which it can be developed. As we have pointed out it is based upon an understanding of the wishes of the other person. Beyond this point, tact depends upon a wide range of information, a high general intelligence, and good common sense. In the development of tact as a personality trait, therefore, the one specific thing which can be done is to give training in the understanding of other people, particularly in understanding facial expressions and gestures. This, however, is *only the beginning*. The most important phase of tact is based upon the possession of a wide range of information and high intelligence, which can be obtained only through the process of a wide and complete general education.

The Development of Aggressiveness Requires Understanding of One's Own Ability. Aggressiveness as a personality trait requires an energetic insistence upon the rights of the individual as opposed to the rights of other individuals. A person must develop the attitude that in a conflict between the wishes of himself and another person, his own wishes are of most importance. He must also decide quickly what his wishes are so that he may take the initiative. This does not mean that he must lack tact in attaining his ends, but he must never be satisfied until he has found the means for influencing the other person to change his wishes in conformity with his own. In developing this trait of aggressiveness, training should consist primarily in teaching a child to act quickly and to continue trying to obtain his own ends regardless of opposition which may arise.

As a specific example, when children are organizing a baseball game, one boy may decide that he wants to be the pitcher. Training in aggressiveness consists in inducing him to continue his insistence upon being the pitcher until he gains his end. This gaining of his end should, however, be made to depend upon something besides mere insistence. He should be able to find reasons why it is to the advantage, not merely of himself but of the other players, that he should pitch. If it happens that he is not a good pitcher and that he ought not to pitch, he may fail in gaining his end.

In developing this trait of aggressiveness, therefore, it

is desirable to control the training situations to the extent that the child will be led to insist upon his own rights as opposed to those of others, primarily in those situations in which he can be expected to prevail by virtue of ability. Whether there will be many such situations or only a few will depend upon the level of ability which a child possesses. Aggressiveness as an undesirable character trait consists in the development of this insistence upon one's own rights at times when it is not to the best advantage of the social group as a whole, while aggressiveness as a desirable character trait consists in insisting upon one's own rights at the time when one has something of real value to contribute to the social group. Aggressiveness, then, as a desirable character trait depends not merely upon the insistence of one's own right at the expenses of others, but upon the possession of a high degree of ability and the knowledge that the proper occasion has arisen for the display of this ability. The training in aggressiveness, then, should consist in putting a child into situations where he really has the ability to dominate others, and then inducing him to continue his efforts to prevail until the other individuals permit him to have his way.

Loyalty Is Based upon Specific Habit Formation. Loyalty consists of the willingness to subordinate to some extent one's own wishes for the sake of aiding another person. It consists further of the willingness to work for the advancement of the wishes of another person against the opposition of third parties. Such training in loyalty at a primitive level may be found when two boys are playing together with a ball. Some other boy or group of boys may appear and demand the ball to play with. If the owner of the ball objects, the boy who has been playing with him has two courses of action open to him. He may support the owner of the ball in his refusal to give it to the other boys, or he may decide that the opposition is too great and that he will join in with the majority against his former playmate. Loyalty demands that he support his playmate against the group of outsiders. Training in loyalty consists in furnishing many such opportunities to support friends and companions in their difficulties with third parties, and in arranging these conditions in such a way that the choice will ordinarily be made in favor of the friend against the outsider. This trait does not require the exercise of any great amount of intelligence and does not require the possession of any wide range of information. It is in this sense much more specific in character and much more easily developed than such personality traits as sympathy and tact.

In a similar way we could show how other personality traits grow out of the particular experiences which arise from day to day during the child's life. The development of desirable personality traits, then, consists in having a wide range of social contacts, under such conditions that the child learns to act in a way which meets with the approval of those people with whom he comes into contact. The possession of undesirable character traits may depend merely upon this lack of wide social contacts, with the resulting lack of habit formation, or it may depend upon the existence of a narrower range of social contacts which have developed habits that were satisfactory in these particular situations but which are not satisfactory to the social group as a whole.

Development of Personality Depends upon Breadth of Experience. The procedure to be used in developing those right social responses which we call good personality is the same procedure which needs to be used in all habit formation. It consists primarily in providing opportunity for the social activities. This opportunity must not be so narrowly prescribed that mistakes are impossible. We do not develop desirable personality traits merely because we have been in situations which rigidly limit our behavior to the desirable responses. We have previously shown that learning requires possibility of error. The good personality can be considered to be firmly established only when there has been opportunity for the showing of bad personality traits. Ordinarily this opportunity for making undesirable social responses must not only have been present, but the undesirable responses must have occurred before the desirable responses can be formed so that they may be depended upon.

The person with good personality, then, is the person who has had a great variety of social contacts, and has made use of his opportunities to do things which have both pleased and displeased those with whom he has come into contact. As a result of his mistakes as much as because of his correct responses, he has developed socially desirable ways of acting which we call a good personality. The person with a good personality is not the one who has led a sheltered life, but the one who has actively participated in life both good and bad as it is certain to be found in our social system.

III. SUMMARY

The belief that good character can best be developed by a disciplinary process is gradually giving way to the concept that there must be freedom of action. We are giving up the belief that man is essentially evil in his desires; we are developing a faith in the essential worth of human nature. While it was formerly believed that knowledge of the important moral principles was intuitive, we now recognize the necessity of information concerning right and wrong. We have relied upon information as a means of moral education, but now recognize that information can furnish only a more or less valuable background for habit formation.

The essential feature of moral training is habit formation. In our anxiety to guard against errors in matters of morality we have exercised such close supervision of children that we have many times defeated the ends of education. Effective teaching and learning require the presence of situations containing the possibility of error. We learn from mistakes as well as from correct actions. Moral education, to be effective, requires supervision to set the goals and to suggest methods of attack upon problems, but demands progressive relaxation of supervision so that the child may come to have confidence in his own unaided ability to meet moral situations.

A good personality requires the possession of habits which are pleasing to other people. To have a good personality we must have developed a sensitiveness to the wishes of other people and in addition must have gained social intelligence and a group of habits which enable us to respond effectively. Such habits and this type of social intelligence can be developed only by wide social experience. Narrowly restricted social contacts may lead to the development of a personality which is pleasing to a limited social group, but the well-rounded personality grows out of varied contacts with all the types of people to be found in the social community.

CHAPTER XVI

MENTAL HYGIENE

Mental Hygiene as a Problem in Habit Formation. The problem of mental hygiene is frequently made difficult because of the vagueness with which it is stated, or because the fundamental problem is not stated at all. Mental hygiene has a positive and a preventive aspect. The positive aspect of mental hygiene is concerned simply with the formation of good habits, while its preventive aspect is concerned with the avoidance or breaking of bad habits. Mental hygiene as a whole then deals with the technique of avoiding bad habits and forming good ones. By good habits we mean those which are socially acceptable; this means ordinary habits, the *usual* habits that are found in the community in which we are living. By bad habits, we mean those which are anti-social or unsocial, the habits which get us into difficulty. These habits are ordinarily those which are *unusual* and purely individual. When we fail to conform to the customs of the community in which we live, we get into difficulties.

Difficulties caused by social maladjustment may produce effects which are broader than the mere failure to secure the approval of the people around us. This failure may cause mental disturbances of a far-reaching kind. Mental hygiene, then, is concerned with the attempt to avoid those mental disturbances which are an outgrowth of failure to conform to the social customs of the community in which we live.

The Approach to Mental Hygiene Is Ordinarily Made from the Standpoint of the Psycho-analytic School of Psy-

chology. This school believes that we have important instinctive tendencies which are the driving forces of human life. When these driving forces meet with opposition, mental disturbances may result. The demands of the social world in which we live are constantly running counter to instinctive urges. If this conflict between the demands of life and the instinctive tendencies can be met satisfactorily, the individual develops in a normal fashion. If the instinctive tendencies can be directed into channels which are socially acceptable and useful, difficulty may be avoided. If, on the other hand, an instinctive tendency is directed into a channel which is not acceptable socially, the conflict between social custom and the internal urge is likely to become acute, and far-reaching mental disturbance may be the outcome.

Driving Forces Which Are Factors in Mental Hygiene. Freud points out that the instinctive tendency which is most likely to gain an expression not approved of socially is the sex instinct. Adler believes that the desire for power is the most probable source of such difficulties. Jung believes that there are many instinctive tendencies which may get us into such difficulties, but especially the group of tendencies which are centered around the instinct of self-preservation. The technique of mental hygiene from this point of view consists in determining in the first place what instinctive driving forces we have that are likely to cause difficulty, and in the second place what life situations are most frequently the starting points for conflicts between social custom and internal driving force. The contribution to mental hygiene of the psycho-analytic psychology consists in a description of the circumstances in which conflict between external circumstances and internal desires is likely to take place.

Mental Hygiene from the Standpoints of Functional and Objective Psychology. When we approach the problem of mental hygiene from the standpoint of functional psychology, we are prone quickly to drift into the psychoanalytic point of view, since the functional psychology also makes extensive use of the concept of instinctive tendencies as real driving forces in human nature.

From the standpoint of recent objective psychology, this conflict between driving forces (instinct) and custom cannot be used as an explanation for the occurrence of mental disorder, since the concept of instinct has been minimized or discarded. From this point of view, conflicts can occur only between different systems of habits. Mental hygiene from this viewpoint is concerned with the establishment of good habits and with the establishment of sets of habits which are consistent with one another. If bad habits are established, they sooner or later get the individual into difficulties. If an individual has contradictory habits, difficulty may be expected to arise. The technique of mental hygiene is simply the technique of habit formation based upon an understanding of the demands of the society in which the child is living.

A Typical "Bad" Habit of Childhood. It is desirable to point out the kind of bad habits which are most likely to be developed, and to explain their development from these two different points of view. A kind of bad habit which is becoming very common among children at the present time is refusal to eat. Many children who have parents well able to provide the proper kind of food and who have the proper kind of food placed before them daily, are nevertheless badly undernourished because of their refusal to eat this food in the right quantity or the right variety. In many cases this refusal to eat goes to such an extreme that there is difficulty in maintaining a sufficient degree of health to keep the child alive. The child is desperately hungry, is literally starving in the presence of an abundance of food.

Explanation of "Refusal to Eat" in Terms of Interference with Driving Forces. Adler explains such a habit by reference to desire for power. When the child is still an infant he is quite helpless. He must depend for the satisfaction of all his wants upon the people surrounding him. Out of this state of helplessness the child develops a great desire for power. He sets as a goal in life the gaining of superiority over the people around him. This problem of gaining superiority over the surrounding people does not become acute so long as the parents are willing to defer constantly to the wishes of the child. Sooner or later, however, conditions are likely to arise under which he will feel neglected. Such a situation may be produced by the appearance of a younger child in the family, or by the parents becoming absorbed in any other activity which results in a real or apparent neglect of the child. The child in this situation begins to hunt about for some means of regaining his lost position as the center of interest of his parents. By chance he discovers that refusal to eat will cause the parents to be greatly concerned and cause them to once more give him their undivided attention. Having made this discovery, the child at once adopts this device as a means for gaining power over the parents.

As a means of forcing their attention, many other bad habits may be established as well, for example, biting finger nails, sucking the thumb, abnormal fears, etc.

Freud explains such habits on the basis of interference with sex instinct. He says that the first sex attachment of children is for the mother. This is true because the mother is the one who is primarily concerned with caring for the children. In handling the children she is certain to produce many accidental stimulations of sex zones, resulting in a gradual development of an affection on the part of the children which is based upon this sex stimulation.

Early in life, ordinarily at about five years of age, the children are forced to make a readjustment in their sex attachment for the mother. They have now reached an age at which they can understand that the mother is not a proper object of sex attachment on their part. They are forced to make some substitution for this early sex attachment. This substitution may or may not be satisfactorily made. Undesirable substitutions for early sex attachments of this kind are found in such activities as thumb-sucking, biting finger nails, refusal to eat, and abnormal fears.

Jung proceeds in a similar manner to show that these habits are merely undesirable outlets of instincts concerned with self-preservation. The thing which makes these habits undesirable is that they are purely individual and frequently anti-social. Proper training should result in the securing of outlets for these instinctive driving forces which are not merely individual but which conform to social usage.

Typical Effects of Mental Conflict. If habits are established which are purely individual, these habits are certain to lead to conflict with social custom and the result of this conflict may appear in many undesirable ways. Examples of undesirable results of mental conflicts are to be found in chronic indigestion, anæsthesias of parts of the skin, hysterical blindness, shell shock as found among soldiers, chronic imaginary ill health, etc. Other effects of such conflict are to be found in many types of special motor disorder, especially stuttering. The bad boy in school is frequently merely a boy who is suffering from a mental conflict.

As an example of the extreme to which the bad effects of social conflicts may go, we may cite the case of a woman of middle age who constantly sought out physicians for the treatment of imaginary illnesses. She was able to describe her imaginary pains so vividly that she had succeeded in having many operations for the removal of various organs which showed no evidence of disease aside from her description of pain. One physician discovered that her illness was purely hysterical and refused to operate, but she succeeded in misleading many others.

The Function of the "Subconscious" in Mental Disorder. Psycho-analysts explain abnormalities of behavior as the result of the suppression of instinctive desires by environmental circumstances. It is supposed that some event which has strong emotional characteristics leads to the suppression of an instinctive desire. This suppressed tendency does not disappear completely from the mind of the child, but is merely pushed back into the subconscious. There it is stored away along with other such tendencies which have been suppressed in the past. These tendencies, living in the subconscious, lose none of their driving power. Indeed, they may become more powerful merely because of their suppression.

It is, however, impossible for suppressed desires to escape into the conscious life of the child under ordinary circumstances. The psycho-analysts suppose that between the conscious and the subconscious mind there stands a metaphysical entity, the "censor." It is the duty of this censor to prevent the escape from the subconscious mind of any tendencies which would be unacceptable in the conscious life of the individual. In order to escape the censor, these subconscious tendencies take on various disguises. The disguise in one case may take the form of chronic indigestion, in another it may take the form of loss of sensitiveness in some part of the skin, and in another it may be an abnormal fear, a slip of the tongue, a dream, etc.

Sometimes it happens that these subconscious tendencies become rather well organized and coördinated among themselves so that there gradually develops a subconscious personality. This subconscious personality may become sufficiently important so that it is able now and then temporarily to take possession of the body of the individual and overcome the resistance offered to it by the censor and the conscious mind. When such a situation arises, there is a case of dual personality.

In a case of dual personality, the secondary or subconscious personality, while it may be well organized, is invariably somewhat defective. The person while under the influence of the subconscious personality is likely to show lack of sensitivity to pain, to show lack of fatigue, to have the general level of behavior of a person many years younger, etc. This means that the tendencies which have been suppressed into the subconscious, although they are very numerous and may occasionally become quite well organized, are, nevertheless, quite incomplete, and taken by themselves are incapable of carrying on a normal life.

In the case of apparently normal individuals, these subconscious tendencies are supposed to be present. They do not, however, have the strength or the importance that they have in the abnormal cases. Certain specific kinds of behavior have been recognized as due to the working of the subconscious mind. These tendencies have been assigned definite names, such as *compensation, rationalization, sublimation, Œdipus complex, inferiority complex,* etc.

Compensation. By compensation is meant the attempt to cover up some defect of personality or ability by over-reacting in some other way, usually in a manner opposite to that which would result from the defect of personality or character. For example, a person who is inclined to lie may attempt to cover up his defect by talking much about his honesty. He is very ready to protest that he is telling the truth, although no one has questioned the truth of his remarks. A person who has small physical stature is inclined to engage in as much vigorous physical activity as possible and to pride himself upon the fact that he has physical strength as great as that of people much larger than he is. Or the person of small physical stature may be very talkative or he may be self-assertive in his relations with other people. Such a manner of act-ing is attributed by psycho-analysts to the suppression of instinctive tendencies, resulting from personality, charac-ter, or physical defects, and to the attempt of the suppressed tendencies to escape into the conscious life of the indi-vidual.

For the objective psychologist, it seems unnecessary to introduce a driving force or tendency which has pre-sumably been suppressed and, having been suppressed, attempts to escape. To the objective psychologist such repressed tendencies are purely fictitious and have no real existence. He would explain the behavior of the person who lies frequently, and therefore constantly harps upon his own honesty, purely in terms of habit formation. The behaviorist would say that such a person, having told lies frequently and in consequence having been forced to defend himself against the consequences of his lying, has developed a well-organized set of habits concerned with defense of his own actions. These habits have be-come so well established and firmly fixed, and have become connected with so many situations as stimuli, that they are very easily and readily set into action. The person, then, who is constantly protesting his honesty, has simply developed a set of verbal habits which have many adequate stimuli, so that they function frequently. This set of verbal habits is unusual in the sense that it is not built up in the great mass of individuals who seldom lie, but usually tell the truth; in their case there is no occasion for the establishment of such a set of habits.

The person of short stature likewise builds up habits concerned with physical exercise, self-assertiveness, talkativeness, and the like, simply as a result of the conditions under which he is forced to live. These habits are of exactly the same nature as all the other habits of which he is possessed, in the sense that they have been formed according to the same principles. It is not necessary to assume any special driving force lying back of them to explain their formation and continued existence. Compensation is merely a name for a set of conditioned responses built up in just the same way and according to exactly the same principles as other conditioned responses, and it is unnecessary to assume a driving force which has been suppressed and is trying to escape.

Rationalization is another kind of behavior which has been explained upon the basis of subconscious tendencies. By rationalization is meant the making of excuses or the finding of reasons for an action which are illogical and not the real reasons which lie back of the person's behavior. Classical examples of rationalization are such as (1) the father taking his child to the circus on the grounds that the child will enjoy it, making no reference to the fact that he himself would also like to see it; (2) the fable of the fox and the grapes—the fox, being unable to get the grapes, decides that they are sour so that he doesn't want them anyway.

Such rationalizations occur on a large scale in times of war. The real reasons for war are frequently of such a nature that we could not justify our participation in it by them alone. For example, if the causes of a war are purely economic, purely the desire for more territory or more commercial power on the part of a nation, the majority of the people will refuse to participate in it. If, however, they can give themselves some additional reason of a religious or social nature, they can justify their participation. The stories of wartime atrocities and cruelties on the part of the enemy are for the most part manufactured and intended simply to furnish reasons which will make an appeal to the mass of the population.

According to the theory of psycho-analysis, we have subconscious tendencies which cause us to want to engage in the specified activity. These tendencies, however, are of such a nature that we would turn away from them in disgust if we only recognized them. As a means for influencing our behavior, they adopt disguises in the form of legitimate reasons for engaging in the act. These reasons, however, on close examination are seen to be false. They are reasons which cannot logically be applied to the situation.

The objective psychologist would explain rationalization in just the same way that he explains all habit formation, without the aid of any subconscious or other spiritual tendencies. He would say that the average person is not well trained in logical forms and processes of reasoning, that the average person is not well able to distinguish in many circumstances the real causes which produce certain effects. Rationalization is merely a type of faulty reasoning based upon lack of information on the one hand, and already existing well-established habits on the other. In the case of the father who takes his child to the circus really because he wishes to go himself, the objective psychologist would say that in the first place the father built up, as a child, well-established habits concerned with attendance upon and enjoyment of a circus. He has also built up habits concerned with furnishing entertainment to his child and he has discovered that it is sometimes unwise to give the real reasons for his actions. He has formed a definite series of habits concerned with getting results in which he is interested in a roundabout fashion. Making of the excuse that he must take his boy to the circus represents merely the working out of some of these definitely established habits of evasion which he has formed. Such a habit does not need a driving force back of it to cause it to work to any greater extent than any other habit needs such a driving force. As was pointed out earlier in the discussion of learning, the objective psychologist finds such driving forces wholly unnecessary in habitual action in general.

Sublimation represents a socially desirable way in which subconscious tendencies may express themselves. The emphasis of psycho-analysis in general is upon socially undesirable forms of response. This emphasis upon socially undesirable actions is merely an outgrowth of their attempts to explain mental abnormalities. Mental abnormalities, however, are comparatively rare when compared with normal human behavior. If psycho-analysis could tell us nothing about normal human activity, its value and its application would be greatly restricted.

In sublimation, suppressed wishes and desires find a method of getting by the censor and escaping from the subconscious, which is socially good and worth while. It has been claimed, for example, that much creative art in the form of music, painting, sculpture, etc., is an expression of suppressed sex desires. Likewise, the interest of many men and women in religion has been attributed to the sublimation of sex tendencies. This is supposed to be especially true of the Christian religion, which has traditionally assumed a negative attitude toward sex. The Christian religion has supposed sex tendencies to be essentially evil and has taught that the expression of sex desires should be avoided whenever possible. The constant effort to suppress such tendencies results in storing up in the subconscious mind many suppressed wishes and desires dealing with sex. These subconscious tendencies are constantly attempting to escape, and many of them do so in the form of socially acceptable participation in religion, art, etc.

The advice which we give a person who has suffered from some strong emotional upset, to "work hard and forget it," is presumably based upon this view, that the emotional disturbance can be suppressed but must still have some kind of outlet. This outlet may be a desirable one in the form of increased energy in business life or play, or it may be an undesirable one in the form of mental disorder or abnormality of some kind.

From this viewpoint, so far as education must deal with some of the instinctive tendencies which cannot be permitted direct expression, its primary aim is not merely to suppress these tendencies but to provide desirable outlets for them. This process has been called sublimation.

For the objective psychologist, this process of sublimation is like compensation and rationalization, merely a matter of habit formation according to the usual principles. The guiding force of instinct is supposed to be lacking except as we have bodies which are physically adapted to certain kinds of activity. We also have physiological processes which normally stimulate our physical structures in such a way that activity results. The kind of activity which follows upon this physiological stimulation depends in the first place upon our hereditary equipment in the form of a body mechanism which is capable of certain activities. It depends in the second place upon the kind of conditioning which has taken place.

The sublimation of sex tendencies is explained by the objective psychologist in terms of habit formation in the following way. As the child develops, its body as a whole (and sex organs in particular) gradually attains functional maturity. As this functional maturity is attained, and indeed even before it is attained, there is frequent internal organic stimulation resulting from physiological processes which are almost inevitable accompaniments of the process of living. These physiological changes stimulate the sex structures and the body as a whole in such a way that activity of some kind is certain to occur. In the beginning the activity which occurs is almost a matter of chance, in the sense that it is highly unpredictable on account of the complexity of bodily make-up. It is not wholly a matter of chance, because some nerve patterns are more closely connected with the sources of sensory stimulation than others. These connections, however, need remain more closely connected with the source of stimulation than other patterns only until there has been an opportunity for conditioning the behavior of the child. It is possible by a process of conditioning to connect up any type of activity that we please with the original physiological stimulations attributable to sex development. The process of conditioning to physiological stimuli, then, for the objective psychologist explains all cases of so-called sublimation of sex instinct. The spiritual driving force is entirely left out. The only thing present which could possibly justify the concept of the driving force is the fact that physiological stimulations, such as those associated with sex, are likely to be persistent and are likely to reappear frequently. They have no other element of drive than just this persistency and frequent reappearance.

Complex. The word "complex" has had a wide usage following the development of psycho-analysis. It can best be explained by citing one of the most common examples. According to the psycho-analysts, the *Œdipus complex* appears very early in life, usually at about five years, and is present in most children, the normal as well as the abnormal. This complex refers specifically to the attachment of a boy for his mother. The attachment of a girl for her father is of exactly the same nature, although given a different name (*Lysistra complex*).

The psycho-analysts point out that during the early years of childhood the mother is made responsible for the care of the children. In the case of the boy, all the types of stimulation which Watson has pointed out as giving rise to love responses are produced by the mother but not usually by the father. This type of stimulation includes gentle stroking, warmth, patting, fondling, etc. The mother's handling of the child both during play and while caring for it by bathing, etc., is likely to furnish the stimuli for love responses on many occasions. There is likely also to occur much accidental stimulation of specific sex areas. As a result of this stimulation, the boy gradually develops an affection for his mother which is primarily sexual in nature. This affection has reached its height by the time the boy is four or five years of age. At about this time he has forced upon him the fact that the father is also a source of sexual interest to his mother.

He is forced to recognize that his father occupies a place in his mother's affections which from a sexual point of view is superior to his own. He is therefore forced to suppress his own infantile sex interest in his mother. This forcible suppression of his infantile sex interest results in the formation of the *Œdipus complex*.

This complex is of extreme importance because of the fact that it involves such strong emotional reactions and such strong instinctive tendencies; also, because of the fact that it is so universal. Practically no boy escapes it in some form. If the parents are wise or if circumstances are otherwise favorable, the readjustment which is forced upon every boy at about five years of age can be made without permanently unfavorable consequences. If this readjustment is wisely handled we may speak of the infantile sex interest as being properly *sublimated*. On the other hand, if the readjustment is not properly made, the infantile sex interest in the mother is merely suppressed and will inevitably reappear in undesirable forms at some time in the child's later life. This reappearance may be in the highly undesirable form of sex perversion of one kind or another. It may be in the form of total lack of interest in women which results in the boy remaining a bachelor all his life. It may appear in some form not apparently directly related to sex, such as stammering, chronic invalidism, etc.

The objective psychologist would agree with the psychoanalyst in his description of the course of development up to the point where he begins to speak of the suppression of the instinctive tendencies of sex. The boy does undoubtedly form many habits of a kind which can properly be classified as sexual in connection with his mother. Sooner or later many of these infantile habits must be discarded and replaced by others. It is entirely possible that in the process of replacing these infantile habits by others of a more mature and more desirable nature, mistakes may occur. These mistakes may be due to the ignorance of the parents which leads them to fail in their responsibility of providing proper training. The whole matter, however, is identical with that of replacing one habit by another at any time during life. It is merely a matter of breaking certain habits which we recognize as being bad or outgrown, and replacing them with others which are thought to be better and more desirable. This matter of breaking undesirable habits and replacing them with more desirable ones proceeds in the opinion of the objective psychologist in the same way that all conditioning of responses proceeds. It is merely a matter of bringing stimuli and responses into the right sequence and combining them a sufficient number of times until the right connection has been formed.

From the viewpoint of the objective psychologist, the great contribution which has been made by the psychoanalyst is that he has pointed out the fact that such readjustment does occur. He has shown that contrary to earlier opinion, sex habits are present in very small children and that readjustments in these sex habits are necessary as the child grows older. The *Œdipus complex* is merely a name which is given to bad habits growing out of the process of readjustment which takes place in the habitual relations between a boy and his mother at about five years of age. We have pointed out that a similar readjustment takes place between a girl and her father, although it is likely to be less important because the relationship between the girl and her father during the early years has not ordinarily been so close as that between the boy and his mother. This means simply that a smaller number of infantile sex habits join the girl and her father, and that they are less strong and therefore more easily broken than in the case of her brother.

For the objective psychologist, complex in general— superiority complex, fear complex, etc.—refers to the existence of a group of habits, more or less contradictory in nature, that are brought into existence when external circumstances force the breaking of old habits and the formation of new ones.

In Conclusion, Then, There Are Two Widely Different Approaches to the Problem of Mental Hygiene. The facts which make necessary a program of mental hygiene are the same from both points of view; they are, however, interpreted differently. The procedures used in the treatment of children so as to secure a normal mental life are in large part the same from both points of view. The essential difference beween the viewpoint of psychoanalysis and the objective psychology is, up to the present, theoretical rather than practical. The psychoanalysts insist that the facts indicate the existence of spiritual forces (instinct and emotion) which have been suppressed. The objective psychologists insist that the facts do not require this interpretation, that we need not assume the existence of these suppressed forces but that the explanation can proceed entirely in terms of the well-recognized principles of habit-formation and learning.

Choice between the two points of view depends not so much upon immediate practical consequences as upon the effect which the point of view will have in determining future development of knowledge. The primary objection to the psycho-analytic point of view is that it is based upon an undue emphasis upon instinctive and emotional driving forces. If we can make a complete catalog of the instincts and the emotions, then the remaining task of mental hygiene is to perfect the details of practical procedure in controlling and directing their development. The objective psychologists minimize or discard instinct and emotion as motivating forces. For them mental hygiene is a problem in learning and habit-formation. Progress will depend upon perfecting theories of learning and techniques of training. Both groups of psychologists agree in emphasizing the importance of environmental control as a determiner of right mental development.

Summary

The problem of mental hygiene is to secure social rather than purely individualistic development. From the standpoint of psycho-analysis instinctive desires must be directed into socially useful channels; if they get a purely individualistic expression they are certain to cause mental conflict which will result in their suppression. The next step will then be mental disorder, in consequence of the continued activity of the suppressed instinctive desires. Annoying habits of childhood, such as refusal to eat, thumb sucking, abnormal fears, and temper tantrums are manifestations of driving forces which have been relegated to the subconscious. Adult activities such as rationalization, compensation, sex perversions, and chronic invalidism are based upon bottled up instinctive forces. When these forces are properly directed into useful channels, the abnormalities disappear.

From the standpoint of objective psychology mental hygiene is a problem in habit formation; mental "driving forces" are not recognized. The service rendered by the psycho-analysts has been in pointing out the occasions which are likely to give rise to troublesome habits and in showing their far-reaching effect. Good habits (*i.e.*, socially acceptable ways of action) must be formed, and bad habits must be broken according to the usually accepted principles of learning.

CHAPTER XVII

EXPERIMENTAL EDUCATION

The Need for Experimental Education. Common practice in education is a condensation of the experiences of the human race in controlling and directing child development. Curricula and methods used in the educational systems of civilized countries represent the best thought of the race. Their diversity is due in part to the variety of demands of adult life in the various countries; but after making due allowance for differences in objectives in education, there are left over a multitude of conflicting opinions concerning educational matters. In some cases practice is highly standardized and dissenting opinions are few, in others there is much disagreement. The standard practice of one generation is challenged by the next. Educational fads and fancies succeed one another without end. Vested opinion rightfully holds its place as being the outgrowth of racial experience; but new theories are adopted, often without adequate reason, because of dissatisfaction with old ideas.

Experimental education is an attempt to apply to educational problems the methods of investigation that have been found useful in natural science. It attempts to resolve differences of opinion by experimental observation rather than by appeal to *a priori* argument. It tries to find a basis in scientific law for choice of curricula and methods; then it tests out the wisdom of the chosen practice by controlled observation.

Experimental Education Is a New Development. The attempt to solve educational problems by controlled experiments is an affair of the present century. Although we have a fair understanding of the nature of the problems involved and although a definite experimental technique has been worked out, there are so many difficulties in the way of carrying on experiments designed to solve educational problems that comparatively little has been accomplished. Educational experimentation is an affair of the past few years, because it had to wait upon the development of psychology. Until the general psychological methods for experimenting objectively with human beings were worked out, educational experimentation was impossible.

Introspective Psychology Did Not Favor Educational Experiments. The structural psychology was purely subjective. Its interest was solely in states of consciousness and their relationship to one another. These mental processes and their interrelationship could be studied only by people who had had a considerable amount of training in introspection. The only individuals who possessed such training in sufficient degree to make their work scientifically valuable were graduate students or instructors in universities. Their school life was practically finished, so that almost the whole range of educational problems was closed to direct investigation. The only possible way to investigate child psychology and the problems of learning as found in childhood was by means of retrospection. If these graduate students and instructors in the university who were attempting to work out the problems of psychology were able to remember correctly the details of their mental life while children, they might be able to build up a system of child psychology and an understanding of the learning of children; but if with the passage of years they had forgotton the details of their mental life as children, a real understanding of child development would remain impossible. Whatever understanding of child life could be gained by the structural or any other introspective psychology must be obtained always from the adult point of view. The problems of teaching and of learning as found in the elementary grades and high school must continue to be solved from the adult point of view rather than from the point of view of childhood.

The Pioneer Work of G. Stanley Hall. Those people who were interested in understanding the development of children and in improving the work of the school, were not satisfied to continue to approach the problems of childhood from the adult viewpoint. They believed it possible to make a direct study of the facts of child development which would be worth while. This direct study could not be introspective but must take place by observation of the behavior of children. The leader of this child study movement in America was G. Stanley Hall. Although most of his theories have been challenged by modern psychologists and educators, the interest in child study which he fostered has been one of the most important psychological and educational movements of the century.

Objective Method in Psychology Furnished the Basis for Educational Experiments. At the same time that psychologists and educators were attempting to study objectively the facts of child development, other psychologists had become interested in studying the behavior of animals. The early experimenters in this field were Lloyd Morgan and E. L. Thorndike. These experimenters worked out an objective method for studying the behavior (especially in learning situations) of animals. Pavlov's work upon the conditioning of reflexes in animals was very suggestive. When the technique of observation had been rather well worked out, it occurred to a number of investigators that the same technique could be used in studying the development of children. J. B. Watson was one of the first to apply methods of conditioning to the study of the early behavior of infants. Arnold Gesell has developed and made extensive use of objective methods for observing the behavior of children. By about 1915, psychologists and educators had become thoroughly committed to objective procedures in studying children, and objective procedures have come to dominate the entire field of psychological and educational experimentation.

The Application of Statistical Method to Educational Experimentation. At the same time that this objective technique for observing the reactions of children was developing, the applications of mathematics to problems of biology and psychology were being worked out. Beginning with the work of Sir Francis Galton, the application of statistics to biological and psychological problems was understood to be valuable and necessary. With the development of psychological and educational tests, the need for applying statistics to education became apparent and statistical procedures for treating the results of educational experiments were rapidly developed. By about 1915, knowledge of the methods to be used in carrying on objective experiments for the study of child behavior and knowledge of the statistical principles to be used in treating the results of these experiments had both developed to a sufficiently high point so that really valuable experimentation in educational procedures became possible. Nevertheless the amount of such experimentation has been disappointingly small.

Difficulties in the Way of Educational Experiments. There are several reasons for failure to carry on the much needed experimental work. Such experiments require the coöperation of large numbers of research workers. Due to the diversity of interests of educators and to their absorption in the immediate problems connected with their particular jobs, this coöperation has been difficult to obtain. It is also necessary in carrying on any educational experiment to make use of a large number of children as the learners in such an experiment. There has been a general feeling among laymen, and to a considerable extent among teachers as well, that children should not be made the subjects of experiments.

It is easy to show that this prejudice against using children in experiments is not well founded, but it nevertheless exists. Educational experiments which are concerned with comparing two different methods of instruction should ordinarily be concerned with making comparison between two methods, both of which are good. Ordinarily both of the methods will be found to be already in use somewhere in the educational system. The comparison is intended merely to discover which of the two methods is better. Such comparison need not radically change the treatment of any child, need not waste any of his time and cannot possibly harm him. Sometimes a new method of instruction may have been worked out which is believed to be better than any existing method, and the desire is to try it out in such a way that comparisons can be made with existing methods which it is designed to replace. Whenever such a comparison needs to be made, it seems unwarranted to be greatly concerned about harm to the children who participate in the experiment. Unless the method is introduced experimentally, those who have originated it are likely to secure its adoption in some schools on *a priori* grounds, without any direct proof of its value. It would seem much more sensible to try out the new method alongside the

old, under controlled conditions, so that the next generation of school children could be taught according to the
method which proves to be better. Prejudice against
experimenting with children results merely in the introduction of new "plans" of instruction as fads. Such fads
come and go with no proof ever being furnished of their
merit or lack of merit.

Experimental testing of new "plans" involves a considerable amount of work in addition to the usual work
of teaching. The teachers themselves are ordinarily not
fitted by their training to carry on the statistical analyses
and comparisons which are needed. They also cannot
spare the time from their instructional work for this experimentation. This extra work must be carried on by an
extra staff who require funds for their maintenance. Such
money is not often available.

*Failure to Experiment Has Had Undesirable Educational
Consequences.* As a result of these difficulties in the way
of carrying on controlled experimentation, educators have
ordinarily been content to adopt the one method or the
other, whichever happens to appeal to them. Some educator works out a scheme of instruction or a curriculum which
he believes to be good. Having convinced himself by
a more or less logical process of reasoning that his new
scheme is better than the one that has previously been
in use, he proceeds to introduce it into the school system
that is under his charge. When he has made no special
provision for comparing the results of his new system
with the results of the system which it has displaced, he
is unable to state even after his new plan has been in
use for years whether it is really better than the one that
it superseded. That is, he is unable to make any such
statement upon the basis of scientific proof. He ordinarily does claim that his new system is better than the

one which preceded it, and he furnishes many arguments to support his view. These arguments, however, remain merely matters of opinion, since no provision was made for any definite scientific comparisons. We are always left with the impression that an administrator who has introduced a new plan without making provision for comparing it with any other plan feels that he must find the new plan better in order to justify his own judgment in having introduced it in the first place. The teachers who are working with him as his subordinates in the new plan are likewise prejudiced in its favor, because they wish to remain in good standing in the school system and feel that support of the new plan will increase their favor in the eyes of the administrator.

When such new plans are introduced into a school system, they are frequently called experiments. They are experiments only in the sense that they are the use of a new method or a new curriculum, but they lack the essential features of scientific experimentation.

What Is an Educational Experiment? The essential feature of scientific experimentation which is concerned with deciding upon the merits of a new method for teaching children or of a new departure in the curriculum involves the comparison of the new method or curriculum with some other method or curriculum which it is designed to replace. This comparison has several aspects. (1) It is necessary that there shall be one group of learners who are proceeding under the one plan of instruction; there must also be another group of learners who are proceeding under the second plan of instruction. (2) Some provision must be made for insuring that the two groups of learners have the same initial general ability, the same initial skill, and the same initial amount of information. (3) Provision must be made so that during the period of time while the comparison of the two plans is being made the two groups of learners shall have equal opportunities and shall be treated in the same way in all other features of their educational life, except the one special feature which is being tested. (4) Provision must be made for some satisfactory (objective) means of measuring the education-changes which take place in each of the two groups of learners. This evaluation of the educational changes which occur in the two groups must be made in such a manner that unprejudiced and accurate comparison between the two groups is possible. (5) This comparison must make use of the best statistical techniques. (6) The result of the period of experimentation should be a decision in favor of the one plan or the other which is independent of the opinions and mere general impressions of the people who are concerned with conducting the learning of either of the two groups of children.

So-called Educational Experiments. All too frequently administrators have become convinced of the value of some new plan or scheme of instruction, such as the Dalton plan or the Winnetka plan, or some other variety of unit or contract plan of education; or they have become convinced of the value of some new departure in the curriculum, such as emphasis upon the manual arts, or a course in general science, or an orientation course, and have adopted the new procedure or new curriculum without making any provision for an actual test of its value.

At the University of Wisconsin, for example, an Experimental College has been established, which is experimental only in the sense that it is an attempt to apply the project method of teaching to college education. It lacks the essentials of an experiment because adequate provision has not been made for securing a similar group of students for purposes of comparison, and for satisfactorily measuring the outcomes of the new educational procedure. The decision whether the new educational procedure is more valuable than the one which it is designed to replace has been left to the opinion of prejudiced observers. The result has been that those who in the beginning were prejudiced in favor of the plan have decided that it is very valuable, while those who in the beginning were prejudiced against the plan have decided that it is a failure. Nowhere is there any sufficient objective information to enable a disinterested observer to form an opinion of its value.

The Need for Educators Who Are Trained in Scientific Method. The failure of educators in general to make provisions for objectively evaluating the results of new educational procedures is probably due to the fact that they have little knowledge of modern objective methods in psychology. Many of them are remarkably ignorant of psychology as a whole. Those who have had training in psychology have ordinarily been trained in the older introspective method. The psychology with which they are familiar is the older structural psychology, which does not make use of objective experimentation but depends entirely upon introspection, or it is the somewhat more recent functional psychology, which in its beginnings remained primarily introspective in nature. Being familiar only with one or the other of these two types of subjective psychology, educators can hardly be expected to recognize the importance or even the possibility of objectively evaluating the results of a new educational scheme. If not wholly ignorant of the methods for making such objective comparisons, they are at least more or less unfamiliar with them, and therefore skeptical of their values. They are likewise usually not well trained in mathematics, especially in statistics, as a foundation for scientific method. Before educational experimentation can be carried on extensively, it seems necessary to develop a body of educators who are trained in the newer objective psychology, who are familiar with the possibilities for experimenting with the behavior of human beings, and who have a sufficient acquaintance with mathematical and statistical techniques.

Which Schools of Psychology Favor Educational Experimentation? It will be well at this point specifically to relate each of the modern schools of psychology to the work of educational experimentation. It has been pointed out that the structural school is not at all adapted to experimenting with educational procedures. The functional school of psychology grew up in part as a result of the attempt to carry on such experimentation. It still retains so much of the older introspective attitude that it is only partially adapted to making comparisons between different plans in education. The behavioristic or objective psychology has completely discarded the subjective approach to the study of human behavior and is well adapted to the study of child development and the making of comparisons between schemes for directing this development. The school of psycho-analysis is highly subjective in its theory, and is not adapted to making comparisons; it represents rather a means for making individual case studies and for aiding individuals in making adjustments. The Gestalt psychology is so new that its meaning is theoretical rather than immediately practical. It may develop a new attitude toward human nature and human behavior which will help us to determine the kind of experiment we should like to set up; but it will not introduce any new principle for conducting educational experiments.

Summary

Experimental evaluation of techniques is a new development in education. It was impossible until the subjective attitude in psychology was replaced by objective method. Although the technique of experimentation is well understood by a few leaders, few extensive and conclusive experiments have been carried on. The difficulties which have been largely insurmountable are lack of time on the part of educators, who are absorbed in the routine of their jobs, lack of funds, and opposition based upon prejudice and misunderstanding. Failure to experiment favors the introduction of fads into education.

Wider use of the experimental method in evaluating educational procedures must wait upon a more general training of educational leaders in psychological method and statistical technique, and upon the development of a favorable attitude on the part of the educated public.

CHAPTER XVIII

PSYCHOLOGICAL PRINCIPLES AND EDUCATIONAL PROBLEMS: A RÉSUMÉ

I. Principles of Contemporary Psychology

Restraint vs. Freedom in Education. In this discussion of psychology and education it is proposed that the current educational system is always based directly upon the beliefs which are held concerning human nature in general and concerning the nature of children in particular. The attitude toward childhood that has dominated the thinking of the Christian era up to the present century is that a child is essentially a miniature adult. Education during the Christian era has usually made the additional assumption that the child is essentially evil in his inner nature. Rousseau proposed the theory that the child comes into the world as a perfect being and is spoiled by contact with civilization. Based upon the former view, educational institutions have relied mainly upon a process of discipline, restraint, and external direction. The culmination of this point of view is the statement of the aim of education as social efficiency. The latter view requires a complete change of attitude; it demands an educational procedure in which children are given complete freedom, the teacher being merely an onlooker who prevents interference with the child's own inner growth.

Education as a Creative Process. The emphasis upon the importance of child nature contained in the theories of Rousseau demands investigation to determine what the facts of child nature actually are. This fact-finding study began with G. Stanley Hall near the beginning of the twentieth century. Since his time many data have been collected which are causing profound modification of the former conception of the nature of children. The belief that children are miniature adults is being challenged. Such a belief does not fit with the facts of child nature as they are now understood. It appears, rather, that children must be accepted as being, in a sense, a different kind of creature from adults. They are to be thought of as living a life of their own with maturity as a goal to be attained in the distant future. We may liken them to raw material which can be made into civilized adult human beings in good time, if it is put through the proper processes of manufacture. The business of education is understood to be essentially a creative industry in which children, regarded as raw material, are subjected to manufacturing processes. Parents and teachers are to be regarded as workmen who are engaged in a constructive manufacturing process bringing to bear upon their problems whatever skills and tools they possess.

Conflicting Tendencies in Contemporary Psychology. For the sake of understanding this modern scientific attitude toward children and education, it is necessary to understand the psychology of the present day. It is true that the opinions concerning the nature of adult man and of the child which are held by present-day psychologists do not yet furnish the basis for established educational procedures, because they are new and not yet familiar to the public. We may expect them to influence most profoundly the educational system in the near future.

The psychological systems of contemporary importance are commonly called structuralism, functionalism, objective psychology (often called behaviorism), purposive or hormic psychology, psycho-analysis, and Gestalt psychology. Among these six schools of psychology, we can distinguish four important tendencies: (1) the tendency toward objectivity and materialism; (2) insistence upon the existence and the importance of spiritual or mental driving forces; (3) the trend toward analysis of mind and behavior into parts or elements; (4) the belief that analysis into parts leads to an oversimplification and a misunderstanding of mind and behavior.

Objectivity and Materialism in Psychology. At the beginning of the century in America the prevailing psychology was structuralism. It was essentially a dualistic system, assuming mind and body to be separate entities that existed in a kind of parallelism. The interest of the structural psychologists was in the mental side of this dualism. They were absorbed in the analysis and synthesis of mental states, and because of this absorption they neglected to be concerned about the utility of their science.

In part because of the barrenness of the structural psychology, a change in attitude occurred near the beginning of the century. Interest shifted from mind as a static thing to mind as an active agent in the process of adaptation to environment. Interest in the applications of psychology to education and business and to the study of the actions of animals and children made necessary a departure from the introspective method, which had been characteristic of the structural psychology. These changes in interest led to the development of a new psychological point of view—functionalism. Functionalism, in keeping with the earlier psychology, was interested in mind as distinct from body. It was concerned, however, with the manner in which mind aided man to maintain himself in the world. This interest in adaptation required a study of man's bodily activity as well as of his mental states. With the functional psychology, therefore, objective method found a legitimate place in psychology.

During the second decade of the twentieth century, a new psychological movement appeared—objective psychology. It was created by a logical extension of the same tendencies which created functionalism. Applications of psychology require an objective method of investigation; animal and child psychology likewise require an objective approach. The first step toward behaviorism was taken when investigators in animal and child psychology pursued their work, neglecting to interpret their findings concerning child and animal activity in terms of conscious mental processes. Having met with some success in understanding the behavior of children and animals without using the concept of mind, they came to the conclusion that mind was not only unnecessary, but did not, in fact, exist. Objective psychology thus became materialistic.

In this manner, out of structuralism that was a truly mental science, there came into existence a tendency toward objectivity and materialism. It first manifested itself in the functional psychology and has reached its extreme in the objective psychology of the present day.

Mental Forces in Contemporary Psychology. There are two groups of psychologists who believe that human beings cannot be understood without supposing the existence of mental or spiritual driving forces of a non-material character. In America, William McDougall is the leader of the purposive group. He believes that desires, purposes, cravings, and the like are natural to human beings. He is opposed to the mechanistic and materialistic trend of the three previously mentioned psychological groups. He believes that the mental machinery described by the structuralists and functionalists and the bodily mechanism described by the behaviorists would remain inert and motionless unless driven by instinctive and emotional forces. These mechanistic psychologists, however, believe that the things which he classes as desires and purposes are themselves mechanisms—the products of learning—and that the only driving force needed to operate the mental and physical machinery is normal environmental stimulation.

The second group of psychologists who lay great emphasis upon internal driving forces are commonly called psycho-analysts. This type of psychology was originated by Sigmund Freud. He emphasizes the importance of sex instinct as a motivating force which dominates human life. Disorders of this instinct are stated to be responsible for most mental abnormalities, and proper direction of sex impulses is believed to be responsible for most worthwhile human actions. Other psychologists who have the same general attitude toward the importance of driving forces are not willing to attribute such great importance to sex instinct, but they are all agreed that it is instinct in some form which furnishes the motive force of human life.

Are Mind and Behavior Merely Collections of Mental Elements and Reflexes? The structuralists took as their task the analysis of complex mental processes into elements and the discovery of the laws of their combination. The elements were found to be sensations, feelings, and images. There was some controversy concerning the existence of a fourth, namely a thought element. The laws governing the organization of the complex processes such as ideas, perceptions, and emotions were found to be the laws of association. The general goal of this group of psychologists was to be found in working out a mental mechanics, in which each part of mind was nicely cataloged and labelled and located with reference to each of the other parts.

The typical procedure of the functional psychology is,

likewise, that of analysis of mental activities into their elements, but it has added on a similar analysis of bodily movement. Interest in bodily movement led functionalists to give great importance to instinct as a phase of adaptation.

The procedure of objective psychology is similar to that of the two earlier systems in that it is concerned with the analysis of behavior into elements and the discovery of laws governing the combination of these elements into the more complicated activities. The behavior elements that are found are reflexes. The laws of combination of these elements are the laws of learning. The conditioned reflex is taken to be typical of all learning, and all the complex activities of adult life are believed to be built up from a complication of a comparatively small number of original reflexes.

These three schools of psychology—structuralism, functionalism, and behaviorism—have in common the belief that analysis of mind or of behavior into its parts or elements together with the discovery of the laws governing the combination of these parts is the primary business of psychology.

Critics of "Atomistic" Psychology. Recently there has arisen a school of psychology which objects to the atomistic explanation of mind and action which is characteristic of structural, functional, and objective psychology. This psychological viewpoint originated in Germany at about the time that behaviorism was developing in America. The movement has been received with great interest in this country, although the number of its followers remains comparatively small. The distinguishing characteristic is an emphasis upon the essential unity of mind and of behavior. It presents the doctrine that the attempt to analyze mental and physical activity into elements has resulted in a misunderstanding of human mind and behavior. Human activities are believed to exist as units which cannot be analyzed into smaller parts or elements without losing something of importance. The chief tenet of this school is that in human activity, the whole is usually greater than the sum of its parts—it is greater because it includes an organization that is not present in any or all of its parts.

Does Instinct Furnish a Foundation for Learning? So long as psychologists were interested exclusively in mind, they had little interest in instinct. It represents a form of action which has relatively little mental content. When psychological interest shifted from mind, in a static sense, to mind as a factor in adaptation to environment, instinct became a topic of considerable importance. Instinctive tendencies were believed to furnish the basis for all learned actions. They were believed to be all-important factors in motivating school work and every kind of learning. Long lists of instincts were prepared and attempts were made to discover the age at which each might be expected to appear so that it could be properly utilized by parents and teachers. When careful observations of behavior were made, it was soon discovered that the definiteness and invariability which had been supposed to exist in instinctive activity were lacking. This discovery led to profound modification of opinion concerning instinct. Some psychologists have now gone to the extreme of asserting that there are no instincts at all, in the sense of complex inherited behavior patterns, but that all complex activities are built up by a process of conditioning from a few simple reflexes. The purposive psychologists, the psycho-analysts, and many functionalists hold fast to instinct as an inherited mental driving force of great importance in human life. The Gestalt psychologists tend to agree with the behaviorists in discrediting instinct as an inherited form of action.

The Nature of Emotion. Emotion was first treated as a mental state characterized chiefly by its confusion. Such is the opinion of structural and functional psychologists. The purposive psychologists think of emotion as being the mental aspect of instinct. The psycho-analysts sometimes use the words emotion and instinct interchangeably. In their system, however, emotion seems to be truly mental, while instinct may refer to bodily action.

Among these psychologists an important theoretical question has been,—whether emotion comes before and causes bodily activity or whether it is to be thought of as the consequence of bodily disturbances. The former view is the common-sense one and has gained wide acceptance. The latter was proposed by James and Lange. Experimental tests of the validity of the James-Lange theory are inconclusive. Dana and Cannon have proposed that emotion is characterized by nervous discharge from the diencephalon. Bodily activity is produced by motor impulses from the diencephalon, while the peculiar quality of emotional consciousness is added when cerebral processes are influenced by thalamic discharge. Emotion as a mental state and the bodily aspects of emotion are believed to be parallel. Neither precedes nor causes the other.

The behaviorists have proposed that emotion consists of widespread visceral and glandular response in contrast with instinct, which consists of activity of the skeletal muscles. It is characterized by a considerable change in the energy output of the body. It has been recognized that there is nothing in visceral behavior to distinguish between two strong emotions such as fear and anger. Emotions are apparently differentiated from one another more by the external goal of the bodily activity than by the character of the visceral responses. Carr and Meyer have proposed that an additional distinguishing feature of emotion is lack of coördination, a kind of awkwardness. Emotion is to be classed with unskilled activity.

Emotion and Education. It is commonly believed that emotions can be used as motivating forces to secure the doing of school work. Purposive and functional psychologists subscribe to this view; it fits with the theories of the psycho-analysts. The technique of making an appeal to emotions as motive forces is not clearly stated; we are told merely that it should be done. We should somehow get the learner emotionally excited about the task to be performed, but no explanation is given of the underlying mental processes which connect the emotions with the task.

Objective psychologists think of emotion as being, in part, a disturbance of the energy regulating mechanisms of the body. This is a fact of importance for the teacher. Each learning situation demands a given level of energy output, a level that is too high or too low may be undesirable. Whatever emotions are used in the classroom must be very mild affairs.

Emotion is classed as a mental disturbance by the subjective psychologists. Orderly processes of thinking and reasoning are interfered with. It is, therefore, undesirable in learning situations. Some objective psychologists make emotional behavior equivalent to lack of skill. Training in the correct modes of response, then, will reduce emotion. As a person's education progresses, the vigor, frequency, and variety of emotional responses will be decreased. Emotions do not motivate learning; they indicate rather that learning remains to be accomplished.

The production of machine-like precision and skill in doing useful work is not the only objective of education.

Æsthetic interests are believed worth-while. The latter demand the preservation of a certain readiness for emotional response, both in the performer and in the audience. Emotions add to the color and variety of life; we must learn to keep them within conventional limits, but they should not be eradicated—if that were possible!

Conflicting Opinions concerning Learning. Subjective psychologists are interested in the laws governing the association of mental processes. The order and sequence of thinking and reasoning are explained by the association of ideas, images, feeling, and the like. The Laws of Frequency, Recency, and Intensity determine the strength of an association. Functionalists place emphasis upon the importance of the association of mental processes with motor activity. They have formulated the Law of Effect to explain exceptions to the Law of Frequency. The study of motor activity has made these exceptions apparent. The behaviorists have translated association into objective language and have furnished an over-simplified description of motor learning. They have added the word "conditioning" to psychological terminology, but have discovered no new laws. Gestalt psychologists disapprove the atomistic tendencies of orthodox psychology, but they have not replaced the theories that they decry with better ones of their own. They give us little comfort with their hazy concepts of "insight" and "maturation."

At the present time we know very little about the neurological basis of learning. We have been forced by the weight of experimental evidence to give up the belief that habit-formation, or association of ideas, consists of the building up of nerve pathways of low resistance. Relatively large portions of the nervous system are clearly involved in even the simplest activity. We are convinced only that learning requires relatively permanent changes.

Concerning the nature of these changes we may scarcely hazard a guess.

In the absence of an adequate theory of learning, teaching must remain an empirical procedure. We must continue to try out experimentally those procedures that seem worth-while, checking the one against the other. The immediate hope for improvement in the techniques of learning and teaching lies in experimental education.

Mental Tests and Standardized Educational Tests. The great development in the use of mental tests has occurred under the leadership of functional psychologists. They, at first, believed that it would be necessary to test each mental function separately, thus getting a kind of mosaic picture of an individual's mental worth. Binet assumed that all mental functions developed at approximately the same rate. Out of this assumption grew the concept of mental age and the general intelligence test, as we know it to-day. Objective psychologists have discarded the concept of mental functions; tests, therefore, are from their viewpoint samples of behavior. If the samples are carefully taken and treated, they may be used as the basis for estimating the character of the rest of the child's behavior. From the objective point of view, mental-test scores are never measures of native ability as distinct from achievement, and educational subject-matter tests are not measures of achievement as distinct from native ability. All tests alike give a basis for estimating the present behavior status of an individual. By relating present status to other known facts of development—such as age, educational opportunity, social status, etc.—predictions concerning the child's future can be made. Objective psychology, therefore, is less fatalistic in its attitude toward mental measurements than is functionalism.

II. Psychological Views of Educational Problems

Provisions for Individual Differences in Education. Subjective psychology is not adapted to the study of individual differences; individual psychology is necessarily objective. The three systems that are adapted to the study of individual differences are functionalism, objective psychology, and psycho-analysis.

The facts of individual difference which have an important bearing on education are: (1) a child may have a high degree of ability for one kind of work and a low degree of ability for another; (2) some individuals can and do learn more rapidly than others; (3) children differ in their methods of study and learning; (4) children differ in specific preparation for learning a given activity. Educational adjustments demanded by these facts are: (1) individual freedom in choice of subject matter, courses, curricula, etc.; (2) provision for different rates of progress in a given unit of subject matter; (3) variation in methods of instruction, freedom for choosing different methods of study; (4) provision for a graded curriculum. School systems make these four provisions in varying degrees, influenced by tradition, fad, and fancy. The many new "plans"—the Dalton plan, the Winnetka plan, supervised study, the contract plan, etc.—differ from one another in the relative degree of emphasis that they place upon the one or the other of these necessary types of adjustment to individuals.

Vocational and Educational Guidance. Guidance of individuals in choice of education and vocation requires an understanding of the abilities possessed by each individual and knowledge of the demands made upon human abilities by a multitude of school subjects and vocations. Psychologically, an objective approach is essential; a training in subjective psychology seems of little value to an advisor. It seems impossible that one person should combine all the abilities needed for giving educational and vocational advice. Coöperation among teachers, parents, vocational practitioners, and guidance experts is essential.

Pre-school Education. Pre-school education is based psychologically upon the importance of the early years of childhood in the development of personality, character, and intelligence. Psycho-analysts first pointed out the extreme importance of the conditions of early life in avoiding mental disorder; objective psychologists believe that the circumstances of the first few years go far toward determining the future intellectual worth of an individual. Nursery schools rightly place great emphasis upon motor training, for it is through the environmental contacts made possible by motor control that intellectual development occurs; they properly stress social adaptation, for many of the important social attitudes are determined very early in life.

Adult Education. Adults do learn; apparently they learn easily and well. The reasons why a man becomes old-fashioned, conservative, and out of date are social and economic rather than psychological. Modern life demands a re-adjustment in educational institutions, so that we will cease crowding so much training into the early years of life far in advance of the time when it is needed, and so that we will encourage men and women to continue their education all through the middle period of life.

Extra-curricular Activities. We must recognize that much education goes on outside of the classroom. We must stop the practice of making an arbitrary class grade a prerequisite to participation in out-of-class education. We must rather guide students into those activities which have greatest educational value for them as individuals. We must utilize knowledge of individual differences for extra-curricular as well as for curricular guidance.

Education in Character and Personality. Objective psychology teaches that effective learning requires freedom to make mistakes. We do profit by errors as well as by correct actions. Present character training programs must be examined to discover whether we are not imposing too many restrictions upon children, because of our anxiety to protect them. Too close supervision and too long continued protection defeat the ends of education. There must be progressive relaxation of restraint so that at last the individual is free to try himself out in all situations before he can reach that kind of dependability and responsibility which is the goal of character education.

Personality develops primarily through social contacts. Children must learn through their own experience how to conduct themselves in social situations. The parent and the teacher can furnish them with opportunities for learning and can aid them in developing important concepts such as loyalty, aggressiveness, tact, etc. Nevertheless, with personality as with character, proper development requires freedom for personal contact with the varying situations in life, both good and bad, so that the child can develop ways of acting which are based upon a firmer foundation than words. Mental hygiene is concerned with developing right personal habits.

Psycho-analysis explains character and personality as the external expression of the important instinctive driving forces. Environmental circumstances determine whether they are well directed or whether they go astray. Individual and anti-social expressions are indications that normal outlets have not been found; they are symptoms of a condition that may well lead to mental disorders. Mental hygiene is concerned with the technique of finding useful outlets for bottled up instinctive forces.

What Have the Several Psychological Systems Contributed to Education? Structuralism was the first well-developed experimental psychology. In itself it was barren of educational value; as a necessary step in the development of mental science, it paved the way for the objective method which appeared in functionalism.

Scientific child study began with the functional psychology and was made possible by the introduction of objective method. Through its interest in adaptation to environment, functionalism favored an educational psychology. It added the Law of Effect to the earlier Laws of Association. This law must be revised, but it contains an element of truth. The outstanding contribution of the functionalists is the testing movement, including both mental and standardized subject-matter tests.

Objective psychology has contributed no new principle. It is rather the culmination of the tendencies which appeared in functionalism. It has contributed detailed fact-finding studies of infancy and childhood. Innumerable learning experiments have been conducted in the attempt to solve both practical and theoretical problems. Interest has shifted from the analysis of adult human behavior to the attempt to understand the origin and development of human actions. The contributions of the objectivists are in matters of technique rather than principle. Education starts where objective psychology leaves off, and practices the control and direction of human development.

An appreciation of the great importance of early childhood in education remains as the primary achievement of psycho-analysis. Its emphasis upon the value of environmental control presents a challenge to educators. The importance of instinctive driving forces is a debatable question. Through weakening somewhat the taboos against discussions of sex, the Freudians have aided in the solution of the problems of sex education.

Purposive psychology is the last stand of those who believe that there is more to human beings than matter and motion. It boldly asserts that desires, wishes, strivings, etc., are basic to human action. The value to education of these forces—if we may accept their existence—is in the motivation of learning. We have only to tap the instinctive sources of power to secure unlimited effort to learn.

The meaning for education of the Gestalt psychology is not yet clear. Probably it places first emphasis upon making clear to pupils the goals for which they are striving. It requires, too, that these goals shall not be set beyond their reach—beyond their level of insight. It minimizes the value of drills and routine procedures and favors a unit plan of learning.

From psychology as a whole, it is clear that development from infancy to maturity is an orderly process. Each new phase of development is understandable and predictable, if only we have the skill and the patience to follow the clues that are furnished by a close and unprejudiced observation of children as they grow in a social environment.

INDEX OF AUTHORS

SUBJECT INDEX